W9-CLJ-970

The Episcopacy in American Methodism

KINGSWOOD BOOKS

Randy L. Maddox, Director
Seattle Pacific University

EDITORIAL ADVISORY BOARD

Justo L. González
Hispanic Theological Initiative, Emory University

W. Stephen Gunter
Candler School of Theology

Richard P. Heitzenrater
The Divinity School, Duke University

Thomas A. Langford
The Divinity School, Duke University

Robin W. Lovin
Perkins School of Theology, Southern Methodist University

Rebekah L. Miles
Brite Divinity School, Texas Christian University

Mary Elizabeth Mullino Moore
Claremont School of Theology

Jean Miller Schmidt
Iliff School of Theology

Harriett Jane Olson, *ex officio*
Abingdon Press

Neil M. Alexander, *ex officio*
Abingdon Press

The Episcopacy in American Methodism

James E. Kirby

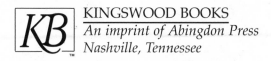

KINGSWOOD BOOKS
An imprint of Abingdon Press
Nashville, Tennessee

THE EPISCOPACY IN AMERICAN METHODISM

Copyright © 2000 by Abingdon Press

All rights reserved.

No part of this work may be reproduced or transmitted in any form or by any means, electronic or mechanical, including photocopying and recording, or by any information storage or retrieval system, except as may be expressly permitted by the 1976 Copyright Act or in writing from the publisher. Requests for permission should be addressed in writing to Abingdon Press, P.O. Box 801, 201 Eighth Avenue South, Nashville, TN 37202-0801.

This book is printed on recycled, acid-free, elemental-chlorine–free paper.

Library of Congress Cataloging-in-Publication Data

Kirby, James E.
  The episcopacy in American Methodism   /   James E. Kirby.
    p. cm.
  Includes bibliographical references and index.
  ISBN 0-687-07333-2 (alk. paper)
  1. Methodist Church—United States—Bishops—Appointment, call, and election—History. 2. Methodist Church—United States—Government—History.   3. Methodist Church—United States—Doctrines—History.   I. Title.

  BX8345.K57   2000
  262′.127—dc21   99-048368

This volume contains material that originally was published as chapters 1 through 3 in *The Methodists*, by James E. Kirby, et al. Copyright 1996 by Greenwood Press. Used by permission.

00 01 02 03 04 05 06 07 08 09—10 9 8 7 6 5 4 3 2 1

MANUFACTURED IN THE UNITED STATES OF AMERICA

FOR

J. Edmund and Ruth H. Kirby,
*who served with their bishops for
forty-four years in
the Northwest Texas Annual Conference.*

We are an office, not an order.
We are not prelates on the one hand,
nor diocesan officers on the other.
We exist for the connection and are a kind
of cement uniting the whole denomination.

Bishop James K. Mathews

Contents

Introduction

This is the story of the "itinerant, general superintendency" of episcopal Methodism, that unique part of the movement that gave Methodism shape and form. It begins as it should with a brief look at the form of the office authorized by John Wesley when he sent Thomas Coke to organize an independent body of Methodists in America, and traces its evolution as Francis Asbury and his successors led a movement committed "to reform the Continent, and to spread scriptural Holiness"[1] across the lands in the New World called America. No individual was more significant in shaping Methodist episcopacy than Asbury. He both held and personified the office of bishop in American Methodism for the first three decades of its existence. It was Asbury who refused to accept Wesley's nomination to act as a general superintendent without the consent of the body of preachers, and in so doing shifted Wesley's personal power to the conference; he administered, promoted, defended, and modeled itinerant ministry, the key to Methodist success in America. And it was Asbury and his successor bishops who held the denomination together in the face of threats to its unity as it grew, by the middle of the nineteenth century, to become America's largest Protestant denomination. The episcopacy was the linchpin of early American Methodism.

The story of episcopal Methodism in America is built around two foci—the episcopacy as it was created and its practice estab-

9

lished by Francis Asbury, and the division of the church North and South in 1844. Although living in the climate of a nation on its way to civil war, and caught up in conflict over the institution of slavery, the Methodists who formed themselves into the Methodist Episcopal Church, South, did so in defense of the "Asburian" ideal of episcopacy as a co-equal branch of church government. Their brothers and sisters in the North affirmed the concept of a strong General Conference directing an episcopacy conceived as an "abstraction" to be shaped in literally hundreds of ways to meet changing circumstances. Bishops were considered to be officers of the General Conference, serving at its pleasure. The history of both branches of episcopal Methodism from 1844 until 1939 is influenced primarily by questions concerning regional autonomy and episcopal authority related to these divergent expressions of a common past.

The reader will see quickly that although the story contained in these pages continues into the present and even dares to speculate about the future of the episcopal office in the life of the church in the twenty-first century, it lacks any consideration of the experience of the Evangelical United Brethren, who joined with the Methodist Church in 1968 to create The United Methodist Church. If one understands the thesis that is the basis of this essay, it will be recognized that the history of the United Brethren, the Evangelical Association, and the EUBC is separate and unique. They were, in effect, grafted in 1968 into an institution whose history with regard to the episcopacy they did not share. A part of the difficulty on both sides in conducting the negotiations that finally led to union was related to the awareness that this was the proposal. African American brothers and sisters in their respective branches of episcopal Methodism, despite having modeled their episcopal offices after those in the MEC and the MECS, likewise have shared only a part of that history, and when the day comes, as well it may, when all of American Methodism seeks to be rejoined into one body, a new understanding will have to be articulated based on those parts of the past that are shared and this history rewritten. To some extent, this revision was done when the Methodist Protestants, who had rejected episcopacy altogether, joined the Methodist Church in 1939 and began their new life in it by electing, for the first time, two bishops. Likewise, in 1968 the EUBC agreed to grant its active bishops life tenure as United Methodists and turned the page on their traditional understanding of the episcopal office.

Both the northern and southern branches of Methodism evolved their understanding of the episcopal office separately for the better part of a century. Practice and custom, driven often by the necessity of meeting significant needs, such as finding a way to provide episcopal supervision for their missionary outposts in other lands, were at least as important in shaping the office as deliberate modifications. In Methodist history, there have always been movements determined to limit the scope and power of the bishops, some of which actually divided the denomination. They shaped it as well. These changes, whether resulting from deliberate attempts to modify the office or evolution in response to need, all shared a role in the inexorable march away from "itinerant, general superintendency" toward diocesan and localized episcopacy. This culminated in the formation of the Methodist Church in 1939, whose jurisdictional structure located the place of episcopal elections in regional bodies, limited episcopal service both in time and space and, thereby, changed the office of bishop and the characteristics of those who occupied it more than any single act in Methodist history.

This is the story of the unique office that has been central to the life and self-understanding of the people called Methodists in America. What is left yet to be known is how in the future it will serve what has become a world church. One active bishop, in responding to the last chapter, put it well: "If the way ahead is not corporate executive or personal power, how do we do this impossible job?" The basic arrangement followed in telling this story is chronological, but occasionally the story can be better understood thematically. These shifts will be apparent and, it is hoped, useful to the reader. The book was designed with seminary students, clergy, and informed laypersons in mind, and offered with the sincere expectation that it can enable us all better to appreciate and appropriate the grand story of American Methodists.

Many persons have been of assistance in this project. It is impossible to thank them all, but special help was provided by my colleagues Russell E. Richey of Duke Divinity School and Ken Rowe of Drew University, with whom I have worked for years and whose knowledge and understanding of Methodism always inform and challenge me. I would be remiss not to acknowledge the help given by the director and staff of the Bridwell Library of the Perkins School of Theology. They opened its rich resources to me and gave me a place to work in peace during some very hectic years. My special

11

thanks to its director of the Center for Methodist Studies, Page A. Thomas, who found material on short notice, answered questions, hunted lost references, and suggested helpful ways to illuminate the story. He, like the library itself, is a rare gift.

My old friends and colleagues who served in the episcopal office—Eugene Slater, McFerrin Stowe (now deceased), James S. Thomas, and John Wesley Hardt—spent hours in conversation and in reading what I have written. We have not always agreed, but their support has never wavered. Many other bishops, with whom I was associated in the eighteen years I worked with them as a member of the Association of United Methodist Theological Schools, have helped in ways they do not even know, and I am grateful to them too.

The Perkins School of Theology of Southern Methodist University has generously enabled me to take leave to have uninterrupted time for work on this project and provided me with the able assistance of Ken Dahlberg, who worked long hours on the final draft. For the better part of thirty-five years since I first began to write about Matthew Simpson, Patty Kirby has patiently heard more about bishops than she ever wanted or needed to know, and she deserves special recognition and thanks.

July 29, 1998
Dallas, Texas

CHAPTER 1

American Episcopacy

John Wesley's Methodists made their way to the American colonies around 1760. Although not fully organized, nor empowered to function as an autonomous ecclesiastical body until 1784, they flourished in the New World and grew to be America's largest Protestant denomination by 1840. In those years, many persons provided leadership and influenced the shape of the new denomination. But in the final analysis, two distinct and unique forces defined American Methodism: the first was the powerful hand of Francis Asbury, who guided its fortunes in the early years, and the second was the form of itinerant general superintendency that Asbury created, supported, and defended—which became the linchpin of denominational stability and the key to the success of its ministry. Had either of these been lacking, Methodist history in America would be quite different. The story of Methodism in America is inseparable from its episcopacy, and episcopacy cannot be seen apart from Francis Asbury.

The Roots of American Methodism

The early historian of Methodism, Jesse Lee, gives the society organized in New York City the honor of being the oldest in America, but others give that place to one established under the leadership of Robert Strawbridge at Sam's Creek in Frederick County, Maryland.

The New York society was led by Philip Embury, an Irish local preacher whose family belonged to a group of German Lutherans who fled the armies of Louis XIV invading the Palatinate in southern Germany, went first to Ireland, and then later immigrated to America. Embury was born in Ireland, converted there under the preaching of John Wesley, and became a class leader and local preacher. He came to New York in August 1760, and after some years began preaching to a small group in his home. From this modest beginning the society grew to require larger quarters and moved to a new meeting place in a rigging-loft on Horse-and-Cart Street. Eventually they purchased land and built the John Street Methodist Church. The new building, Jesse Lee said, would hold twelve hundred to fourteen hundred people. In time a society also was organized in Philadelphia. However, Embury never rose to prominence as a leader in the connection, and for a time ceased preaching entirely.

Robert Strawbridge, like Embury, seems to have arrived in America around 1760. The society he organized in the southern colonies eventually built a log meetinghouse near Sam's and Pipe Creeks that some claim to be the first Methodist building in America.[1] Under Strawbridge and his associates, indigenous American leaders such as Jesse Lee, William Watters, and James O'Kelly joined the Methodists. In contrast to Embury, Strawbridge did exercise leadership over a number of societies in the southern colonies and eventually challenged both Wesley's practice and Asbury's leadership.

In addition to the American preachers, there were individuals sent by Wesley to work in America. In 1767 George Whitefield, who was already well known in the colonies for his preaching, asked Wesley if he could spare preachers for work in America but was offered none. The following year, Thomas Taylor, a member of the New York society, wrote Wesley asking for money to help in the building of the new chapel on John Street and requesting an experienced preacher for the society.[2] Robert Williams and John King joined Strawbridge in 1769. Both received Wesley's permission to come to America, but neither had the support of the conference and both were required to work under supervision. Williams managed to get his passage paid by a friend and arrived in the colonies without either money or promise of support.

Then with strong encouragement from Wesley, Richard Boardman and Joseph Pilmore (Jesse Lee spells his name "Pillmore") agreed in 1769 to accept an appointment in the New World. The conference from which they were sent also agreed to provide fifty pounds to assist in repaying the debt on the John Street building in New York City. Shortly after their arrival they too appealed to Wesley for more help, and in the 1770 Minutes of the Wesleyan Conference, the first in which "America" is listed among the places being served, two additional persons are named, Williams and King. The following year, the societies reported to the conference a membership of three hundred sixteen. Between 1769 and 1774 Wesley sent eight itinerants to America, but Asbury was the only one among them who fully committed himself to the work in America. The others were present in the colonies only for a time and returned to England.

From these modest beginnings the foundation was laid for the remarkable explosion of Methodism into American society. When the Methodist Episcopal Church was organized at the Christmas Conference held in Baltimore in 1784, it had almost fifteen thousand members. Eighty-four preachers served forty-six circuits, which were located mostly in New York, New Jersey, Maryland, and Virginia. From there it moved with even greater success onto the Western frontier, and by 1840 the Methodists were the largest Protestant denomination in America and its mainline religious body. Considering this rapid growth and geographic expansion during the first few decades of its existence, it is significant and surprising that American Methodism in different places, under a variety of leaders, and in a climate of rapid change did not fragment. And it was not because they did not exemplify the characteristic propensity of American religious organizations to divide. As Russell Richey has argued, divisions and/or near divisions constitute the story of virtually any denomination or denominational family, a fact Richey then demonstrates by a careful outline of the Methodist experience of them.[3] They were numerous, and some of them have been wrenching enough to give Methodists a great deal to overcome.

At the time of the American Revolution the Methodists were connected in the public mind with Tory sentiments associated with John Wesley, whose "Calm Address to our American Colonies" had called into question the loyalty of Methodists to the American cause and created considerable animosity. In addition to this unfavorable political climate, Methodism suffered a variety of internal disputes that threatened to divide it even before it was formally organized in 1784. Robert Strawbridge disregarded the strict prohibition of the first American Conference in 1773—and Wesley's own well-established practice—which required Methodists to receive the sacraments from the Church of England, defiantly administering the sacraments of baptism and the Lord's Supper in the societies under his direction. Eventually preachers in the South determined to organize themselves into a church and went so far as to ordain several of their number. Had Strawbridge and his supporters been successful in this effort, it is obvious that Methodism would either have been governed under a presbyterian system or one like that characteristic of the Moravians and United Brethren. It was a significant challenge, and recognized at the time by the preachers in the connection to pose a genuine threat to their unity. Francis Asbury marked the occasion of Strawbridge's passing by noting in his journal, "Upon the whole, I am inclined to think the Lord took him away in judgment, because he was in a way to do hurt to his cause. . . ."[4]

Richard Allen, in 1787, walked out of St. George's Methodist Church in Philadelphia to protest its treatment of African American members and began the African Methodist Episcopal Church. James O'Kelly demanded rights for preachers, protested the monarchical behavior of Asbury, and left in 1792 to form the Republican Methodists. O'Kelly, like Strawbridge, was potentially a leader of the connection. He was respected and had influence among the preachers. His appeal in 1792 for a more democratic form of church government clearly was in accord with the post-Revolutionary climate, and his protest of Asbury's autocratic style of leadership was attractive to many. But in the end, O'Kelly was not able to remove Asbury. Although William McKendree, the true successor to Asbury, followed O'Kelly out of the connection for a year, he never joined the Republican Methodists.

Despite all of this, Methodism spread across the land and grew to immense size without having its power or mission blunted by divisions. In part this success can be attributed to the organizational structure that was given by Wesley. It combined the features of strong central control with an infinite capacity for expansion. The itinerant system of ministry and the basic organization of bands, classes, societies, and conferences functioned to undergird the preaching of the doctrines of personal holiness and perfection. Wesley's practice of utilizing laypersons as itinerant preachers was well suited to the con-

16

ditions in America. This system could accommodate massive turnover in its ranks and still provide large numbers of preachers, able to go wherever people could be found, who were at home with those they sought to serve. Their theology and revival methods were compatible with the spirit of the new nation. Moreover, the population of the nation at the end of the Revolution, with its vast numbers of unchurched, provided a fertile field for a zealous group whose stated mission was to "reform the continent, and to spread scriptural holiness over these lands."

Francis Asbury, Craftsman of American Episcopacy

For all of the advantages that it brought from England, the linchpin of Methodism in America proved to be the itinerant general superintendency, and its form and practice were established and personified in the life and work of Francis Asbury. From the beginning the chief task of that episcopacy was to nourish and protect the itinerant system of ministry. Asbury established the functions of the episcopal office in American Methodism by his own example, and in a single act shifted the power of the connection to the hands of the body of its preachers. He more than any other single individual defined, administered, and defended the itinerant system. One of Asbury's biographers wrote:

> No other man exerted such constant, resistless pressure to establish the itinerancy; no other man gave so forceful an example of the thing itself. If one particular service of a life of singular devotion as father and founder of American Methodism were to be selected for its preeminent value, it would have to be . . . Asbury's success in persuading the preachers to itinerate.[5]

When Asbury successfully forced the preachers out of their more comfortable surroundings in the cities, they extended "the work into the country towns and villages"[6] where the denomination was eventually to have its greatest influence. He was committed to this from the time he arrived. While still in New York he observed, "I judge we are to be shut up in the cities this winter. My brethren seem unwilling to leave the cities, but I think I shall show them the way."[7] Asbury "not only had the genius to lead, but he had the will to govern."[8] Frank Baker describes him correctly as the "master craftsman of American Methodism."[9] Without his forceful presence, long tenure,

17

and constant movement through the conferences in the three decades after the church was organized in 1784, powerful forces led by influential preachers, generated by a desire for democratic reform and sectional interests, might have overcome and scattered the connection.

Francis Asbury (b. August 1745) joined John Wesley's Methodist revival as a local preacher in 1766. At the Conference of 1771 in Bristol, Asbury and four others offered themselves for service in America. Only he and Richard Wright were chosen. Both were young; Asbury, the more senior in experience, had only four years in the conference. None of the preachers Wesley sent or authorized to go to America in these early years were ordained.[10] Traveling with Wright, Asbury landed in Philadelphia on 27 October 1771 to begin work.[11] He was never to return again to England. A year later Wesley named him "assistant in America" and urged him to be attentive to the "discipline" of the church.[12] Historian Nathan Bangs is mistaken when he writes that Wesley here named Asbury a "general assistant" and thereby "constituted him the head of the preachers and societies in America, with power to station the preachers under the general direction of Mr. Wesley himself."[13] This happened later. Lee tells us in his historical account that the person designated "assistant" in America was generally the oldest or senior preacher in a circuit.[14] This designation was more appropriate to Asbury's level of responsibility. Only later was he actually given authority over all the Methodist work in America and functioned in the role of a "general assistant." With respect to enforcing discipline, about which Wesley was most concerned, Asbury failed to satisfy Wesley's expectations, and the following year he was replaced by Thomas Rankin, who had a reputation as a disciplinarian. It is hard to imagine what Methodism would have become with Rankin as its leader. He was older than Asbury, senior to him in experience, and had worked directly with Wesley. He came to America with the expanded title of "general assistant." In English Methodism, that title designated the preacher who was in charge of all the circuits and who had power to appoint others to their stations without himself being located in a specific appointment. Rankin's actions made it abundantly clear that he understood his authority from Wesley in this way.

Immediately upon his arrival in 1773 he gathered the preachers in the connection at St. George's Church in Philadelphia and held the first Methodist conference in America.[15] Asbury, who arrived at the conference a day late, called it a "general conference," the first time the designation was used. This was to distinguish it from the regular "quarterly conference" and to indicate that all the preachers were invited to attend.

Rankin, a Scotsman converted under the preaching of George Whitefield, first decided to become a minister in the Church of Scotland. Unable, for lack of funds, to secure the necessary university education required for ordination as a Presbyterian, he went to work for an Edinburgh firm, which in the late 1750s sent him as its agent to Charleston, South Carolina. It was while on leave at home in Edinburgh in 1761 that he heard John Wesley preach and offered himself for service with the Methodists.

Rankin worked for eleven years as an itinerant preacher assigned to circuits before Wesley sent him to oversee the work in America. Following closely his mandate from Wesley to establish discipline and perhaps the allegiance of the Americans to the founder, Rankin attempted to ensure that the societies followed the rules laid down by Wesley for both members and preachers. The conference under Rankin's leadership reaffirmed its loyalty to Wesley and agreed to follow his practice of not administering the sacraments. This clarification, as has already been noted, was necessitated by the practice of Robert Strawbridge in Maryland, who, despite being warned to cease, continued giving the Lord's Supper to the members of his flock and refused to stop. The issue was an old and divisive one on both sides of the Atlantic, exacerbated by Wesley's determination for Methodists not to separate from the Church of England. In the long run, Rankin's discipline may have been effective and useful to the growing societies, but the immediate result was a sizable exodus of both members and preachers from the fold. Of sixty traveling preachers in the connection when Rankin arrived, only twenty-eight remained in 1778, including ten who joined that year. And as might have been predicted, he was soon in conflict with Asbury. When Rankin refused to appoint him to Baltimore in 1774, Asbury appealed directly to Wesley. Wesley supported Rankin and told Asbury it would be best for him to return to England. When Asbury failed to appear, Wesley renewed his directive to come home but confided to Rankin, "I am not sorry that Brother Asbury stays with you another year." Perhaps Wesley knew that getting Asbury back to England would not be easy, and he may have had mixed feelings about having him around anyway. One of the reasons that Asbury never returned to England even for a visit was that he, and later the American Methodists, feared Wesley might not allow him to come back to America. Asbury was not fond of Rankin but at least had the grace to say of him, "He will not be admired as a preacher. But as a disciplinarian, he will fill his place."[16] Rankin clearly could not command enough popular support to be a viable leader for Wesley's flock in America.

In 1775 Wesley created great animosity for himself and his followers in America by publishing a wildly popular paraphrase of Samuel Johnson's "Taxation no Tyranny" under the title "A Calm Address to Our American Colonies." It sold one hundred thousand copies. The basis for Wesley's "calm" advice was his conviction that the Americans were not being treated differently from other British subjects and therefore had no cause for their complaints about taxes. His advice was for them to get on with the business of being loyal subjects of the Crown. Patriotic sentiment like that which prompted the Boston Tea Party in December 1773 ran strongly against his advice and often directed its disapproval at Wesley's followers in the colonies. This led Asbury to lament: "I . . . am truly sorry that the venerable man ever dipped into the politics of America."[17]

Asbury's difficulties with Rankin were finally resolved when, on the eve of the American Revolution, Rankin and the other preachers sent by Wesley to America returned to England, leaving Asbury alone in the colonies. After experiencing the increasing threat of persecution from loyalists, Asbury decided to "lye by at Thomas White's, in the Delaware state, where he shut himself up."[18] In that place he had the added advantage of not having to take the state oath of allegiance. Asbury went into seclusion on 10 March 1778 and confessed a few days later in his journal, "I was under some heaviness of mind. But it was no wonder:—three thousand miles from home,—my friends have left me—; I am considered by some as an enemy of the country;—every day liable to be seized by violence, and abused."[19] Despite being unable to travel or preach for over a year, his influence and leadership continued, especially among the northern preachers. The situation was different, however, in the South.

Consolidating Asbury's Power

In 1779 two conferences were held. The regular session was scheduled to convene on 18 May at the Broken Back Church in

Fluvanna County, Virginia.[20] But a group of northern preachers loyal to Asbury, plus William Watters, the oldest American preacher and the presiding officer at the 1778 session of the conference, gathered in "irregular" session earlier in April at White's and resolved "that brother Asbury ought to act as general assistant in America."[21] The gathering was held in anticipation of the challenge that would come from the southern wing of the connection. In anticipation of questions about why this "Delaware Conference" was held, Lee described their gathering as "preparatory to the conference in Virginia."[22] The *Minutes* of the meeting list the following reasons why Asbury should be recognized as general assistant: "1st, on account of his age; 2d, because originally appointed by Mr. Wesley; 3d, being joined with Messrs. Rankin and Shadford, by express order from Mr. Wesley."[23] With the exception of Watters, none of the preachers who attended the meeting with Asbury went to Virginia for the regular session of the conference. They were opposed to the administration of the sacraments in Methodist societies, and considered themselves faithful followers of Wesley and the ways of "old" Methodism. But they constituted only a small segment of Methodism. Bishop Neely correctly describes Asbury's conference as "irregular, if not absolutely illegal."[24] Richey argues that "far more of the thematic agenda of Methodism flows through . . . Fluvanna, than Methodism's historians have been willing to concede."[25]

The regular conference in Virginia, which Asbury was unable to attend, did not affirm his leadership. Instead, it challenged the established practice of Methodists in America, and Wesley's authority, by deciding to continue the administration of the sacraments. This southern conference, presided over by Philip Gatch, "represented the majority of the circuits, preachers, and members of the American Methodists. Ignoring the action of the northern conference, it elected a new committee of supervision and established a presbytery to administer the ordinances and to ordain other approved preachers."[26] The committee of supervision, composed of Philip Gatch, James Foster, Le Roy Cole, and Reuben Ellis, first ordained themselves elders and then ordained others who had been selected by the conference. The seriousness of this innovation was not lost on anyone. Jesse Lee knew that although they considered themselves loyal Methodists in connection with John Wesley, "they had practically formed a temporary Presbyterian Church." He goes on to say, "There was great cause to fear a division, and both parties trembled for the ark of God, and shuddered at the thought of dividing the church of Christ."[27] According to Neely, the southern preachers did not desire a division in American Methodism.[28] However, they thought that their action was essential to the mission of Methodism in the South. Aside from their wanting to receive the sacraments in their own congregations, the Revolutionary War had diminished the presence of the Church of England, and it was impractical—if not impossible—for Methodists to receive the sacraments from Anglican priests even if they had preferred it.

The action of the preachers in Virginia was deplored by their counterparts in the North, who met again the next year in another irregular "conference before the conference." At this meeting, Asbury, who was now free to travel, was delegated to try to work out a compromise.[29] In the company of Freeborn Garrettson and William Watters, he set out for Manakintown in Virginia to meet the conference when it opened on 8 May 1780. He read to them Wesley's thoughts on separating from the Church of England and proposed that for one year they suspend the measures they had taken.[30] After making his presentation, he adjourned to his lodgings to await their decision. It was not an easy proposal to accept, for some of the most prominent members of the connection were in favor of administering the sacraments and had good reasons for doing it. "After an hour's conference," Asbury reported, "we were called to receive their answer, which was, they could not submit to the terms of the union." There was no choice but to accept the decision and Asbury said he left the meeting "under the heaviest cloud I ever felt in America."[31] The last word, however, was yet to be spoken. Whether due to Asbury's powers of persuasion, a fear of dividing the connection, the gracious and conciliatory spirit of his Virginia colleagues, or (as Asbury claimed) the power of prayer, Asbury's plan "took with the Virginia preachers, and they consented to the proposal."[32] Asbury's journal does not tell us why the preachers changed their minds and accepted this compromise, only that he was surprised they did so. Perhaps he did not know the reason. He had been getting ready to return to the North and learned of their decision only when he went by the conference to say good-bye, leading him to reflect, "Surely the hand of God has been greatly seen in all of this."[33] Neely says that Edward Dromgoole acted as a mediator in the dispute, and the journal of William Watters, who was present for the discussion, reports that the original proposal was changed to give it two provisions instead of one. The first was to suspend the ordinances for a year in order to allow time to seek John Wesley's advice. The second was that in the interim they would agree to request Asbury to superintend the work as a whole in order to promote unity. "The proposal in a few minutes took with all but a few."[34] Shortly thereafter, the conferences returned to the practice of meeting together, and in 1782 the first reunited conference gave an affirmative answer to the question "Do the brethren in conference unanimously choose brother Asbury to act according to Mr. Wesley's original appointment, and preside over the American conference, and the whole work?"[35] With this affirmation, Asbury emerged as the leader of American Methodism.

After the American Revolution

By now the situation in America was improving. The actual fighting in the Revolutionary War ceased with the surrender of General Cornwallis at Yorktown on 19 October 1781. Although the Treaty of Paris was not signed until two years later, life in the colonies returned to normal, and Asbury's ability to travel through the connection strengthened his authority. Wesley added the weight of his influence by sending word that anyone coming from England or Europe to work in America ought to be approved by Asbury and agree to be subject to the American Conference. He added, "I do not wish our American brethren to receive any who make any difficulty of receiving *Francis Asbury* as the General Assistant."[36] There had been problems with certain individuals coming to America who were unwilling to be subject to the discipline of the conference, and by his letter Wesley gave explicit approval of the regulations contained in the American *Minutes*, and made them binding upon any who would preach in America. He also reaffirmed his earlier appointment of Francis Asbury as the general assistant in America. By the time the societies were ready to organize themselves into a church in 1784, Asbury was recognized both by the preachers and officially by John Wesley as the leader of the connection.[37] Asbury remained the undisputed leader of the Methodists in America until his death in March 1816. The amount of work he did and the example he set by doing it are little short of astounding. Nathan Bangs claimed that in forty-five years of ministry in America, Asbury traveled two hundred seventy thousand miles, mostly on horseback, preached sixteen thousand four hundred twenty-five sermons, and ordained more than four thousand ministers. In the process, he crossed the Alleghenies sixty times and established the Methodist Episcopal Church in America.[38]

At the close of the American Revolution the Methodists were in a critical situation. It was clear to everyone that they could not continue to exist, much less hope to fulfill their mission of spreading scriptural holiness through the land, without being organized into an independent church with full authority to function as a church. They could not expect to receive significant numbers of their preachers from England. Even Wesley himself was understandably reluctant to offer encouragement to persons wishing to come to America. He wrote to James Barry in July 1784, "It is an invariable rule with me not to require any one to go over to America—nay, I scruple even to advise them to it."[39] The societies in the newly formed United States of America were now separated from the conference in England and Wesley was persuaded the time had come to provide them with the only thing they yet lacked: ordination and the power to administer the sacraments. Whatever else John Wesley may have been, he was pragmatic. He would do what had to be done to safeguard their mission.

CHAPTER 2

Wesley's Ordination for America

Following the end of the American Revolution, with the signing of the Treaty of Paris, Asbury appealed to Wesley on behalf of persons under Methodist care who remained unbaptized and had not received the sacrament of the Lord's Supper in years. In order to minister to them, he asked Wesley to give his preachers in America the power to complete the organization of an independent church by providing them with an ordained ministry. Since it was not the first time such an appeal had been made, and given the situation in America, Wesley could not have been surprised by the request. He had in fact discussed the American Methodists with Thomas Coke during the fall and winter of 1783–84. At least by early 1784 Wesley was convinced that his followers in the new nation had to be given separate and independent status.[1] There was no longer any way American Methodists could be expected to operate as societies dependent upon the ministry of the now banished Church of England or on the Methodists in England.

The Need and Basis for Ordination in America

The Methodist societies in America already embodied two marks of a Christian church: (1) they were congregations of faithful men and women, in which (2) there was the preaching of the pure word of God. Wesley determined to supply the societies with the other two marks: holy orders, to provide for an ordained ministry; and the sacraments.[2]

Wesley's chief adviser in this decision was Thomas Coke. Coke, the child of an affluent family, had been born in Wales. At five feet one inch tall, two inches shorter than Wesley, Coke was a likable individual whose contribution to the growth of Methodism in America may be undervalued. He was educated at Oxford where he took a degree in civil law, and eventually was ordained a priest in the Church of England. Coke first met Wesley in 1776. After being dismissed from his position as a curate in Sommersetshire he joined the Methodists, serving in the London Circuit. In a short time he won Wesley's confidence and, in addition to other duties, directed the Tract Society, which printed and distributed free literature. Drawing on his knowledge of the law, Coke helped Wesley draw up the "Deed of Declaration," which provided for a legal center of authority for the movement after Wesley's death. The Deed established the "conference" as a legally defined body of named preachers. And Coke was behind the early efforts to initiate foreign mission projects in Africa and the East Indies.

Wesley told Coke in February 1784 that he wished to ordain him for leadership in America.[3] His reasons for taking the step that effectively separated the Methodists in America from the Church of England were practical and specific: (1) the Revolution had forever divided England and America; (2) the Episcopal establishment was abolished; (3) the Methodist societies were in a deplorable condition; and (4) Asbury had appealed to him to provide a form of church government suited to their needs, and Wesley was willing to assist them.[4] Writing on the subject a year later, Wesley said,

> But since the late revolution in North America, these have been in great distress. The Clergy [of the Church of England], having no sustenance, either from England, or from the American States, have been obliged almost universally to leave the country, and seek their food elsewhere. Hence those who had been members of the Church, had none either to administer the Lord's supper, or to baptize their children. They applied to England over and over; but it was to no purpose. Judging this to be a case of real necessity, I took a step which, for peace and quietness, I had refrained from taking for many years.[5]

He might have added, as he did in his "Letter to the Brethren in America" (10 September 1784), that he had unsuccessfully approached the bishop of London, Robert Lowith, who had jurisdiction over the colonies, about providing ordination to Methodist preachers there.[6] The bishop, he said, "peremptorily refused it. All the other bishops were of the same mind; the rather because (they said) they had nothing to do with America."[7] "It's not my problem" is the modern version of their reply.

Wesley spoke to confidants of his plan to ordain persons for work in America at the July 1784 meeting of the English Conference in Leeds. One of these confidants was John Pawson, who remembered: "The preachers were astonished when this was mentioned, and to a man opposed it. But I plainly saw that it would be done, as Mr. Wesley's mind appeared to be quite made up."[8] Wesley did not consult his brother Charles, for he knew without speaking to him that Charles would be strongly opposed. Wesley also appealed for volunteers to serve in America at the Leeds meeting, and chose Richard Whatcoat and Thomas Vasey from those who came forward. Coke, who had been ordained a priest in the Church of England in 1772, was at first lukewarm to the idea of receiving ordination as a general superintendent for America, but gradually accepted it and wrote Wesley:

> The more maturely I consider the subject, the more expedient it appears to me that the power of ordaining others should be received by me from you, by the imposition of your hands; and that you should lay hands on brother Whatcoat and brother Vasey for the following reasons: (1) It seems to me the most scriptural way, and most agreeable to the practice of the primitive churches. (2) I may want all the influence, in America, which you can throw into my scale.[9]

Coke's reference to the likelihood that he would need support in America is explained in the same letter. "Mr. Brackenbury informed me at Leeds that he saw a letter from Mr. Asbury, in which he observed that he would not receive any person deputed by you with any part of the superintendency of the work invested in him, or words which evidently implied so much."[10]

The First Ordinations

Any concerns raised by speculation about Asbury's response did not long deter either Wesley or Coke. The ordinations took place in

27

Bristol on 1 and 2 September 1784. With the assistance of James Creighton, Coke and Wesley ordained Vasey and Whatcoat deacons the first day, and elders the next. The second day Coke, already a priest, was given authority, through the laying on of Wesley's hands, to exercise administrative leadership as a "superintendent" in America. The meaning of this term is likely that of "overseer of the whole," which is how Wesley defined the office of bishop.[11] When Charles heard what his brother had done, which to him was nothing less than the separation from the Church of England, what he had long feared, he expressed his displeasure in a few lines of a now-famous verse:

> So easily are Bishops made
> By man's, or woman's whim?
> W[esley] his hands on C[oke] hath laid,
> But who laid hands on Him?[12]

The more moderate expression of Charles's disapproval is found in a long letter to Dr. Chandler, an Anglican priest on his way to America, dated 28 April 1785.

> I can scarcely yet believe it, that, in his eighty-second year, my broth-er, my old, intimate friend and companion, should have assumed the episcopal character, ordained Elders, consecrated a Bishop, and sent him to ordain our lay-Preachers in America! I was then in Bristol, at his elbow; yet he never gave me the least hint of his intention. How was he surprised into so rash an action? He certainly persuaded himself that it was right.[13]

In a postscript appended to the same letter, Charles offers his opinion that the Methodists in America were nothing more than "a new sect of Presbyterians" and predicted that after his brother's death "they will lose all their influence and importance; they will turn aside to vain janglings; they will settle again upon their lees; and, like other sects of Dissenters, come to nothing!"[14]

Charles was convinced that John could not, or simply would not, see his ordinations for America as separation from the Church of England. He also mistrusted Coke and was afraid Coke had used his brother to further his own ambitions. In a letter written in 1785, after the ordinations, Charles responded to John's earlier question of him: "What then are you frighted at?"[15] "At the Doctor's rashness,"

28

Charles replied, "and your supporting him in his ambitious pursuits; at an approaching schism, as causeless and unprovoked as the American rebellion."[16]

While Charles may or may not have been correct in believing his brother was being used or was simply unwilling to see the consequences of his actions, it is clear that John Wesley had determined, to his own satisfaction, that ordination of persons for America was necessary, right, and within the scope of his powers as a presbyter in the Church of England. He saw no alternative but to put the Methodists in America on an independent footing.

On 18 September 1784 Wesley's three newly ordained and commissioned emissaries sailed from Bristol and headed for America. For Coke, this was the first of nine trips in the span of twenty years to the United States (and he would die at sea on yet one more voyage headed to India). Since their mission was to establish a separate church in America, Wesley sent with his preachers a set of Articles of Religion (modified from the Anglican Thirty-nine Articles), an abridgement of the *Book of Common Prayer* (which he called the *Sunday Service for the Methodists in North America*), and *A Collection of Psalms and Hymns for the Lord's Day.* "They are now at full liberty," Wesley said in his accompanying letter to "Our Brethren in America," "simply to follow the Scriptures and the Primitive Church"; and, in a final benediction, he admonished them to "stand fast in that liberty wherewith God has so strangely made them free."[17] Ironically, one of the first ways that the American church exercised its liberty was in basically laying aside the *Sunday Service*—despite, or perhaps partly because of, Coke's staunch advocacy of it.

It is hard to imagine why William Warren Sweet, in his *Methodism in America History*, argues that Wesley did not intend to begin a new church in America. This assumes that Wesley was less aware of the situation in America, and of the implications of his own actions, than seems likely. It is true that Wesley continued to maintain his loyalty to the Church of England until the end of his life. He could hardly have been unaware that what he had done would result in the creation of a church, free and independent of the Church of England. (Of course, he may have been less aware of how soon its preachers would also assert their independence from his authority.)[18] Wesley's claims about the ordinations for America must be classed with his protests that he had not varied from the Church of England "in one article either of doctrine or discipline." Both must be balanced by

29

Wesley's concession that he had made a number of innovations over the years that severely diminished Methodist ties with the Church of England.

> We have in a course of years, out of necessity, not choice, slowly and warily varied in some points of discipline, by preaching in the fields, by extemporary prayer, by employing lay preachers, by forming and regulating societies, and by holding yearly Conferences. But we did none of these things till we were convinced we could no longer omit them but at the peril of our souls.[19]

Norman Spellman states it clearly and correctly: "John Wesley deliberately inaugurated a Church in America."[20]

Wesley's Theological Rationale for the Ordinations

Despite his pragmatism, necessity and compelling urgency might not have been sufficient to convince a man like Wesley to assume the powers of a bishop and ordain preachers for a new church in America. He required a theological rationale for doing it as well. The ordinations came near the end of a lifetime of theological reflection and change, during which Wesley became convinced that he, a presbyter in the Church of England, could legally exercise the power of ordination normally reserved to bishops. One of his early biographers says that "his right to ordain . . . was no new assumption. . . . It was a firm conviction of forty years standing."[21] But it is clear that in so doing Wesley broke with a long-standing interpretation of episcopacy that had dominated the practice of the Church of England, of which he claimed to be a loyal minister. It is hard to imagine that he was not fully aware of the gravity of his action.

In his letter to "Our Brethren in America," Wesley notes that "Lord King's *Account of the Primitive Church* convinced me many years ago that bishops and presbyters are the same order, and consequently have the same right to ordain."[22] For one who considered himself a loyal member of the Church of England and of the "high church" persuasion, this was a significant change. Wesley first read Peter King's *Inquiry into the Constitution, Discipline, Unity, and Worship of the Primitive Church* (London, 1691) in January 1746.[23] The challenge of King's argument to Wesley's existing beliefs is evident from a letter he wrote just weeks earlier defending apostolic succession to

Westley Hall, his brother-in-law, who was disgruntled with both the Methodists and the Church of England. In this letter Wesley easily affirmed:

> We believe it would not be right for us to administer either Baptism or the Lord's Supper unless we had a commission so to do from those bishops whom we apprehend to be in a *succession* from the apostles. ... We believe that the threefold order of ministers ... is not only authorized by its "apostolical institution," but also by the "written Word."[24]

It is significant that Wesley claims never to have modified the position he took after reading Peter King. The seed of this idea, planted four decades earlier, finally germinated and matured in American Methodism in their concept of bishops as elders (presbyters) consecrated to a higher "office" rather than as a third order of ministry.

In addition to King, Wesley's thinking was influenced by reading Edward Stillingfleet's *Irenicum, or Pacificator: Being a Reconciler as to Church Differences* (London, 1659). Bishop Stillingfleet, attempting to find middle ground between the Puritans and the Church of England, argued that no particular form of church government was required by Scripture. On reading him, Wesley judged that "he has unanswerably proved that neither Christ or His Apostles prescribed any particular form of Church government, and that the plea for the divine right of Episcopacy was never heard of in the primitive Church."[25]

The Puritans had argued that the single proper form of church government was given in Scripture and that no true church could exist without it. They identified form of government as of the *esse* (very being), not just the *bene esse* (well-being), of the church. In his search for the middle ground where agreement could be found, Stillingfleet identified three general principles that should inform and regulate any form of church government:

> [1] that prudence must be used in settling the government of the church. .... This hath been the whole design of this treatise, to prove that the form of church government is a mere matter of prudence, regulated by the word of God; [2] that form of government is the best according to principles of Christian prudence, which comes the nearest to apostolical practice, and tends most to the advancing the peace and unity of the church of God; [3] the determining of the form of government is a matter of liberty in the church.[26]

31

Stillingfleet's argument had convinced Wesley. On 3 July 1756 he wrote:

> As to my own judgment, I still believe "the Episcopal form of Church government to be both scriptural and apostolical": I mean, well agreeing with the practice and writings of the Apostles. But that it is prescribed in Scripture I do not believe. This opinion (which I once heartily espoused) I have been heartily ashamed of ever since I read Dr. Stillingfleet's *Irenicon* [sic].[27]

Stillingfleet also advanced a claim about ordination that would be crucial to Wesley's eventual decision to offer it. In standard Anglican practice, there was one ordination of presbyters to convey the power of "order" (the right to do sacraments), and a further ordination of bishops to convey the power of "jurisdiction" (supervision of the larger church, including the right to ordain). Stillingfleet found warrant only for a single ordination, which would convey both the power of "order" and the power of "jurisdiction." While he argued for retaining the restriction of the right to ordain to those in jurisdiction, it was again now more on prudential grounds:

> For our better understanding of this, we must consider a twofold power belonging to church officers, *a power of order*, and *a power of jurisdiction*; for in every *presbyter*, there are some things inseparably joined to his function, and belonging to every one in his personal capacity . . . both as to the *right* and *power* to do it, and the *exercise* and *execution* of that power; such are preaching the word, visiting the sick, administering sacraments, etc. But there are other things which every presbyter hath an aptitude, and *jus* to, in *actu promo*, but the limitation and exercise of that power doth belong to the church in common, and belongs not to any one personally, but by a further power of choice or delegation to it; such is the power of visiting churches, taking care that particular pastors discharge their duty; such is the power of ordination and church censures, and making rules for decency in the church; this is what we call the *power of jurisdiction*.[28]

The potential implication of Stillingfleet's position is that there are the *power* and *right* for anyone who has been ordained to offer ordination, given sufficient prudential considerations. That Wesley recognized this implication is clear from a letter he wrote to his brother Charles in June 1780: "Read Bishop Stillingfleet's *Irenicon* [sic] or any impartial history of the Ancient Church, and I believe you will think as I do. I verily believe I have as good a right to ordain as to administer the Lord's supper. But I see abundance of reasons why I should not use that right, unless I was turned out of the Church."[29]

Stillingfleet's implication echoes in Wesley's defense of his continuing loyalty to the Church of England shortly after ordaining Coke, Whatcoat, and Vasey for work in America: "I am now as firmly attached to the Church of England as I ever was since you knew me. But meantime I know myself to be as real a Christian bishop as the Archbishop of Canterbury. Yet I always resolved, and am so still, never to act as such except in case of necessity."[30]

Henry Rack, Wesley's recent biographer, disparages the idea that Wesley was convinced by King and Stillingfleet's arguments, while admitting that Wesley was often inclined to reach and act on unorthodox conclusions after reading just one book. Rack believes it is more likely that Wesley used respectable authorities to fortify or justify positions he wished to hold for other reasons. He correctly notes that Wesley did nothing in the 1740s and 1750s based on the alleged influence of either King or Stillingfleet, leading Rack to conclude that "they were only used for apologetic purposes in the 1780s to support actions he had decided to take for practical and not theological reasons."[31]

There can be no doubt that Wesley was determined above all else to meet the needs of his flock in the new American nation, and to assist them, as he was able, in their mission of reforming the continent and spreading scriptural holiness in the land. At the same time he was deeply committed to adherence to the practice of the early church, so far as possible, as he understood it. As such, Frank Baker seems justified in taking at face value Wesley's claims about the influence of his earlier study upon his decision to ordain:

> Based on his study of the primitive church, Wesley claimed that for the first two hundred years the presbyters of the Alexandrian church had ordained as bishop one of themselves rather than dilute their ecclesiastical purity by seeking aid from a foreign bishop. . . . Wesley himself was not only a presbyter with a presbyter's inherent right to perform the office of the presiding presbyter or bishop; by his extraordinary call to found and rule the Methodist societies it had been demonstrated that in function he was the equivalent of a scriptural bishop. . . . Both in *ordine* and *gradus* he was a scriptural *episcopos*.[32]

33

Luke Tyerman, another of Wesley's biographers, suggests that Wesley might also have been influenced near the time of his decision by the actions of members of the Countess of Huntingdon Connection, who stood in the same relation to the Church of England, as did Wesley's Methodists. Some of her chapels, like some of Wesley's, were supplied by ordained priests of the Church of England. Their claim was that "they varied, not dissented, from the Church." However, two of them were cited in a civil suit for "their irregularity in preaching in a place not episcopally consecrated, and for carrying on Divine worship there, contrary to the wish of the minister of the parish"; they were found guilty. After the verdict was sustained in the ecclesiastical courts, they became subject to prosecution and had to suspend their services in the chapels of the Countess. Eventually the Countess and her leaders determined that two persons should formally secede from the Church of England, place themselves under the protection of the Act of Toleration, "and should take upon themselves to ordain others." This was done, and on 9 March 1783 they proceeded to ordain six persons. Tyerman highlights the fact that "during the service, Mr. Wills addressed the congregation, and assigned his reasons for believing that he had the right to ordain, namely, that presbyters and bishops were the same order, and that, as he and Mr. Taylor had been ordained presbyters, they had really been ordained bishops and had as much right to ordain others as any bishop in the land."[33]

There was a significant difference, however, between Wesley and the New Connection of the Countess. Her chapel in Spa Fields had been registered as a dissenting house of worship, a step that Wesley refused to take with his own chapels. Although Wesley's ordinations were irregular, to say the least, he was more comfortable standing on what he regarded as valid and ancient tradition and practice than in accepting the relief he might have gained by acknowledging any form of dissent.

Once having taken the step for America, Wesley ordained three persons for work in Scotland in 1785. He defended this action by claiming that the church in Scotland, like the one in America, was not under the Church of England. He did not finally ordain persons for work in England until 1788, but by that time it was clear that every action necessary to enable all Methodists to continue as independent organizations after Wesley's death had already been taken. These ordinations did little to change the situation, and they did not enable the Methodists in England to avoid serious controversy over their relation to the Established Church after Wesley's death.

There is no escaping the fact that Wesley himself functioned for those in his connection as a bishop when measured by his exercise of the traditional tasks of the office. Since the time of Leo the Great, who was pope from 440 to 461 C.E., in addition to their sacramental powers, bishops had exercised the responsibility to judge, administer, and teach in the church. Wesley's leadership at various times clearly embodied all three of these. He was the author of the rules of the societies and the final judge in their application, it was he who devised an administrative structure for the societies and oversaw it throughout his entire life, and he was the supreme teacher and interpreter of doctrine and theology among the Methodists. By means of his writings, sermons, and personal example, he taught the meaning of Methodism and gave definitive expression to its theological self-understanding. He was its bishop.

It is more difficult to estimate the degree to which he served as the model of episcopal practice for Coke and Asbury. No person could assume Wesley's role among the Methodists in either America or England. Frank Baker describes Asbury as Wesley's "episcopal apprentice," and makes it clear that in the first third of Asbury's life he learned much from his association with Wesley and from those who had learned from him.[34] Asbury read widely from Wesley's writings and learned from him the methods of successful evangelism and the workings of the itinerant system of ministry. There is no question, however, that he went beyond anything he had learned from Wesley in adapting all of the methods to suit the Methodists in America. "Yet the apprenticeship was certainly of inestimable influence, probably of inestimable worth. Without it Asbury could never have learned Wesley's spirit and methods; without these American Methodism could not have developed as it did—might never have developed at all."[35] It must also be said that in moving beyond anything he found in Wesley, especially in the area of episcopal administrative practice, Asbury created a new and innovative understanding of episcopacy that matured and flourished in America. It was this that established him forever in a unique place among American Methodists, not unlike the place occupied by Wesley in English Methodism.

Ironically, Wesley provided more adequately for the future of the church in America and Scotland than he did for the Methodist Connection in England. Immediately following his death, a controversy arose among British Methodists, similar to the one that threatened the unity of American Methodism following the end of the American Revolution, created by the increasing demand from both preachers and laypersons to allow the Lord's Supper to be administered in their chapels. The first conference after Wesley's death, in July 1791, passed a vague and general resolution to "follow the plan of Wesley." Since there was, however, no agreement among them about that plan, this did nothing to prevent a conflict. As had happened in America, senior preachers in the connection began to ordain persons without the consent of the conference. In 1792, rules had to be passed that forbade both ordinations without the consent of the conference, and the administration of the Lord's Supper in any of the societies with the exception of those in London. Moreover, it was stipulated that services were not to be held in Methodist chapels during "church hours." The process used in the conference to decide whether to administer the sacrament is interesting. After debating the subject thoroughly and finding themselves unable to reach a consensus, the conference members cast lots, and all agreed to abide by the results. "Mr. Adam Clarke was then called on to draw the lot, which was, 'You shall not administer the sacrament in the ensuing year.' All were satisfied. All submitted. All was peace. Every countenance seemed to testify that every heart said, 'It is the Lord: let Him do what seemeth Him good.'"[36]

Despite the claims of peace and unity, in the following year the number of societies demanding to receive the Lord's Supper from their preachers increased. In addition, there was a new controversy about the use of titles, ministerial dress, and the distinctions between ordained and unordained preachers. The unresolved questions of the relation of the societies to the Church of England in turn raised suspicions about the loyalty of English Methodists to king and country—a very dangerous thing in England in 1793. A resolution was passed in conference that forbade the wearing of gowns, cassocks, bands, or surplices; proscribed the use of the title "reverend"; and stipulated that any distinction between ordained and unordained preachers should be dropped. A concession was made allowing any society whose members were unanimous in their desire for the sacrament to have it, but it had to be given in the evening only and according to the form of the Church of England. A letter to the members of the connection, signed by conference president John Pawson and by secretary Thomas Coke, once again affirmed "that we have no design or desire of making our Societies *separate churches*." It went on to say, "We have never sanctioned ordination in England either in this Conference or in any other, in any degree, nor ever attempted to do it."[37]

The number of societies desiring the sacraments from Methodist preachers was reported at the next meeting of the conference to be forty-five out of a total of one hundred thirty-eight circuits. The concessions made in the interest of promoting harmony served only to create dissension, and the controversy over the sacrament boiled until it came to a climax in 1794. Many members saw the innovations as a definite step toward final separation from the Church of England. Others, without particular loyalty to the Church of England, saw them as disloyal to Wesley. After a bitter struggle following the Conference of 1794, the Conference of 1795 drafted a "Plan of Pacification" that allowed a Methodist chapel to have the sacrament if a majority of trustees, stewards, and leaders all favored it. The same proviso applied to the administration of baptism, the burial of the dead, and the conducting of services during church hours. The ordinances were to be administered only by persons authorized by the conference, and only on Sunday evenings. If services were conducted during "church hours" on Sunday, the preacher "shall read either the service of the Established Church, our venerable father's abridgment, or, at least, the Lessons appointed by the Calendar."[38]

The differences between what Wesley allowed in America and his unwillingness or inability to address the issues surrounding the relation of Methodists in Great Britain to the Church of England serve clearly to illustrate the ambiguity that he felt on the subject. They also show the degree to which Wesley had come to believe that the ties between the Methodists in America and the Church of England, though never strong, had been forever cut by the Revolution and the creation of a new nation. He was sufficiently prescient to know that the successor to the Church of England, the Episcopal Church in America, could not fill the void either. He was clear in his belief that he had no choice but to resolve the matter for his American brothers and sisters, but he could not bring himself to do the same for England. In a real sense, British Methodists did not finally resolve their relation to the Established Church until 1836, when, for the first time, the conference began the practice of ordination using the traditional and ancient method of laying on of hands. Though the two bodies remain separated, talks about a possible reunion continue.

CHAPTER 3

American Episcopal Methodism

Coke and his newly ordained traveling companions, Vasey and Whatcoat, arrived in New York on 3 November 1784. After a brief stay in the city they set out for Philadelphia, where they expected to meet Asbury. The meeting actually took place on 14 November at Barratt's Chapel in Delaware.[1] Coke preached; after the sermon, his biographer reported he saw "a plainly dressed, robust, but venerable-looking man moving through the congregation and making his way to the pulpit; on ascending the pulpit, he clasped the doctor in his arms and, without making himself known by words, accosted him with the holy salutation of primitive Christianity. This venerable man was Mr. Asbury."[2]

Coke and Asbury, 1784

In his journal, Asbury related his surprise at seeing Whatcoat take the cup during the service and participate in the administration of the Lord's Supper.[3] He clearly was not yet aware of the exact news that Coke was bringing from Wesley. This was not because Coke had kept his mission a secret. He had discussed it in New York with John Dickins, who was stationed at the John Street Church. Dickins had assured Coke that Wesley's decision to enable the Methodists in

America to become a new and independent church would certainly meet Asbury's approval and urged him to make it public immediately. But Coke declined to follow this advice in favor of talking first with Asbury. He had never met Asbury and felt he owed him the courtesy of hearing the news before it was disseminated abroad.[4]

While Asbury was unaware of the exact content, he obviously anticipated that Coke was bringing some important announcement from Wesley. When he received the information that Coke had arrived and might be found at Barratt's Chapel, he contacted several preachers and requested them to gather for the occasion, in case Coke had anything of importance to communicate. After the service, when Coke made him aware of what Wesley had directed, Asbury immediately called together the preachers who had gathered. Eleven preachers joined him and Coke in the home of Mrs. Philip Barratt and were informed about the authority with which Coke was empowered, and the outlines of the plan with which he was entrusted. The response of this council of preachers to the news they received was to suggest that it would be prudent to schedule a conference as soon as the other preachers could be collected together from the various states.[5]

Asbury's description of this initial council sounds rather matter-of-fact: "The design of organizing the Methodists into an independent Episcopal Church was opened to the preachers present, and it was agreed to call a general conference, to meet at Baltimore the ensuing Christmas."[6] But the language of "opening" the matter to the preachers is significant. In effect, Asbury's response to Coke's plan to ordain him a general superintendent was to submit the proposal to the discretion of his preachers and their conference in a way that Wesley could never have imagined. Asbury went so far as to vow to this initial gathering that he would not move into the role of general superintendent unless it was the unanimous desire of the preachers at the proposed conference that he should "not act in the capacity I have hitherto done by Mr. Wesley's appointment."[7] By this one act, Wesley's independent and unique power over the church in America was ended.

Although there is no record of Coke's response, he must have been surprised by this turn of events, if not astonished. As Norman Spellman notes, Wesley's plan had not envisioned the creation of a conference of the American preachers to have authority over the new church. He "had intended that his superintendents should ordain whom they chose, and that they should be the sole ecclesiastical rulers, under himself, of both preachers and people in America."[8]

This meant that the role of those Wesley had chosen was roughly analogous to his own among the British Methodists. Yet for some reason Wesley thought the Methodists in America needed two general superintendents. The comparison with the situation in England is informative in this regard, since there were many more members in England and Wesley had never considered adding persons to assist him in his work as superintendent. The obvious explanation is probably the correct one. Even blessed with Wesley's authority, the preachers in America would never have been willing to serve under Coke alone. In addition to the fact that Asbury was the acknowledged and accepted leader of American Methodists, Coke was ill-suited to the task. As late as 1859, one of Coke's episcopal successors, Bishop James O. Andrew (MECS), could still reflect:

> I have often thought it was well for Methodism in this country that Bishop Coke returned to England and ceased his episcopal oversight of the American Church; for with all his acknowledged ability, zeal and piety, he did not understand the genius of the American people. He was an English gentleman, and could not very promptly accommodate himself to the circumstances of the Church in this country.[9]

Despite Wesley's apparent maneuvering, Asbury emerged to play a role in American Methodism that was unique and quite analogous to Wesley's in England. Although an adopted son, he had completely identified with America and was the right person at the right time for its leadership. Calling the preachers together in anticipation of Coke's arrival and agreeing in advance to abide by their decision for Asbury to lead are arguably the two most important steps taken by Asbury or anyone else in shaping American Methodism and its episcopacy.

What motivated him to do it? In the first place, he had little to lose. Of the preachers Wesley had sent to America, he was the only one who was still in the country. He was the unchallenged leader of the American Conference, and this position had been affirmed in a series of events prior to 1784. Although his initial appointment to superintend the work had come from Wesley, it had been ratified by the Americans. Given the choice of having Thomas Coke as the sole superintendent in America, it was unthinkable that the preachers

41

would reject Asbury. In turn, Asbury knew their affirmation would enhance his authority and independence vis-à-vis both Wesley and Coke.

But we should not ascribe too much to such strategic motives. It is not unreasonable to assume that after almost a decade and a half in America, Asbury had actually become convinced that the power in the connection properly resided in the body of preachers. In any case, as Bishop Neely notes, his act of submitting the question of his super-intendency to the traveling preachers

> conceded power to the Conference such as it never possessed before, and, whatever may be thought of his motive, the Church owes much to Asbury for this act. Even if his purpose was to strengthen his own personal power, its effect was the destruction of supreme personal government on the part of Wesley, Coke, Asbury, or any other individual. It destroyed personal government and placed the governing power in the Conference.[10]

The unexpected organization of the Christmas Conference called an American Conference into existence, granting it independence from Wesley and the English Conference.[11] As Richey has said, "As for Asbury the bishop, so also for The Methodist Episcopal Church as a whole, power and authority derived both from Wesley and from the existing American conference."[12] From this moment on, exercised through the Conference, the supreme power in American Methodism was lodged in the body of traveling preachers. Over the years that power has been delegated to bishops, to the General Conference, and even shared with laypersons, but there is no question that from 1784 to the present it finally resides with the body of preachers.

The Christmas Conference, 1784

Asbury sent Freeborn Garrettson to summon the preachers to gather in Baltimore at Christmastime 1784 for what has come to be known as the "Christmas Conference." Although he rode twelve hundred miles in six weeks, Garrettson was never able to resist the temptation to stop and preach along the way; therefore a number of preachers failed to get the word. One of them was Jesse Lee. Writing of Garrettson with some frustration, Lee said, "Being fond of preaching by the way, and thinking he could do the business by writing, he did not give timely notice to the preachers who were in the extremities of the work; and of course several of them were not at that conference."[13] Lee did not receive the call to the conference until 12 December. When it came, he was in poor health and five hundred miles from Baltimore, so he decided not to attend.

To fill the interim before the conference, Asbury organized a preaching tour for Coke that covered a thousand miles. Asbury sent with him Harry Hosier, known as "Black Harry," a local preacher who knew the way and who could preach to African Americans. Vasey and Whatcoat accompanied Asbury himself, preaching through western Maryland.

The Christmas Conference assembled in Baltimore in late December 1784.[14] It remained in session for ten days. Although all eighty-one preachers in the connection were eligible to attend, Coke reports that "nearly sixty" were actually present. While no journal of the proceedings was kept, everyone knows what was accomplished. As Jesse Lee later summarized it, "We formed ourselves into a regular church, by the name of *The Methodist Episcopal Church*; making at the same time the Episcopal office elective, and the elected superintendant [sic] amenable to the body of ministers and preachers."[15]

Before the gathered preachers took action to create an independent organization for America, the first order of business was to affirm their allegiance to Wesley.

Quest. 2. What can be done in order to the future union of the Methodists?

Ans. During the life of the Rev. Mr. Wesley, we acknowledge ourselves his sons in the gospel, ready in matters belonging to church-government, to obey his commands.[16]

This "binding minute" would soon create considerable problems for the Americans and sour their relation to Methodism's founder—or, in the more moderate words of Jesse Lee, it "was afterwards the cause of some uneasiness."[17]

As the published *Minutes* record: "The second action taken was to form ourselves into an Episcopal Church, under the direction of superintendents, elders, deacons and helpers, according to the forms of ordination annexed to our Liturgy, and the Form of Discipline set forth in these Minutes."[18] They were to be called "The Methodist Episcopal Church." Thomas Ware credits John Dickins with suggesting the name.[19] Having settled the form of government, and following the directive of Wesley to Coke, they proceeded to elect Coke and Asbury superintendents, thirteen preachers as elders, and three preachers as deacons.[20] Although Asbury writes, "We spent the whole week in conference, debating freely, and determining all things by a majority of votes," he does not describe the process used to choose persons to be ordained elders and deacons.[21] For this we must turn to Coke's report: "To the office of deacon every other preacher in full connection was chosen; and in the choice of presbyters or elders all partiality seemed to give place to superior considerations; namely to qualification and character, such as might tend to promote the glory of God, and the welfare of immortal souls."[22]

Lest this sounds too idyllic, Coke adds, "But how rigorously soever they adhered to the principal of impartiality; it was not in their power to give universal satisfaction."[23] Some were obviously angry at being omitted.

On 27 December 1784, Coke, assisted by Philip William Otterbein (a German Reformed pastor and friend of Francis Asbury living in Baltimore) "and other ministers," "set apart" Francis Asbury for the office of a superintendent.[24] Asbury had been ordained deacon and then elder over the previous two days. He was apparently quick to adopt the trappings of his new office. In the latter part of January 1785, at the first meeting after the formal organization of the new church, Jesse Lee expressed his surprise "and no little mortification" to see Asbury "in full canonicals, gown, cassock, and band."[25]

Having created an episcopal organization, the conference outlined in its *Minutes* the duties of a superintendent and the lines of accountability.

Quest. 26. What is the office of a Superintendent?

Ans. To ordain Superintendents, Elders, and Deacons; to preside as a Moderator in our Conferences; to fix the Appointments of the Preachers for the several Circuits; and in the Intervals of the Conference, to change, receive or suspend Preachers, as Necessity may require; and to receive Appeals from the Preachers and People, and decide them.[26]

A note is added that "no person shall be ordained a superintendent, elder, or deacon without the consent of a majority of the conference, and the consent and imposition of the hands of a superintendent," giving the superintendent veto power over all persons elected to ministerial orders or office.[27] This was later changed so that a United Methodist bishop cannot now refuse to ordain any candidate presented to her or him who has been recommended by the Board of the Ordained Ministry and duly elected by the body of preachers in executive session at the annual conference.

The general superintendents were made amenable to the conference for their conduct, and the conference given "power to expel him for improper conduct, if they see it necessary."[28] The collective power of the body of preachers assembled in conference clearly exceeded that of the general superintendent.

Wesley and His Bishops

Although the nature of Wesley's relation to his brethren in America was soon to be tested, the outcome had been predetermined by Asbury when he submitted his election and Wesley's plan for the church in America to the preachers for ratification. Wesley had not anticipated that a conference would be established. Exercising his authority, he named Coke and Asbury to oversee the work in America and gave them full power to do it, including the power to organize a church, to ordain and appoint the preachers, and to manage its business affairs; but he assumed they would remain subject to him alone.

The first crisis challenging this assumption was not long in coming. In September 1786 Wesley wrote to Coke, who was in England at the time, "I desire that you would appoint a General Conference of all our Preachers in the United States, to meet at Baltimore on May the 1st, 1787. And that Mr. Richard Whatcoat may be appointed Superintendent with Mr. Francis Asbury."[29] No one should doubt that Wesley assumed his right to issue such a directive, and the appropriateness of the request he made of Coke. He regarded himself as head of the church in America, and had their pledge of loyalty to him in the "binding minute." He had named the other general superintendents and assumed he was doing nothing out of the ordinary in adding a third. This may indicate both the extent to which the venerable Wesley was out of touch with the sentiment of his followers across the Atlantic and how little consideration he had given to Coke's suitability to lead in America.

The conference was quick to react. Jesse Lee reports:

> When this business was brought before the conference, most of the preachers objected, and would not consent to it. The reasons against it were, 1, That he [Whatcoat] was not qualified to take the charge of the connection. 2. That they were apprehensive that if Mr. Whatcoat was ordained, Mr. Wesley would likely recall Mr. Asbury, and he would return to *England*.[30]

John Emory concurred with Lee's evaluation: "And had the conference considered themselves obliged, as Dr. Coke contended, to receive Mr. Whatcoat merely by virtue of Mr. Wesley's authority, they might have been equally required by the same authority to submit to the recall of Mr. Asbury."[31] Coke argued that the affirmation of loyalty to Wesley made in 1784 obligated the American Conference to follow his directive and ordain Whatcoat. But the growing independence of the body of preachers made itself felt. Both Coke and his plea were ignored. The preachers not only refused to accept Whatcoat, but they also rescinded their earlier acceptance of Mr. Wesley's authority by removing the "binding minute" from the *Discipline*. In a final personal rejection, they took Wesley's name out of the list of superintendents for the church in America. Lee, who was fully supportive of these actions, says, "They had made the engagement of their own accord, and among themselves, and they believed they had a right to depart therefrom, when they pleased. . . ."[32]

Having settled matters with respect to their relation to Wesley and his authority in America, they clarified the scope of the powers they were willing to grant Coke. While still in Europe, Coke had immediately followed Wesley's directive, both mandating the election of Whatcoat as a bishop and changing the previously agreed-upon date for the next meeting of the conference. These actions exceeded the power given him by the preachers. In his defense, none of this was of Coke's own making, but loyalty to Wesley had placed him squarely in the middle. The preachers were unsympathetic with his plight and determined to ensure that it could never happen again. They required Coke to sign a certificate affirming that he would not, "by virtue of my office, as superintendent of the Methodist church, during my absence from the United States of America, exercise any government whatever in the said Methodist church."[33] Coke further agreed to limit his work as a superintendent, when in the country, to ordination, presiding in the conferences, and traveling through the connection.[34] He lost his power to station the preachers, leaving Asbury the sole episcopal leader with the full powers of the office. Almost from the beginning (to borrow from George Orwell), all Methodists bishops were equal, but one was more equal than others.

When news of these conference actions reached Wesley, he was displeased, and he blamed Asbury specifically for the decision to remove his name from the *Minutes*.[35] Asbury admitted taking no part in the debates, thereby revealing much about his own position, since he probably had sufficient influence among the preachers to have defeated the resolution had he wanted to do it. We can only conclude that he agreed with what was done. This point was not lost on Wesley, who wrote to Whatcoat:

> It was not well judged of Brother Asbury to *suffer*, much less indirectly encourage, that foolish step in the late Conference. Every preacher present ought both in duty and in prudence to have said, "Brother Asbury, Mr. Wesley is *your* father, consequently ours, and we will affirm this in the face of all the world."[36]

Wesley was frustrated and angry, which is understandable, but he had little sensitivity to the spirit of independence of his preachers in America, and perhaps less understanding of the implications of their actions in 1784 in organizing themselves into a General Conference. During the debate, as he remained silent, Asbury may have been remembering his earlier words concerning Wesley's "Calm Address to Our American Colonies": "I . . . am truly sorry," he said, "that the venerable man ever dipped into the politics of America."[37] The majority of American preachers agreed with Jesse Lee's comment: "If there was any thing improper in the business [of the "binding minute"], it was in entering into the engagement, and not in departing from it."[38] The conference eventually elected Whatcoat a bishop, and in 1789 it returned Wesley's name to the *Minutes*, listing him with Coke and Asbury as one of the persons who "exercise the episcopal office in the Methodist Church in Europe and America," but they never replaced the "binding minute."[39]

Placing Wesley in the ranks of the bishops was ironic, to say the least. Following the adjournment of the Conference of 1787, Asbury, assisted by John Dickins and Thomas Coke, revised the form of the *Minutes* and published them in the *Discipline*. It was in this edition, without the consent of conference or consultation with Wesley, that they changed their title from "superintendent" to "bishop."[40] In the

47

Minutes of the previous Conferences of 1785, 1786, and 1787 the question concerning the leaders of the church reads, "Who are the superintendents of our church?"[41]

Spellman contends that "Asbury is probably more responsible than any other person for the use of the term 'bishop' within The Methodist Episcopal Church."[42] It is unlikely, however, that Coke opposed the change. Everything we know about Coke would compel us to believe that he would have assumed the title proudly. The most positive explanation for the change is that Asbury understood both terms to be scriptural and synonymous. He used them in an interchangeable manner in his "Valedictory Address to William M'Kendree,"[43] his "Last Will and Testament,"[44] and his long letter to Joseph Benson.[45]

The change was significant to Wesley. He was furious when he learned of the decision to begin a college in America and name it "Cokesbury," in honor of Coke and Asbury. He quickly dispatched one of his best-known epistles, the "Dear Franky" letter:

> But in one point, my dear brother, I am a little afraid both the Doctor and you differ from me. I study to be little: you study to be great. I creep: you strut along. I found a school: you a college! nay, and call it after your own names! . . . One instance of this, of your greatness, has given me great concern. How can you, how dare you suffer yourself to be called Bishop? I shudder, I start at the very thought! Men may call me a knave or a fool, a rascal, a scoundrel, and I am content; but they shall never by my consent call me Bishop! For my sake, for God's sake, for Christ's sake put a full end to this![46]

The title never caused the concern for Americans that the practical questions of power and practice surrounding the office presented. More than half a century later Leonidas Hamline spoke before the 1844 General Conference and argued that "our Church constitution recognizes the episcopacy as an abstraction, and leaves this body to work it into a concrete form in any hundred or more ways we may be able to invent."[47] The unique form of Methodist episcopacy evolved; it was worked out over the years, in a variety of situations, and through a series of sometimes unrelated challenges and events. The pattern in Methodism, from its beginning in America to the present, has been to alter substance by modifying practice or reorganizing. Although the Third Restrictive Rule—part of the constitution adopted at the conference in 1808 and designed by Joshua Soule to

protect and define the Asburian model of itinerant general superintendency—remains the law of the church, the form of its episcopacy
and the practice of bishops in The UMC bear little resemblance to the
original.[48] This observation applies equally to doctrinal issues. The
Articles of Religion prepared by Wesley and sent to America in 1784
have not been amended either, but the substance of the doctrines
affirmed by them has often been modified. For example, Article VII,
"Of Original or Birth Sin," declares a doctrine of original sin that is
not reflected in the liturgy used to administer the sacrament of infant
baptism. To answer the question of how such things have come to be
requires an examination of "peaks" of innovation in practice.

CHAPTER 4

The Bishops and the Conference

The official organization of the MEC could not have been better timed. It provided an immediate church home for many former Anglicans and set in motion a method of itinerant church planting that proved to be remarkably suited to the new nation, with its ever-expanding frontier. The result was a time of rapid growth, both in terms of members and of itinerating elders. While this was a cause for celebration, it posed an increasing problem of how all of these elders could be gathered from their widely dispersed circuits to participate in the yearly conference. The initial solution was to hold multiple smaller regional annual conferences. But as the number of these annual conferences increased—there were eleven held in 1789, scattered from Charleston to New York—so proportionately did the difficulty of presenting for approval every issue to every annual conference. As Abel Stevens observed: "The rapid multiplication of sectional or 'annual conferences' facilitated the local business of the denomination, but rendered legislation on its general interests difficult, if not impossible."[1]

Asbury's Council

In response to this situation, Asbury devised an organization that he called "The Council," and presented it to the conferences for their approval in 1789. The Council was to be composed of the bishops and presiding elders chosen by the bishops who would serve as representatives of the entire connection (note that this plan is the origin of the title "presiding elder," which is then taken up in the *Minutes*[2]). The Council would require consensus in its decisions, and nothing that it passed would be binding until it was ratified in every conference. Asbury's ability to get this proposed council, which one of his biographers calls "an experiment in organization," through the annual conferences offers testimony to his influence.[3] As a strategy, however, it was programmed to fail. Although it was approved by a majority of the preachers, the organization of The Council was quickly opposed by influential persons like Jesse Lee and James O'Kelly, who were made members of it.[4] The shortcomings of the plan were obvious: (1) it enhanced Asbury's power, since it gave him, along with the other bishops, the authority to select the members of The Council; (2) the provision requiring unanimous assent to all matters brought before The Council before they could become binding in the various conferences assured Asbury of a veto on all proposed legislation; and (3) acts of The Council had the force of law only in the conferences that affirmed them.[5] Lee recognized that The Council model had the potential to divide the connection: "If then, one district should agree to any important point, and another district should reject it; the union between the two districts would be broken: and in process of time our *United Societies* would be thrown into disorder and confusion."[6]

Describing the plan as "entirely new, and exceedingly dangerous," Lee wrote Asbury immediately to complain and to urge in its place the creation of a General Conference.[7] O'Kelly's reservations were of a more personal nature and were influenced by his dislike for Asbury. He suspected Asbury's real motive in creating The Council was further to enhance his power. He wrote Asbury threatening to use his influence against him if he did not "stop for one year."[8] But Asbury went ahead in spite of the opposition, and The Council met for the first time Thursday, 3 December 1789. The first order of business was to amend some of its most glaring faults. They determined, for example, to blunt the power of The Council by making it advisory and stressing that the real power remained with the annual conferences. Twelve persons, including Asbury, were present. Asbury judged "all our business was done in love and unanimity."[9]

Their actions, even if well intended and conducted in love, were unable to solve the inherent problems of the council plan. The requirement that all items must pass unanimously was amended to require only a two-thirds majority and the consent of the bishop; resolutions presented to the annual conferences were made binding on all if passed by a majority of the conferences.[10] These modifications were presented to the annual conferences meeting in 1790, and Asbury reported trouble in several of them. In Virginia, "all was peace until the council was mentioned."[11] Those under O'Kelly's influence passed resolutions in which they refused to send representatives to The Council's next meeting. However, the amendments made in the first meeting passed in a number of conferences, and the second meeting of The Council was convened 1 December 1790. Despite the fact that Asbury described this meeting as one in which "we had great peace and union in all our labours," he also noted that "for the sake of union, we declined sending out any recommendatory propositions."[12] The climate never improved and The Council never met again. Asbury, who had been burned in the southern conferences, was finally convinced that the idea was lost, and urged that it not be mentioned again.

Move to a General Conference

If they were unhappy with The Council, it was incumbent upon Asbury's critics to suggest an alternative to address the issues The Council had been conceived to face. The continuing growth of the connection would bring it to eighteen annual conferences by 1792. This made it practically impossible for each annual conference to act on general church matters. And when they did act, their veto power had the potential to destroy the connection. It was noted above that Lee had recommended a General Conference when he wrote to protest the first meeting of The Council in 1789. By 1791 he had revised this recommendation to a "delegated" General Conference. As Lee's biographer describes it:

> A delegation from each Conference, elected by its members, was the plan he desired to see adopted; and notwithstanding the unceremonious rejection of his letter and himself, by the Council of 1789, he maintained his position and his principles; and in July 1791, submitted a plan for a delegated General Conference in 1792 to Bishop Asbury.[13]

53

Lee's revised proposal could be seen as a compromise between a truly general conference (where all elders in full connection could attend) and Asbury's smaller council. James O'Kelly would have been in no mind for such a compromise. His opposition to The Council and to Asbury had been open and divisive. Having decided not to attend the second session of The Council, he had called a special meeting in his district and persuaded the preachers not to send a delegate in his place. William McKendree, one of those present, wrote: "Monday, 27th, Mr. O'Kelly, the Presiding Elder, came. . . . We had a melting time at sacrament, *and then the poor miserable Council took up all our time until ten oclock at night.*"[14] O'Kelly then wrote to Coke, who was in Europe, arguing for a General Conference open to all elders. By the time of his return to America, the doctor had been persuaded. Asbury wrote of this return with some resignation: "Long-looked-for Doctor Coke came to town: he had been shipwrecked off Edisto Island. I found the Doctor's sentiments, with regard to the council, quite changed. James O'Kelly's letters had reached London. I felt perfectly calm, and acceded [*sic*] to a general conference, for the sake of peace."[15]

It was not easy for Asbury. Sixty days after he wrote of his calm demeanor, he recorded in his journal: "I hope to be enabled to give up all I dare for peace' sake; and to please all men for their good to edification."[16] Asbury preferred The Council arrangement, but the opposition of preachers throughout the conferences, bolstered by the real possibility of secession in Virginia, made it impossible. Nicholas Snethen concluded: "Mr. Asbury submitted to a General Conference for fear of a division in the Connection."[17]

There was one benefit of the move to a General Conference that Asbury may have anticipated: it would consolidate part of his workload. At this juncture there were only two bishops in the connection, and only one of them was functioning in America. Asbury had to attend all eighteen conferences held in 1792 and station all the preachers on their circuits or in their appointments. It took eight months to reach them all and required travel in nearly every state in the Union.[18]

Presiding Elders

The demands that spread episcopal supervision so broadly enhanced the status and power of the presiding elders in the annual conferences. They became in reality the episcopal presence most of the time. Although the presiding elder functioned almost from the very beginning of the connection, the office itself was not officially recognized nor its duties defined until 1792. Chosen by, accountable to, and serving at the pleasure of the bishop, they were, and are, the load-bearing points of the Methodist system.[19] Since they functioned as the de facto bishop in the absence of the general superintendent, presiding elders assumed all episcopal duties save that of ordination, including the role of presiding at annual conference, and assigning the preachers.[20] Asbury's sense of their role is clear: "I wish the most perfect union to subsist between the Episcopacy, and the presiding eldership, and at least a circumstantial account by letter, every half year; that they may be eyes, ears, and mouth, and pens, from the Episcopacy, to the preachers, and people; and the same from the preachers and people, to the Episcopacy."[21]

The General Conference of 1792

The General Conference that O'Kelly and others had pressured Asbury to call convened in Baltimore on 1 November 1792. As the first gathering since the organizing conference in 1784, to which all the preachers were invited, it can properly be described as the first "general" conference of the MEC. A large number attended. Lee says the preachers came both because they believed something important might happen and because they "generally thought that in all probability there would never be another conference of that kind, at which all the preachers in connection might attend."[22]

McKendree's journal records that Coke and Asbury presided conjointly at the sessions of this conference.[23] The preachers who chose to attend because they expected something of importance to happen did not have long to wait. In short order The Council was set aside and the bishops asked that it not be mentioned again. It was then agreed that the General Conference should meet again in four years, "to which, all the preachers in full connection were at liberty to come."[24] It was decided that a two-thirds majority was needed to create a new rule or abolish an old one, but a simple majority could amend. With these preliminary matters out of the way, a challenge was introduced in the session that struck at the locus of the powers of the bishops' making appointments.

The O'Kelly Schism

From the earliest days of Methodism in America until the most recent sessions of its annual conferences the single most significant responsibility of a Methodist bishop has been to station the preachers. But no matter how carefully it is done, the nature of the task always has the potential to create dissatisfaction. And there were those who were dissatisfied with the process from the beginning.

The church was not yet in existence when Asbury confided in his journal that "William Glendenning had been devising a plan to lay me aside, or at least to abridge my powers." Glendenning's plan involved changing the way appointments were made, and prompted the letter from John Wesley to the Americans saying he did not "wish our American brethren to receive any who make any difficulty on receiving Francis Asbury as the general assistant."[25]

In 1792 a more powerful opponent arose again to challenge Asbury. James O'Kelly, one of the persons ordained in 1784 at the Christmas Conference, a member of Asbury's Council, and a presiding elder in Virginia, introduced an amendment on the second day of the conference that was designed to afford the preachers a means to appeal Asbury's appointments.

> After the bishop appoints the preachers at conference to their several circuits, if any one thinks himself injured by the appointment, he shall have liberty to appeal to the conference and state his objections; and if the conference approve his objections, the bishop shall appoint him to another circuit.[26]

O'Kelly's proposed amendment was undergirded by his republican sentiments, his opposition to Asbury's use of power, and a fundamental conviction that the body of preachers had authority to limit and define the work of a bishop. Once the issue was on the floor, powerful forces arrayed on both sides; the debate went on for two or three days.[27] Asbury, who remembered that he "felt awful at the General Conference," commendably removed himself from the chair and recommended the appointment of a moderator to conduct the discussion.[28] He also drafted a masterful letter to the preachers. It read in part: "I am happily excused from assisting to make laws by which myself am to be governed: I have only to obey and execute. I am happy in the consideration that I never stationed a preacher through enmity, or as a punishment. I have acted for the glory of God, the good of the people, and to promote the usefulness of the preachers."[29]

To the letter he attached the comment "I am not fond of altercations—we cannot please everybody—and sometimes not ourselves. I am resigned."

Despite the lengthy debate on O'Kelly's amendment, the final vote was not close. O'Kelly lost and left the conference, along with William McKendree and a few other loyal followers. On the final part of the journey home, McKendree was O'Kelly's only traveling companion. Talking to him, O'Kelly reviled Asbury as "a pope," described the General Conference that he had helped create as a "revolutionizing body," and the preachers as working with the bishop "to gratify their pride and ambition" to the ruin of the church. He also revealed his plan to begin *a republican, no slavery, glorious church!*[30] He made good on the promise in 1793, organizing the Republican Methodist Church. Although McKendree did not take an appointment from the Virginia Conference when it met in November, neither did he follow O'Kelly into the new organization. Had he done so, Methodism would have lost a significant episcopal leader in a critical period of its history.

The defeat of O'Kelly's amendment was not just a vote of confidence in Asbury's leadership. It was a significant renewal of the covenant of itinerant ministry that Asbury, more than any other individual, had helped to establish and defend. Under Asbury's formative leadership Methodist episcopacy became the protector and defender of the itinerant system.

The Itinerant General Superintendent

The 1792 General Conference also took actions that directly affected the shape and practice of its episcopacy. First, the conference determined bishops would be elected in the General Conference rather than in the individual annual conferences. Second, bishops were made amenable to the General Conference for their conduct, and procedures were adopted to govern trials, should any person be charged with wrongdoing. Last, the conference determined that a bishop who should cease to exercise his episcopal duties with the permission of the General Conference "shall not thereafter exercise any ministerial function whatsoever in our Church."[31] Bishops would not be returned to service or membership in their annual conferences.

There were no models of episcopacy in America for Coke or Asbury to follow when the church was organized in 1784. The style and nature of the office in the Church of England was obviously not appropriate either for the new nation or for the Methodists. As it has already been noted, Wesley was himself not a suitable model despite his exercising many of the traditional duties of a bishop. But there was a spirit in the new nation of fresh beginnings ripe with excitement and promise. That spirit equally invigorated the Methodists. As John Locke said earlier, "In the beginning, all the world was America."[32] The first Puritans came as a "new Adam" into a "new world," determined to create in it nothing less than God's "new Israel," a society free from the mistakes and accretions of the past. In that same spirit the Methodists believed themselves to be free in America to reintroduce the government of the primitive church as they understood it. Bishop Andrew summarized this conviction by saying: "The preaching of the gospel and proper church organization were indispensable, and ministers possessing peculiar characteristics were demanded to accomplish the work; and God, who always adapts means to the end of the task to be accomplished, raised up just the class of men needed for the work."[33]

In this new organization, presbyters and bishops were of the same order, with bishops simply being called to a higher office. Bishops, like the apostolic evangelists of the early church, were to itinerate throughout the connection in order to give oversight to it. In nearly every way, the episcopal church government of the American Methodists was framed in the pattern Wesley devised for his societies in England. American bishops served as representative presbyters whose power was derived from and shared with the conference. The locus of power in both was the body of preachers. In the various conferences where bishops functioned, their power gave shape and substance to organization and practice. Yet it must be said that the episcopal office as Asbury expressed it developed independence and powers specific to it that were not dependent on the conferences.

From the beginning, itinerancy and episcopacy have been joined in American Methodism, and a primary task of its bishops has been to ensure the continuation and well-being of the itinerant system.

58

From 1784 until the mid-1820s all Methodist bishops traveled throughout the connection, visiting every annual conference. In order to do this, they were constantly on the road. Richard Whatcoat described one circuit of conferences that he made in 1801 as "about four thousand one hundred and eighty-four miles."[34]

Bishops presided in the conferences, and in the early years they were entitled both to speak and to make motions in them. They selected presiding elders, stationed and disciplined the preachers, and ordained deacons, elders, and general superintendents. In the beginning they had the power to reject individuals presented to them for ordination, authority they lack today. This provision was included in the *Discipline* of 1785 and 1786. The revision, done by Asbury in 1787, removed the provision, but the *Notes* prepared by Coke and Asbury that accompanied the 1798 *Discipline* seem to indicate that in their minds the change was merely editorial in nature. Speaking of the bishops, they wrote: "They have, indeed, authority to suspend the ordination of an elected person, because they are answerable to God for the abuse of their office, and the command of the apostle, 'Lay hands suddenly on no man,' is absolute."[35] The implication is clear that in these matters the early bishops believed they were independent of the conference and subject to the authority of a higher power even than the body of preachers.

In the years following its organization, especially after 1800, the MEC changed rapidly to respond to new challenges it faced in the nation, especially those presented by the opening of the Western frontier. Likewise, the nature and duties assigned to its episcopal leaders were interpreted and sometimes modified by practice. Although formal changes were not enacted, in the successful exercise of the office, modifications were essential. Through it all, however, "the episcopacy had the same essential characteristics all the way down from its inauguration in 1784 to the General Conference of 1808."[36]

The Relation of New Bishops to Asbury

One of the characteristics of the episcopacy was subject to debate prior to 1808. This was the question of whether there would be any seniority of duties and authority for existing bishops over newly elected bishops. It is easy to imagine that had Coke played a significant leadership role in America and exercised power akin to Asbury's, it would have been obvious that new bishops would also exercise the full powers of the office. In fact, Asbury was the only one who had these powers. But the primacy that Asbury exercised by comparison to Coke did not necessarily prejudge the issue at hand, because they had been elected at the same time and their relative roles reflected both the desire of the conference to make clear its independence from Wesley and Coke's frequent absences from America. What would be the role, relative to the powerful Asbury, of the next bishop elected by the will of the conference?

This question came to a head in 1800 when Asbury declared that he planned to resign because "he was so weak and feeble both in body and mind, that he was not able to go through the fatigues of his office."[37] Rather than force him to resign, the General Conference granted him the right to continue as a bishop "as far as his strength will permit." This was the first time the conference gave its permission to a bishop for less than full-time service.[38] While this was happening, the English Conference requested the return of Coke; and after considerable debate, he was allowed to go, with the proviso that if needed in America he would return. With Asbury ill and Coke returning home, it was obvious the time had come to elect another bishop.

The relation of this bishop to Asbury had to be clarified as part of that election. Thus the Friday and Saturday after the opening of the Conference of 1800 were devoted to a lengthy discussion about the authority of the new bishop. The first concern, of course, was his authority to appoint the preachers. Thomas Coke, who had been denied that power, suggested that "the new bishop, whenever he presides at an annual conference in the absence of Bishop Asbury, shall bring the stations of the preachers into the conference and read them, that he may hear what the conference has to say upon each station."[39] Coke later withdrew this suggestion. A similar motion was made by William Wells, who proposed that a small committee of three or four preachers be created to assist in making appointments. It was voted down. This kept the focus on the basic question of whether the next—or any other—bishop would be equal to Asbury. On Saturday afternoon the answer was given in a motion declaring "that the bishops shall have full and equal jurisdiction in all and every respect whatsoever."[40] It passed.

The debate was no doubt influenced by the candidates for bishop. The two major candidates were Jesse Lee and Richard Whatcoat. It seems likely that, given the choices, Asbury would have favored Lee. We know of no stated objections Asbury had to Whatcoat—he described him as a "godly man of great gravity"—but Lee and Asbury had worked together for years. In particular, when Asbury previously became ill in the summer of 1797 and was unable to fulfill his responsibilities, Lee was designated by the New York Conference to travel with him and provide whatever assistance Asbury needed. In this capacity Lee, when required, took Asbury's place in the conference sessions. He records that the "conference at Wilbraham [in New England] made choice of me to preside in that meeting, and to station the preachers."[41] Although he did not station the preachers in other conferences, Lee accompanied Asbury to three of them in which he conducted the business and took the minutes. Asbury would have been comfortable with Lee's preparation for the role of bishop.

Lee, who undoubtedly remembered the experience vividly, reports that there was no election on the first ballot, he and Whatcoat were tied on the second, and Whatcoat was finally elected on the third by a majority of four votes.[42] It is tempting to speculate that Lee may have lost the position he seemed richly to deserve because he was so closely associated with Asbury, but there is simply nothing to establish this was the case. Another possibility is that the conference members wanted to reinforce their commitment that the new bishop be Asbury's equal. Tigert makes reference to a now-lost communication sent by Asbury to the New England Conference in 1797 in which Asbury nominated Lee, Poythress, and Whatcoat to be "assistant bishops."[43] While the conference wisely declined to act on his recommendation, it noted Asbury's preference for a model of a senior bishop with assistants. Those at the Conference of 1800 may have feared that Lee would inevitably become Asbury's assistant. By contrast they recalled that they had shown their independence from Wesley by refusing to make Whatcoat a bishop earlier as Wesley had directed. Perhaps the election of Whatcoat now signaled an attempt to balance Asbury's authority.

Whatever their intent, neither the person elected nor the declaration of equal status of all bishops in the church by the General Conference of 1800 changed Asbury's practice. Tigert correctly says that "despite his legal parity with Asbury, Whatcoat was practically little more than an 'assistant bishop.'"[44] In fact, Asbury spoke of

Whatcoat as the "junior bishop." Despite the fact that Whatcoat was nine years older than his episcopal colleague and senior to him in service in the Methodist connection, Asbury was always "senior" and Whatcoat "junior." When they held conferences together, as they often did, Asbury always stationed the preachers. Whatcoat's *Memoirs* contain many references to conference sessions at which he presided, including the number of persons he ordained deacons and elders, but he never mentions his stationing the preachers. Neither Whatcoat nor any of the others elected during Asbury's lifetime were ever his equal. Only after Asbury's death was real parity achieved among the bishops.

Attempts to Modify the Superintendency

There were a variety of other attempts to modify the nature of the episcopacy prior to the creation of the Constitution of 1808. The more radical and intentional these attempts were, the more likely they were to fail. For example, Jesse Lee tells of a plan originated in the New York Conference "to call a delegated conference of seven members from each conference, chosen by the conference, to meet in Baltimore on the fourth of July 1807, to choose superintendents." He goes on to say that Asbury "laboured hard to carry the point, but he laboured in vain."[45] This scheme, which surprisingly was favored by Asbury, would have effectively converted the itinerant general superintendency into a diocesan episcopacy. The attempt was thwarted in the Virginia Conference but was approved in the New York, New England, Western, and South Carolina Conferences.

In another case, recognizing an opportunity created by the physical weakness of Asbury and Whatcoat, in 1805 Thomas Coke offered to return permanently to the United States on the condition that "the seven Conferences should be divided betwixt us, three and four, and four and three, each of us changing our division annually; and that this plan at all events should continue permanent and unalterable during both our lives."[46] In January 1806, Coke wrote a circular letter to the New York Conference defending the proposal and making a case for his return. In it he complained of Asbury's unwillingness to allow him to function as a "Coadjutor in the Episcopacy." He revealed that he "was not consulted in the least degree imaginable concerning the station of a single Preacher." Present with Asbury in

Georgia, Coke asked for a list of appointments after it had been distributed to all the preachers, but was denied even that. When Asbury was too ill to attend the conference in South Carolina, Coke offered to go, "but he refused me, & appointed Brother Jackson to station the Preachers, & Brother Jesse Lee to sit as Moderator in the Conference."[47] Coke's proposal would have given him authority equal to Asbury's over half of the connection at a time (though it left Whatcoat out of the equation!). It never had any appeal to the Americans, however, so Coke went back to Europe to finish his life and labors promoting the overseas missions of English Methodism.

The journal of the General Conference of 1800 also reveals abortive efforts to establish eligibility requirements for election to the episcopacy and to allow the conference to elect presiding elders. These were presented in addition to the attempts to create an advisory group to assist the bishops in making appointments.[48] The common feature of all these proposals was their obvious intent to limit the power of the episcopacy. The effort to elect presiding elders was to continue until 1828 before being finally defeated.

While these attempts failed, there were more subtle ways in which the role of bishops was modified during this period, specifically in the bishops' relationship to the General Conference. This relationship was a complex and divisive question, which would gradually evolve as the powers and responsibilities of the General Conference were clarified. Some of the changes enacted in conference appeared simple but had large implications for episcopal practice. For example, the General Conference of 1792, which established the office of presiding elder, also placed a limit of four years' service in the position.[49] Although this restriction was specifically related to the presiding elders, by extension it limited episcopal power and prerogative, since they were no longer free to keep persons they selected indefinitely. In 1796, the number of "yearly," or annual, conferences was limited to six.[50] In addition to fixing the number, the legislation described and defined the power of the bishops to add new conferences. In 1800, there was a motion to create a delegated General Conference (as Jesse Lee had recommended earlier).[51] Although the motion failed to pass, the idea's time was soon to come, and when enacted would further limit the power of the bishops to influence its deliberations. Prior to this change, all preachers who had been in full connection for four years were eligible to attend the

General Conference. This, of course, included the bishops, who not only presided but, as preachers, were allowed to participate in the deliberations, make motions, and vote.[52] They lost the latter privileges when the delegated conference was created, since they were ineligible for election as delegates from any annual conference. In 1804, the bishops' power over stationing the preachers was limited by the decision of the General Conference to allow a preacher to remain no more than two consecutive years in the same place. An additional limit on episcopal authority over annual conferences came in the form of a resolution that required each annual conference to be allowed to sit as long as a week.[53] This blunted the ability of the presiding officer to cut debate on any issue by adjourning the conference.

The rapid increase in membership and the geographic spread of American Methodism, all circumstances over which bishops had no control, also changed the nature of episcopacy and its work. When the church was organized in 1784, there were approximately fifteen thousand members being served by eighty-four preachers in forty-six circuits. By 1803, that number had increased to more than one hundred four thousand Methodists in America served by almost four hundred preachers. Although the number of annual conferences had been limited to seven, their size had increased to the point that it was sometimes necessary for preachers to travel long distances and be away from their work for weeks at a time in order to attend the conferences. Nathan Bangs reported that some of the preachers who worked in circuits on the frontier traveled two hundred to four hundred miles to attend the conferences and were away from their work three to six weeks.[54] A general superintendent found it impossible to cover all the territory assigned. The most obvious solution was to increase the number of bishops. This was part of what motivated the proposal in the New York Conference to elect a bishop for each of the seven conferences. Had it been done it would have marked the end of itinerant general superintendency as it had been known and would have dramatically altered the practice and form of itinerant ministry. Despite the debate that took place when Whatcoat was elected to establish his authority vis-à-vis that of Asbury, as the work of the bishops expanded it became obvious that each had to share fully and equally in the powers of the office.

By the end of the first decade of the nineteenth century, the church had considered and rejected most of the alternative models of episcopacy in favor of the original idea of itinerant general superintendency, and had found a way to protect it with the Restrictive Rules of the constitution in 1808. But the issue remained as to how these officers and leaders of the church were to relate to its now-standard policy-making body, the delegated General Conference.

CHAPTER 5

The General Conference and the Episcopacy

Each of the progressive developments in the structure of conference in the MEC affected the nature and function of the episcopal office. The most significant transition in this chain of developments was the move to a delegated General Conference. Consideration of this change must begin with an appreciation of the pressures that brought it about.

Pressures for Modification

The move to a delegated General Conference was encouraged by increasing dissatisfaction with the structure of the General Conference as it had existed since 1792, and an offended sense of fair play and equity. As is often the case in Methodist history, the reasons that led to the change were practical, not theological or doctrinal. After the turn of the century, Methodism expanded to include circuits in Tennessee, Kentucky, and Ohio, and extended from Maine to Georgia in the East. In 1808, the total membership in America exceeded that of the Methodists in England and Ireland combined. The ban that had reduced the number of annual conferences to seven was removed in 1796 by the approval of a proviso that allowed the bishops to create new annual conferences in the interim between General

Conferences as the increase of circuits required. The first conference created under that legislation was the Genesee Conference in 1809, but the decision to organize it fomented a controversy in the church and provoked a formal protest from the Virginia Conference. The enabling legislation giving the bishops power to expand the number of conferences had for some unknown reason failed to be included in the *Discipline*. When the bishop's action was challenged, Asbury asked the annual conferences to express an opinion on the legality of their action. In so doing, he established a precedent that would be followed in the future. The creation of the Genesee Conference was affirmed in the annual conferences and by the General Conference of 1812, but new conferences were never again established in this manner.

Jesse Lee's summary of conferences held, circuits added, and total membership in the years after 1800 provides a clear picture of what was happening. Eighteen new circuits were added in 1802. Fifty preachers were admitted on trial in 1803, and new circuits were added in Quebec, Montreal, and St. John's. By 1812 there were nine annual conferences. Two more were added in 1816. The total had risen to twenty-nine in 1836. This very growth in numbers put pressure on a General Conference where all traveling preachers in full connection with a minimum of four years service were eligible to attend.

In reality, not all preachers did attend. The largest delegations typically came from the conferences in proximity to Baltimore, where the General Conference was usually held. For example, the Baltimore and Philadelphia Conferences had sixty-seven of the one hundred eight delegates at the General Conference of 1804, held in Baltimore. South Carolina, Virginia, and New England, whose delegates had to travel the greatest distance to attend, had a combined total of twelve.[1] Likewise, of the one hundred twenty-nine preachers present in Baltimore at the 1808 General Conference (the last General Conference prior to the creation of the delegated assembly), eighty-two were from the Baltimore, Philadelphia, and New York Conferences.[2] It should be obvious how this disproportionate representation allowed these conferences to control the legislation.

Jesse Lee had first proposed the creation of a delegated conference to Asbury at the time Asbury created The Council. Since Asbury was not in favor, Lee's suggestion was ignored. The idea was presented again to the General Conference of 1800, but, as the language of the *Journal* put it, it was "negatived."[3] Ironically, eight years later it was Asbury who made the motion to create a committee to study a memorial submitted by the New York Conference favoring the creation of a delegated conference. New York passed the proposal in 1807, which left time for only three other conferences to speak to it at their meetings—New England, Western, and South Carolina. The New York Conference resolution called "for the creation of a representative delegated General Conference"[4] and supported the need for the change by stating what everyone already knew:

> When we take a serious and impartial view of this important subject, and consider the extent of our connexion, the number of our preachers, the great inconvenience, expense, and loss of time that must necessarily result from our present regulations, relative to our General Conference, we are deeply impressed with a thorough conviction that a representative or delegated General Conference, composed of a specific number on principles of equal representation from the several annual conferences, would be much more conducive to the prosperity and general unity of the whole body, than the present indefinite and numerous body of ministers, collected together unequally from the various conferences. . . .[5]

The General Conference of 1808

With the concurrence of four conferences, the memorial was forwarded to the General Conference of 1808 for consideration and action. Once again the majority of delegates present were from the Baltimore and Philadelphia Conferences, and they, along with the delegates from Virginia, were opposed to the change. Jesse Lee, despite his early support of a delegated conference, was now negative toward the creation of any rules that might limit the power of annual conferences and was a leading opponent of the measure. That Lee was able to persuade Virginia to oppose it is interesting, since it was always one of the under-represented conferences and clearly stood to benefit from the change.

When the memorial was brought to the floor, the delegates voted to consider it and supported Asbury's subsequent motion to create a committee to study the situation and recommend a specific plan to the conference. In a stroke of political genius, Asbury, who now openly favored the change, proposed that this committee be composed of an equal number of delegates from each annual conference, thereby ensuring that those favoring the memorial would be fully represented and in the majority. Stephen G. Roszel moved that the number from each conference be set at two.[6] The conference elected a distinguished committee composed of Ezekiel Cooper and John Wilson from New York; George Pickering and Joshua Soule (later to be elected a bishop), representing Maine; William McKendree (elected bishop at this conference) and William Burke, on behalf of the Western Conference; William Phoebus and Josias Randle from South Carolina; Philip Bruce and Jesse Lee, representing Virginia; Stephen G. Roszel and Nelson Reed, on behalf of Baltimore; and John McClaskey and Thomas Ware from Philadelphia.[7] In this committee, those favoring the creation of the delegated conference constituted a majority of two.[8] Since New York had already received the concurrence of three other conferences, Asbury safely assumed this would be the case.

The committee was to make its report a week later. In the meantime, according to the only account available, a subcommittee composed of Ezekiel Cooper, Joshua Soule, and Philip Bruce was named to draft a document for consideration in the larger group.[9] Cooper and Soule prepared written documents. With the exception of the section on the episcopacy, there was general unanimity between the two. Cooper favored a form of diocesan episcopacy and earlier had supported the motion to elect a bishop for each annual conference.[10] His version of what became the "Third Restrictive Rule" of the constitution read: the General Conference "shall not do away Episcopacy, nor reduce our ministry to a presbyterial parity."[11] This wording left the specific form of episcopacy open and indefinite, subject to shaping and modification. While Cooper's idea did not prevail in 1808, nor did it get preserved in the constitution, what he advocated has in fact happened over and over again as the church has attempted to reinvent the episcopal office to meet its needs at various places at different times.

Soule's proposal, by contrast, was specific and concrete. The General Conference, he wrote, "shall not change or alter any part or rule of our government, so as to do away episcopacy, or destroy the plan of our itinerant general superintendency."[12] The model that Soule assumed was the Asburian form of episcopacy, "which plan for the last quarter of a century had been operated by three bishops, and which, for the next quarter of a century was to be operated by five others, all of whom had seats in the General Conference of 1808."[13]

70

Elliott says that Bruce, who had prepared no document, supported Soule's version, and it was submitted first to the special committee and then to the conference for its approval.[14]

The report submitted by the special committee is a remarkable document that, with little modification, has mandated the form of the General Conference to the present. It recommended the creation of a General Conference made up of delegates from the various annual conferences. Delegates were to be chosen by written ballot, without debate, in the year previous to the General Conference. The ratio to determine the total number of delegates was decided, and the date of the conference's convening was set for 1 May every four years. The report stipulated the number needed for a quorum and designated the general superintendents as presiding officers. It gave the General Conference "full powers to make rules, regulations and canons for our Church," with six restrictions. These Restrictive Rules provide that the General Conference (1) "shall not revoke, alter, or change our Articles of Religion, nor establish any new standards of doctrine"; (2) change the number of delegates provided for in the report; (3) "change or alter any part or rule of our government, so as to do away episcopacy or to destroy the plan of our itinerant general super-intendency"; (4) "revoke or change the general rules of the united societies"; (5) deny preachers and members the right to a trial before an appropriate body, and of appeal; and (6) allocate the proceeds of the Book Concern and the Charter Fund to any purpose except the support of "travelling, superannuated, supernumerary, and worn-out preachers, their wives, widows, and children." Finally, the report provided that these restrictions could be altered only upon the rec-ommendation of all the annual conferences, with the concurrence of two-thirds of the General Conference.[15]

The process leading to the final adoption of the committee report in the conference was long and complex. The opposition was aided by the venerable Jesse Lee, who diverted discussion from the main topic by moving that the selection of General Conference delegates should be determined by seniority rather than election.[16] As might be expected, the issue of the nature and form of the general superinten-dency in relation to the General Conference was also raised, by Ezekiel Cooper. Cooper managed to postpone discussion of the entire report by making a motion that "each annual conference, respectively, without debate, shall annually choose, by ballot, its own presiding elders."[17] Tigert comments that "as the next best thing to a diocesan episcopacy, Cooper, and those who agreed with him, desired an elective presiding eldership, and this opportunity was considered a good one for carrying a measure that had been frequently defeated, chiefly by those who now sought a Delegated General Conference."[18]

The conference was distracted by the debate on the Cooper motion to elect presiding elders even though the motion had little relevance to any portion of the committee report except for the Third Restrictive Rule. It was a brilliant strategy that, had it been successful, would have imposed a limitation on the power of the bishops and protected the innovation forever under the Third Restrictive Rule as part of the "plan" of the itinerant general superintendency. Everyone understood what was happening, and McKendree rose to oppose the change. He argued that "even the body from whom the delegated Conference derived its existence and powers never elected Presiding Elders, nor stationed the preachers; and there is room to doubt if it ever was the prerogative of the collective so to do."[19] He also noted that "the friends of the proposed alteration thought the constitution would put it out of the power of the Delegated Conference to effect the desired change, and therefore proposed to make the alteration before the constitution was ratified."[20] Cooper's motion was finally brought to a vote on 18 May 1808, after a protracted discussion, and defeated by a majority of twenty-one (73 to 52).[21] The ordination of William McKendree, who had been elected to the episcopacy a week earlier, took place immediately afterward. He was American Methodism's first native-born bishop.

When the conference resumed its business in the afternoon, a debate on the body of the committee report was begun. Its first resolution was to create a delegated general conference. The vote was taken and it failed. Although the large Philadelphia and Baltimore Conferences' delegations voted against it, as expected, the motion was defeated by only seven votes, 64 to 57.[22] Neely suggests that this may have been a calculated parliamentary move to allow the provisions of the committee report to be voted on separately.[23] Perhaps that is so, but some clearly assumed the vote to be final and were frustrated in defeat. Eight of these disappointed preachers, six from New England and two from the Western Conference, prepared to leave the conference, posing again the threat of division in American Methodism. Although there is no mention in Asbury's journal of this incident, Bishop Paine in his *Life of M'Kendree* records that "Bishop

Asbury and Mr. McKendree sought an interview with them and others sympathizing with them, and aided by the wise and prudent Elijah Hedding, prevailed on them to wait a day and see if a reconsideration of the question could not be effected leading to a different result."[24]

The task now before the advocates of the change was to devise a strategy that would allow the conference to reconsider their previous action. The matter remained unresolved from Wednesday until Monday, 23 May, when the new strategy was revealed. The opening gambit came when Leonard Cassell moved and Stephen G. Roszel seconded a motion "that the motion for considering when and where the next General Conference shall be, lie over until it be determined who shall compose the General Conference."[25] It passed. Immediately Enoch George, destined later to be a bishop, moved "that the General Conference shall be composed of one member for every five members of each Annual Conference." After his motion passed, Soule sought to silence the objections (or legitimate concerns) of Jesse Lee and his supporters by moving that "each Annual Conference shall have the power of sending their proportional number of members to the General Conference, either by seniority or choice, as they shall think best." The motion passed and Lee's biographer says that afterward Lee walked up to Soule, "poked him in the side with his finger and whispered, 'Brother Soule, you've played me a Yankee trick.'"[26] And indeed he had.

Asbury then moved from the chair that the General Conference should meet on the first day of May every four years. The first meeting of the new delegated General Conference was set for 1 May 1812 in New York.[27] The Restrictive Rules were next adopted in order, with Lee making the motion to approve Soule's version of the Third Rule;[28] and it was agreed that "no preacher shall be sent as a representative to the General Conference until he has travelled at least four full calendar years from the time that he was received on trial by an annual conference, and is in full connexion at the time of holding the conference."[29]

The Effects of Change

A watershed in the government of the MEC in America had been reached. The powers of the body of preachers assembled in General

73

Conference had been transferred to a delegated assembly with clearly defined and restricted powers. Tigert describes it as a "delegated" conference not only in the sense that its membership was composed of elected delegates but also since the body collectively exercised delegated powers. "It is an agent, not a principal. It is a dependent body, with derived powers. These powers are defined in a Constitution issuing from the body that ordained the Delegated Conference."[30] "The old General Conference," Neely said, "could create a new Constitution and a new kind of General Conference, but the new kind of General Conference could not of itself and by itself do such things."[31] He goes on to say that the General Conference was given "supplementary and concurrent power" with the body of preachers in amending the constitution. But the basic and fundamental right of "constitution making" and "constitution mending" was still reserved to them.[32] The power, as it always had, remained in the body of preachers and now resided in the annual conferences.

Subject to the limits imposed by the six Restrictive Rules, the General Conference was given full power to enact the rules and policies (polity) of the denomination. Quoting Bishop William L. Harris, Neely describes the powers of the General Conference not as a "delegation of enumerated powers accompanied by a general reservation as in the case of the Federal Government, but a delegation of general and sweeping powers under enumerated and well defined restrictions."[33] The provisions adopted in 1808 governing the General Conference remain largely the same today. The size of the conference has been increased as the ratio of delegates to members of the annual conference has been modified, and laypersons now sit as delegates, but in the main the structure remains what was then adopted.

In this change to a delegated General Conference the itinerant general superintendency was preserved, but its power was redefined and limited. The bishops would now sit in the assembly as presidents but not as members, since they were not eligible for election by an annual conference. Asbury and McKendree largely ignored this change in status, continuing to speak and act in the conference. However, it was soon established that this change logically meant that bishops were not allowed to make motions, vote, or to enjoy privileges of the floor. Tigert's interpretation of this change is somewhat less passionate, and less convincing. He says that the constitution did not "formally exclude the bishops from the privileges they had hitherto exercised in the Conference," but when the delegated conference was created, "the bishops ceased to claim the rights of the floor."[34] In either case, this was often a difficult adjustment for those whose prior participation in General Conference had helped them to be elected to episcopal office. One newly elected bishop recently complained during a session of the General Conference that, as a group, they were no different from the potted palms that lined the dais on which they were seated: "just part of the decorations."

In truth, they were more than decorations, they presided over the conference. But the changes of 1808 limited this power as well. Bishops now were able "to rule on points of parliamentary law, but not to decide points of ecclesiastical [law]; for the General Conference was to be the interpreter as well as the maker of church law."[35] The difficult question of whether the General Conference could rule on the constitutionality of its own actions remained to be settled. By 1850 the bishops of the MECS were given the power as a body to veto legislation that they deemed unconstitutional. This authority was eventually shifted to the Judicial Council, an organization developed in the MECS just prior to reunion in 1939, and adopted by the MC when it was organized.

One other matter concerning the episcopacy was reiterated by the conference in 1808. It involved Dr. Coke (who is seldom, if ever, referred to in documents of the time as "Bishop Coke"). Acceding once again to the request of the English Conference and Coke's own preferences, the conference gave him permission to reside outside the United States, subject to the call of the General Conference or annual conferences, but stipulated that he was "not to exercise the office of superintendent or bishop among us in the United States until he be recalled by the General Conference, or by all the annual conferences respectively."[36] Coke's relation to the American church had for all intents been finally determined in 1805 when he attempted unsuccessfully to gain approval to divide the conferences and share equal power with Asbury. The action taken in 1808, however, had significant implications for the future of the episcopacy. The bishops were declared subject to the General Conference, a principle that both Coke and Asbury accepted from the beginning, and they were elected exclusively for service in the United States. By the middle of the nineteenth century this would create a serious problem, as the church was required to provide episcopal supervision for the growing number of missionary conferences outside the continental United States.

CHAPTER 6

After Asbury: Redefining the Episcopacy

Just as the creation of the delegated General Conference changed the nature of Methodist episcopacy, William McKendree's election brought changes in the practices of the bishops. As was discussed earlier, Whatcoat was always regarded by Asbury as a "junior" bishop and actually served only a few years before his death in July 1806. McKendree fared no better in this relation to Asbury, who noted in his journal on 6 May 1808 "the electing [of] dear brother M'Kendree assistant bishop."[1] But McKendree had status because of his service in the Western Conference and was destined to continue in the office for twenty-seven years, only slightly less than Asbury's tenure of thirty-two years. He would quickly prove no "assistant bishop." If anyone should be considered the successor to Asbury, McKendree is the only viable candidate for the designation.

William McKendree

McKendree was born in Virginia, served in the Continental Army during the Revolution, and then joined the Virginia Conference at the age of thirty-one. His first presiding elder and mentor was James O'Kelly, who exerted great influence on him in the early years of his ministry. But when O'Kelly withdrew from the MEC in

1792 to begin his own church, McKendree did not follow him. McKendree's first appointments were all in Virginia, but the bulk of his service was in the West. In 1789, he was assigned as presiding elder in the Cumberland District, which encompassed the entire state of Illinois. McKendree remembered vividly the meeting in which Asbury, who was visiting his circuit in Virginia, had assigned him to the West, and recounted it in the last annual conference he attended before his death. Asbury called him to his room and told him, "Brother M'Kendree, I wish you to go and take charge of such a district, west of the mountains [one which, by the way, included virtually all the stations the Methodists had in that area]." "When do you wish me to start?" McKendree inquired. "In two hours," said Asbury. It took him an hour to pack, mount his horse, and get back to the bishop for final instructions.[2] In 1800, McKendree was sent to Kentucky in the Western Conference as a presiding elder and again had oversight of virtually all the Methodist work. The area encompassed by his district was eventually to become six annual conferences. He remained in the West until his election to the episcopacy, a kind of prelude to the future of the denomination.

When McKendree arrived at the General Conference of 1808, he was unknown to most of the delegates. Early in the session, however, he preached an eloquent sermon that quickly brought him to their attention. Asbury remarked, on leaving the church, that it was a sermon powerful enough to elect McKendree a bishop. He was correct. Fifty-one years old, tall, plainly dressed in the manner of the frontier, McKendree preached with power and simplicity. And once a bishop, he led in the same manner. It fell to McKendree to steer the denomination through some of its most troubled times, and Bishop Andrew, in tribute, described the qualities that equipped McKendree well for the challenge: "The clearness of his mind and his force of character, his keen power of analysis, and his strong and undying attachment to the constitution of the Church, as it had been received from the fathers, all fitted him admirably for the post to which God had called him."[3]

Immediately following his election, McKendree spent the first year of his episcopal service traveling with Asbury, who introduced him to the conferences and the work of a bishop. For eight years they were the only bishops in the church. When Asbury died in 1816, McKendree was alone in the episcopacy. Suffering himself from poor health, he was relieved from active work by the General Conference of 1820, as Asbury had been. But McKendree's health improved sufficiently thereafter for him to continue in an active role until 1828. From the beginning, McKendree exercised the courage and the tact necessary to modify Asbury's practice in order to accommodate it to his own sense of propriety and to the changing needs of the church.

The first example of this willingness to modify Asbury's long-established patterns appeared only three years after his election. McKendree wanted to change the way in which the appointments were made. Asbury had always assigned the preachers by himself; McKendree was more comfortable sharing the task with the presiding elders and relying on them for advice. In a letter to Asbury on the subject, McKendree recognized the senior bishop's opposition to the idea. "I am fully convinced of the utility and necessity of the council of the Presiding Elders in stationing the preachers, but you fear individuals will make it difficult, if not impracticable, for you to proceed on this plan." McKendree then suggested that he was willing to accept a compromise that Asbury had proposed. "If it is still your wish, I will take the plan of stations, after you have matured it—call the Elders to my assistance, and after deliberate council, report in favor, or dictate such alterations as may be thought necessary." But while willing to compromise, McKendree was unyielding in his refusal to make the appointments alone. "I still refuse to take the whole responsibility upon myself, not that I am afraid of proper accountability, but because I conceive the proposition included one highly improper."[4]

McKendree's determination to work with the presiding elders in making the appointments was actually moot at the time, since he and Asbury traveled to the conferences together and Asbury stationed the preachers until 1815 when his failing health required him finally to relinquish the responsibility to McKendree.[5] When, however, the responsibility finally became his, McKendree utilized the presiding elders, meeting as a cabinet to advise and consult with him in making appointments.

McKendree's second innovation came at the session of the first delegated General Conference in May 1812. Prior to the opening of conference, McKendree drew up a plan of business to be brought before the General Conference.[6] His address was read in conference on Tuesday afternoon, 5 May.[7] It obviously came as a surprise to Asbury, for he rose when McKendree finished, and confronted McKendree from the floor, charging him with doing "a new thing."

"I never did business in this way, and why is this new thing introduced?" Standing and facing the venerable Asbury, McKendree tactfully replied, "You are our *father*, we are your sons; you never have had need of it. I am only a *brother*, and have need of it." It is reported that Asbury sat down with a smile and the Episcopal Address became a regular item on the agenda of every General Conference since.[8] Although the address came as a surprise to Asbury, McKendree had in fact consulted a council of selected delegates before he presented it. "And as it was a new thing among us, he asked them to consider it attentively, and give him their opinion without reserve upon the propriety of presenting it; and if they thought an address advisable, to examine it critically, and suggest such alterations or additions as they might think proper."[9]

McKendree's address reported on the state of the church, listed topics for their consideration, urged unity and love, and described how he understood his relation to the conference as a bishop.

> It is only by virtue of a delegated power from the General Conference that I hold the reins of government. . . . I consider myself justly accountable, not for the system of government, but for my administration, and ought therefore to be ready to answer in General Conference for my past conduct, and be willing to receive information and advice to perfect future operations.[10]

McKendree's presentation received a mixed response. John Early's motion to record it in the journal of the conference lost; Jesse Lee's motion to include it with the conference papers carried. However, during the afternoon session, it was referred to the conference sitting as "a committee of the whole."[11] In this discussion, the presentation's various parts were used to establish an agenda for business. The topics were subsequently brought back to the conference separately as items for action, most of which were referred to select committees appointed for the purpose.[12] One of these was a "Committee on Episcopacy."[13]

Electing Presiding Elders

The conference had not been in session long before Laban Clark, a delegate from the New York Conference, reintroduced the familiar question of how presiding elders should be chosen. After a lengthy debate with various unsuccessful attempts to amend, the Clark motion to elect them by popular vote lost by only three votes, 42 to 45.[14] The closeness of this vote is indicative both of the divided mind of the conference on the subject and an omen of things to come. The determination to elect presiding elders was firmly held by many leaders in the denomination and was an issue that took the efforts of four General Conferences finally to resolve. The issue was not simply a question of introducing a more democratic process into the polity of the denomination. It had significant implications for the nature and practice of Methodist episcopacy. From the beginning, the office of presiding elder had been conceived as an extension and expression of episcopal power. As such they were to be chosen by the bishops. Electing those who would serve could only be seen as a limitation of that power.

McKendree was opposed to the innovation and expressed his opinion on the subject in one of his "Essays on Church Government": "A General Superintendency is essentially necessary to perpetuate itinerancy; therefore no judicious friend to the traveling plan will transfer the power of choosing Presiding Elders and stationing the preachers from the Bishops to the Annual Conferences, because in this the power of oversight consists."[15]

He went on to say that if the bishop's power to choose presiding elders were to be removed, "there will remain with them no power by which they can oversee the work, or officially manage the administration; and therefore the Conference must in justice release them from their responsibilities as bishops."[16]

> Therefore, the office of a Presiding Elder is not separate or distinct from that of a General Superintendent, but is inseparably connected with a part of it, and included in it. They are deputized by the Bishops, who bear the whole responsibility of the administration, as their assistants in the Superintendency.[17]

Moreover, McKendree continued, the General Conference has no power to authorize annual conferences to elect their presiding elders. "The General Conference possess [sic] only a delegated power, which is to be exercised under certain limitations and restrictions; but this power is not transferable, for no representative has a right to transfer his delegated powers to another."[18] Despite McKendree's outspoken opposition, the manner of choosing presiding elders was to divide and trouble the denomination until it was finally settled at the General Conference of 1828.

The General Conference of 1816

The year 1816 marked yet another turning point in the history of American Methodism. The delegated General Conference was now a reality. Asbury was dead. Coke had died a year earlier while on his way to India. The episcopal office was for the first time entirely in the hands of American-born preachers. Asbury's death marked not only the end of a remarkable career but also brought to a close "personal" government in the style of John Wesley. During the thirty-two years of his episcopal service, Asbury presided in two hundred thirty-four annual conferences and ordained about four thousand persons in the traveling or local ministry.[19] He laid his hands on seven of the men who were to become bishops in the American church, including one—William Capers—who was elected by the MECS. In most of the years of his episcopal service, he appointed every preacher in the connection. Bishop Paine is fully justified in his claim that "Methodism in America is more indebted to him than to any other man."[20] Perhaps even more important is the fact that Asbury modeled and personified American Methodist Episcopacy. Methodist bishops were expected to be like Asbury. Until Robert Richford Roberts was elected in 1816, they were single, expected to itinerate throughout the connection and attend, in order, every annual conference. This continued for only a short time after Asbury's death. By the mid-1820s, McKendree was the only fully itinerant Methodist bishop.

William McKendree, ill and limited in the service he could render, was the only bishop in the MEC when its General Conference convened in Baltimore on Wednesday, 1 May 1816. McKendree's second Episcopal Address was read, as was Asbury's "Valedictory" to the delegates. In a prior "Valedictory" addressed to McKendree and written in 1813, Asbury advised "that there may be only three effective Bishops, as from the beginning, traveling through the whole continent—each one to preside alternately in the Annual Conferences; one to preside during the sitting of the same Conference, the other two to have charge of and plan the stations and perform ordinations, assisted by the Elders in both branches."[21]

Asbury's concern that there not be too many bishops dominated the thinking of a majority in the connection for years, even though the number of annual conferences was straining the limits of episcopal supervision. In retrospect, it is little short of amazing that during the slightly more than half century of its existence as a united, independent, and organized body in America, Methodism elected only fourteen bishops. And in the same period of time, it grew to become America's largest Protestant denomination.

Three bishops were really no longer enough to oversee the work. Nevertheless, the 1816 General Conference's Committee on the State of the Episcopacy declared that "this conference will, in their present session, elect two additional bishops, and request our present superintendent to consecrate and set them apart for that office."[22] Concurrence was obtained from the delegates, and the first ballot for bishop was taken on Tuesday, 14 May. Enoch George of the Baltimore Conference received fifty-seven of the one hundred six votes cast and was declared elected. A second ballot was taken, and Robert Richford Roberts of the Philadelphia Conference was elected.[23]

Although George was born in Virginia, where his family lived and worshiped in the parish of the Reverend Devereux Jarratt, they soon moved to North Carolina where George began his career as a lay preacher. He was ordained elder in 1794 by Asbury and served eventually in North and South Carolina, Georgia, Maryland, and Virginia. He was a presiding elder at the time of his election and served as a bishop until his death in August 1828.

At age thirty-eight Roberts was one of the youngest persons ever to be elected bishop. Born in Maryland, he grew up on a farm in western Pennsylvania. Roberts was an expert with a rifle, skilled in the ways of the forest, and truly at home on the frontier. He joined the Baltimore Conference in 1802 and, like Enoch George, was ordained deacon and elder by Francis Asbury. Despite feeling ill at ease in the city, he was assigned there for much of his ministry and served well in pastorates in Baltimore, Alexandria, Georgetown, and eventually in Philadelphia at Old St. George's Church. Roberts has the distinction of being the first Methodist bishop to be married at the time of his election. (After Roberts began the trend of having a married episcopate, it would be one hundred fifty-two years before a bishop who had never been married was elected again, William R. Cannon.) Not long after his election, Roberts moved to Indiana, where he lived until his death in 1843. Despite his own lack of formal education, he actively supported the establishment of schools and colleges, one of which is now DePauw University in Greencastle, Indiana.

The advocates of electing presiding elders mounted a campaign again in 1816 to change the manner of their selection and thereby

83

limit the power of the bishops. Although their final objective was the same, the procedure to be used in the elections was slightly modified in the new proposal. Samuel Merwin, a delegate from the New York Conference, moved to amend the section of the *Discipline* related to the method of choosing presiding elders to read:

> At an early period in each annual conference the bishop shall nominate a person for each district that is to be supplied, and the conference shall, without debate, proceed in the choice, the person nominated being absent; and if the person nominated be not chosen according to nomination, the bishop shall nominate two others, one of whom it shall be the duty of conference to choose.[24]

It was further moved that the presiding elders should constitute a council to assist the bishop in the stationing of the preachers. Nathan Bangs amended this motion to stipulate that a presiding elder should serve for four years and could not be removed during that time without his consent.[25]

The conference once again formed itself into a "committee of the whole," a procedure that had been first allowed in the General Conference of 1812, to discuss the motion. Bishop McKendree, who was known to oppose it, relinquished the chair during the entire debate, which went on for a week. At various times Freeborn Garrettson, Philip Bruce, and George Pickering presided. Since the church now operated under a constitution, a new issue had to be resolved prior to the vote. McKendree had argued that the General Conference did not have the power to change the procedure to elect presiding elders. If he was correct, the motion was unconstitutional and, therefore, moot. It was not until late in the conference that the maker of the motion, Samuel Merwin, determined to put the matter of its constitutional status to the delegates. He introduced a resolution that "the motion relative to the election and appointment of presiding elders is not contrary to the constitution of our Church."[26] When the vote was finally taken on 11 May, this Merwin motion was defeated by a large majority, but the matter did not go away.[27]

In a historic move, the delegates made it the duty of the bishops, or of a committee appointed by them, to devise a course of study to be followed by candidates for the ministry who, before being received into full connection "shall give satisfactory evidence respecting his knowledge of those particular subjects."[28] This was a first in the history of the church and a new responsibility for the bishops. They were now established officially in the traditional episcopal function of being the teachers of the church.[29]

McKendree's journal reports that after conference was over, he met with the two new bishops, George and Roberts, and agreed upon how the work should be divided between them. McKendree, perhaps remembering the way in which he had been initiated into the episcopal office by Asbury, proposed that they all attend the first three conferences in order to allow the newly elected superintendents to learn the "peculiarities and difficulties of the Episcopal duties"; afterward they would follow a plan of alternating attendance in the conferences between them. This would make it unnecessary for every bishop to attend each annual conference. Roberts agreed to go with McKendree, but George set out on his own, since he said he did not think it was "necessary for three men to go and do one man's work."[30] They met at the Ohio Conference in September and there began to follow the plan agreed upon earlier for meeting the remaining conferences. The work was divided into three parts, but it was agreed that any one of them was free to attend any conference. McKendree said of this: "Thus was begun the practice of *dividing the work of superintending the Conferences by the Bishops themselves, and also of alternating*—a method which, it is hoped, will be perpetuated as most consistent with the genius of our Church constitution, and best calculated to promote union and perpetuate the itinerancy."[31] In reality, it was the first step in the creation of a modified form of diocesan episcopacy.

After the death of Asbury, the old pattern of itinerant general superintendency was gradually abandoned, the movement toward sectional and diocesan episcopacy was begun, and the church set on the road, which ultimately led to division. In the strictest sense, McKendree was the last itinerant general superintendent in the Methodist Church, but even he modified Asbury's plan in significant ways. Perhaps it was inevitable that it should have happened. No organization is likely to survive, much less prosper, if it does not evolve new ways of being and doing. At the same time, something is inevitably lost in the process of change, and Methodism was no exception to the pattern.

CHAPTER 7

Bishops and Presiding Elders: Limiting Episcopal Power

Although the office of presiding elder was formally defined in the *Discipline* in 1792, it existed in one form or another almost from the very beginning of Methodism in America. Because presiding elders are appointed by bishops, serve at the pleasure of those who appoint them, and then return to the body of preachers when their term is finished, they are in a unique position vis-à-vis both their colleagues and the episcopal leader. Although they remain part of the body of preachers during their service, they are not directly accountable to it but to the bishop who appoints them. Although the preachers have no part in their selection, they are subject to their authority. The elders were and are the load-bearing points in the Methodist structure. Richey characterized these elders as never leaving "the fraternity" of the conference but "for the interim of their tenure in that office, they functioned within and as part of the episcopacy."[1] Bishop McTyeire describes the presiding elder as "the agent or assistant of a Bishop." He goes on to say that the presiding elder is "part of the executive government; and in his district is authorized to discharge all the duties of the absent Bishop, except ordination. The authority by which the Bishop is enabled 'to oversee the business of the Church' consists largely, therefore, in the power of appointing the presiding elders."[2]

Presiding elders are chosen by bishops in The UMC today, in

continuity with the practice of Asbury. The *Discipline* requires the bishop to consult with the cabinet and the Committee on District Superintendency of the district in which the vacancy occurs before making a selection, but the final choice is made by the bishop. Every bishop determines how the selection will be made, but in many instances other presiding elders (now called "district superintendents") nominate individuals for consideration by the bishop. The selection may also be discussed in meetings of the Cabinet. The church has now imposed a six-year term for district superintendents, though it can be extended to eight years "for missional reasons." The limit ended the former practice, especially in the southern church, of moving presiding elders from one district to another to allow continuous service. No elder can serve as a district superintendent for more than twelve years, and no more than eight years in any consecutive eleven.

As we have seen, the principle of bishops choosing presiding elders did not pass down from Asbury to the present without challenge. A campaign to authorize, instead, the election of these leaders by the annual conference occupied every General Conference from 1812 until 1828. This campaign reflected both the growing democratic sentiment of the time and a desire to limit episcopal power. The fact that the height of this effort coincided with the end of the era of personal authority, epitomized by Francis Asbury, shows that it was a reaction to that style of leadership and an attempt to establish a new kind of corporate responsibility and authority in the body of preachers. It was not a movement led by dissidents. Among those who supported the election of presiding elders were such worthies as Ezekiel Cooper, Jesse Lee, Nicholas Snethen, and Nathan Bangs. Since it was not led by a faction, it was a movement that for many years seemed to have a life of its own.

Joshua Soule

On Saturday morning, 13 May, at the General Conference of 1820, Joshua Soule was elected a bishop in the MEC. He was elected on the first ballot, receiving forty-seven of the eighty-eight votes cast. Of the fourteen bishops chosen before 1844, Soule was the only one who was a preacher at the time of his election. He was also the only person who was to have the distinction of being the senior bishop in both the MEC and the MECS. Few individuals had greater impact on the church as a whole. Already known as the author of the Constitution of 1808, Soule was destined to champion and defend the Asburian form of strong itinerant episcopacy almost single-handedly. Admitted to the Maine Conference (his native state) in 1799, he was ordained both deacon and elder by Richard Whatcoat, and served a number of circuits in New England until 1816. At that time he became book agent and editor of the *Methodist Magazine* (which later became the *Methodist Quarterly Review*).

On the Monday following Soule's election, Timothy Merritt, a distinguished member of the New England Conference, made a motion to elect presiding elders in the annual conference. The motion was seconded by Beverly Waugh (who would be elected bishop in 1836).[3] During the lengthy debate on the Merritt proposal, an amendment was proposed by Ezekiel Cooper and John Emory (who would also join the episcopacy in 1836) calling for the bishop to nominate three persons for each vacancy, and for the annual conference to choose the proper number from among those nominees.[4] It is possible that Bishop George was the actual author of their proposal, reflecting the degree to which lack of unanimity existed even among the bishops on this issue.[5] The Cooper-Emory substitute retained the provision that these elders were to constitute a council and advise the bishop in stationing the preachers. While Bishop McKendree was supportive of this provision, he made his opposition to the change of electing presiding elders clear (though from a distance, since he was ill).

The motion was initially laid on the table but later taken off and debated at length. William Capers finally moved that a committee be formed, composed of an equal number of persons known to be on opposing sides of the question, to confer with the bishops to see if the matter could be resolved. Those named to the committee included Ezekiel Cooper, John Emory, and Nathan Bangs, who were in favor; and Stephen G. Roszel, Joshua Wells, and William Capers, all opposed. Caper's manuscript account, which Bishop Paine used as a source in his biography of McKendree, says the committee met with the bishops but was unable to reach an agreement. In time, however, a compromise was struck, which, according to Capers, gained the support of Bishop George. "It met with his (the bishop's [George]) approbation, and, if I am not mistaken . . . was the bishop's motion."[6] The committee report, drafted by John Emory, was presented to the conference by Bishop George and clarified that "when there is more than one [presiding elder] wanted not more than three at a time shall be nominated, nor more than one at a time elected."[7] It also mandated that the presiding elders become an advisory council of the bishops.[8] Five days later (20 May), the resolutions drafted by the committee were considered separately in conference and each passed with a large majority. At this point it appeared certain that in the future presiding elders would be nominated by bishops but elected by annual conferences.

So far as can be determined, no one knew what Soule was thinking, but it changed the future of Methodism. After the votes in favor of the committee resolutions, the next entry for May 20 reports that Joshua Soule, who had not yet been ordained a bishop, was granted permission to leave the conference for the afternoon. It was a routine request from a member of the conference, but it set the stage for some dramatic events.[9]

After leaving the conference, Soule went to his room and prepared a letter, which he sent to the bishops, declaring he could not accept the office to which he had been elected. He wrote:

> In consequence of an act of the General Conference, passed this day, in which I conceive the constitution of The Methodist Episcopal Church is violated, and that Episcopal government which has heretofore distinguished her greatly enervated, by a transfer of executive power from the Episcopacy to the several Annual Conferences, it becomes my duty to notify you, from the imposition of whose hands only I can be qualified for the office of Superintendent, that under the existing state of things *I cannot, consistently with my convictions of propriety and obligation, enter upon the work of an itinerant General Superintendent.*
>
> I was elected under the *constitution and government of the Methodist Episcopal Church* UNIMPAIRED. On no other consideration but that of their continuance would I have consented to be considered a candidate for a relation in which were incorporated such arduous labors and awful responsibilities.
>
> I do not feel myself at liberty to wrest myself from your hands, as the act of the General Conference has placed me in them; but *I solemnly declare, and could appeal to the Searcher of hearts for the sincerity of my intention, that I cannot act as Superintendent under the rules this day made and established by the General Conference.*[10]

It is well to remember that Soule was the author of the Third Restrictive Rule that protected the plan of itinerant general superintendency, which he now thought threatened by an action he judged clearly unconstitutional. McKendree, as adamantly opposed to the legislation as Soule and equally convinced it was unconstitutional, had returned to the city to be present for Soule's ordination. After receiving word of Soule's decision, he wrote to the bishops and delegates, saying, "I extremely regret that you have, by this measure, reduced me to the painful necessity of pronouncing the resolution *unconstitutional, and, therefore destitute of the proper authority of the Church*."[11]

Whatever the delegates may have thought about the authority of their episcopal leaders, the senior bishop in the church believed he had the power to declare actions of the General Conference unconstitutional. Although the sequence of the events that followed Soule's decision is confused, Paine reports that Soule's letter to the bishops reached McKendree before he had finished his letter to the conference.[12] Bishop McKendree's journal, upon which Paine's biography is based, supplies the information about the events that transpired following Soule's dramatic announcement to the bishops.

After receiving Soule's letter, the bishops met and each was asked separately to express his opinion on the constitutionality of the resolutions, the crucial issue for Soule. Bishop Roberts "was of the opinion that the resolutions of the Conference were an infringement of the constitution." Bishop George "chose to be silent." McKendree "considered them unconstitutional."[13] They all agreed that Bishop Roberts, who, along with many of the conference delegates, thought Soule was unwilling to "submit to the authority of the General Conference," should talk with Soule and report the results of his conversation back to the bishops the next morning.

Larger constitutional issues notwithstanding, there was a practical matter that had to be decided quickly by the bishops. Did they expect to go ahead with Soule's ordination? They decided to proceed and set the service for 11:00 A.M. on Wednesday, 24 May 1820. Bishop George was instructed to prepare the necessary credentials. Without full knowledge of the facts, it seems puzzling that Soule gave his approval too.[14] We can only assume that he was convinced that the issues before the conference would be resolved in a way acceptable to him. McKendree, with Soule's knowledge and support, went before the session of the conference on 23 May, requested permission to speak, and outlined what had happened. The conference journal reports only that "the debate on the subject under consideration was

91

suspended, to allow Bishop M'Kendree to make a communication to the General Conference."[15] Other sources report that McKendree read both his and Soule's letters to the delegates. McKendree's letter is contained in Paine's biography, and if it was read to the delegates there could have been no doubt in anyone's mind that the senior bishop agreed with Soule in judging the resolution just passed "unconstitutional, and therefore destitute of the proper authority of the Church."[16]

Their responses to McKendree were spirited and generally critical of Soule for his seeming unwillingness to accept the will of the General Conference. His opponents met and decided to block his ordination. "To the sentiments of Bishop McKendree and Mr. Soule those in favor of a change took exceptions, held a caucus without consulting those not in favor of the change and agreed to arrest the ordination of J. Soule."[17] Debate was suspended on all resolutions and the galleries cleared in order to move the conference into executive session to receive a motion jointly offered by D. Ostrander, a delegate from the New York Conference, and James Smith, a delegate from the Philadelphia Conference. The motion declared that since Soule's letter to the conference had affirmed his intention not to be governed by the resolution on the election of presiding elders, his ordination should be deferred or postponed until he gave a satisfactory explanation to the conference. During the ensuing debate, it became evident that the Ostrander-Smith motion did not have enough support to pass, and they withdrew it. Soule then made a few remarks, which were followed by a motion to reconsider all that had been done previously. The session adjourned without coming to a decision.

The debate was resumed the following morning, with Bishop Roberts in the chair. A heated discussion continued until five minutes of eleven, the time appointed for the ordination of Soule. At his request, the service was postponed and the debate continued until just before noon, when it was determined so many delegates had left the conference that it lacked the two-thirds required for a quorum. Bishop George, who had assumed the chair from Roberts, had no choice under the circumstances but to postpone the ordination again. The mood of the majority was to force Soule to obey the mandate of the conference and abide by its resolutions.

The charge that Soule had refused to submit to the authority of the conference was unfair, misconstruing what the bishop-elect had said. It was actually his loyalty to the General Conference, as he understood it, that caused him to refuse ordination as a general superintendent if the resolution regarding the election of presiding elders went into effect. At no time did he say or imply he was unwilling to abide by the action of the conference, but he would not agree to support an unconstitutional action that violated the Third Restrictive Rule. It must be granted, however, that Soule confused the situation badly when he put himself into the hands of the bishops and agreed to let them decide if he should be ordained.

After lunch, the necessary quorum of delegates returned, no doubt in a somewhat better mood, and certainly having caucused to discuss the subject over lunch. The vote was called for, by written ballot, on the motion to reconsider the election of presiding elders. Two ballots were required, since the first produced a tie vote of 43 for and 43 against; Bishop Roberts, who was again presiding, refused to break the tie. When the second ballot produced the same result, Roberts ruled the motion lost for lack of a majority. The conference moved to a discussion of slavery, which occupied the rest of the day.

At the next morning session, Thursday, 25 May, Bishop George once again announced that the ordination service had been set for noon. Shortly after his announcement, however, Joshua Soule read a statement in which he resigned the office to which he had been elected. Technically, it is difficult to see how a "bishop-elect" could resign an office to which he was never ordained. It was a first in the history of the church, but not the last time that an elected bishop refused ordination.[18] Soule's resignation was promptly laid on the table, where it remained until it was determined on Friday afternoon that Soule would not change his mind and it was formally accepted by the conference.[19] Earlier in the Friday morning session, Edward Cannon, of Virginia, and William Kennedy, of South Carolina, moved that the "rule passed in this conference respecting the nomination and election of presiding elders be suspended until the next General Conference." Their motion also stipulated that in the interval the bishops should continue the old practice of appointing them. Once again there was a protracted debate, but when a vote was taken, it passed 45 to 35. The conference was tired of talking about the issue, and neither side had the strength to prevail. Following that action, Soule was asked once again to withdraw his letter of resignation "and comply with the wishes of his brethren in submitting to be ordained." Despite the fact he had won the day when the offending measure was suspended and had received the approbation of both

93

delegates and bishops, Soule stood and reaffirmed his intention not to be ordained. Although the record states that "his resignation was accepted," there was some confusion among the delegates whether it had been accepted by a vote of the conference or just announced from the chair by Bishop George. "It is difficult to conceive," says Bishop Paine, "the mental agony which such a train of circumstances would produce in an intelligent, conscientious and sensitive mind."[20]

No doubt all the delegates were aware that the question of electing presiding elders in the annual conferences "was now merged in the more important one, whether the episcopacy or the General Conference was to be supreme."[21] Moreover, the attempt had raised a significant related issue—who has the power to rule on the constitutionality of the acts of a General Conference? The conference addressed the latter concerns before adjournment, but both remained on the table for many years to come and had significant implications in the life of the church.

In one last abortive attempt to elect Soule, on the last day of conference, Wells and Capers moved to elect a bishop but had to withdraw their motion for lack of support. Before adjournment, the delegates decided to lay before the entire body of preachers the question of who had authority to judge the constitutionality of actions of a General Conference. They advised the various annual conferences to pass resolutions to give the general superintendents authority to determine the constitutionality of any measure brought to the General Conference. The motion read:

> If they [the superintendents], or a majority of them, shall judge it unconstitutional, they shall, within three days after its passage, return it to the conference with their objections to it in writing. And whenever a resolution is so returned, the conference shall reconsider it, and if it pass by a majority of two-thirds it shall be constitutional and pass into a law, notwithstanding the objections of the superintendents.[22]

The Power of the Body of Preachers Supreme in the Church

Bishop McKendree believed that the precedent of bringing issues before the annual conferences for resolution had been established in 1809, when the Virginia Conference protested the initiative he had taken with Bishop Asbury to form the Genesee Conference.

94

Although they believed themselves to have the legal authority to do it, they responded to the challenge by taking the question to the annual conferences for an opinion. As Bishop Payne suggests, "By this act, the Bishops and the Annual Conferences tacitly declared the Annual Conferences to be the proper judges of constitutional questions."[23] This was done because McKendree believed then, as he did in 1821, that "from the preachers collectively both the General Conference and General Superintendents derive their powers."[24] Although the principle was affirmed that the final authority in Methodist polity resides with the body of preachers, and thus in their assembly the annual conference, the matter is actually more complex, since constitutional questions related to the General Conference involve the acts of a body to whom the power of the body of preachers has been delegated. How can they then rule on the legitimacy of acts made by those to whom they have given legitimate power to act? If the episcopacy is seen as a co-ordinate body with the General Conference rather than simply its officers (as McKendree claimed), then a case can be made that they can be empowered by the body of preachers to make such judgments. This was the position later reaffirmed in the MECS. But if one accepts, instead, the emerging assumption of the MEC, that bishops are officers of the General Conference and entirely subject to it, they clearly would not have the power to judge its actions. This perplexing issue was finally resolved one hundred nineteen years later by the creation of a third, judicial branch of church government, the Judicial Council.

But for now a form of veto power over actions of the General Conference, which required a two-thirds majority to override, was given to the bishops:

By a majority vote, the General Conference of 1820 agreed to the principle of a veto power to be exercised by the Bishops over all enactments of the General Conference, which in the preamble was acknowledged to be no "proper tribunal to judge of and determine such a question." This measure provided not merely a method by which the Bishops might carry an appeal from the decisions of a General Conference to the tribunal of the Annual Conferences—which really lodges the veto power in the body of traveling ministry—but, in the strictest sense, clothed the episcopacy with a veto power, which required a two-thirds majority of the General Conference to overcome it.[25]

It is fascinating that the *Journal of the General Conference* of 1824 gives no official summary of the action taken in the annual conferences in response to the request of the General Conference of 1820 to ratify the veto power of the bishops. A motion offered by the illustrious Peter Cartwright at the conference in 1824 does hint at those results. He says that "a majority of the annual conferences have judged them unconstitutional, and . . . six of the annual conferences have recommended their adoption."[26] Other sources tell us more. In the Baltimore Conference of 1822, Bishop McKendree presented a prepared address in which he explained and defended his ruling declaring the election of presiding elders to be in violation of the Third Restrictive Rule and therefore unconstitutional, but then urged adoption of the suspended resolutions by all the annual conferences for the sake of peace in the church. Ignoring his appeal, "a resolution pronouncing the suspended resolutions unconstitutional was indefinitely postponed by a large vote."[27] Ezekiel Cooper "carried the Philadelphia Conference unanimously in 1822 for the constitutionality of an elective presiding eldership."[28] South Carolina ruled both resolutions to be "contrary to the constitution of The Methodist Episcopal Church, established by the General Conference of 1808."[29] As could easily have been predicted by almost any Methodist, McKendree's journal reports that conference politics flourished when the time came to elect delegates to the General Conference of 1824: "Great were the efforts to secure a majority in favor of the suspended resolutions, but they proved unsuccessful."[30]

Affirming the Episcopal Veto

McKendree's Episcopal Address to the General Conference delegates in 1824 presented two questions: Are the suspended resolutions regarding the election of presiding elders constitutional? If not, should they be adopted, as six of the conferences had suggested, by suspending the Restrictive Rule? On 18 May, Lovick Pierce, delegate from South Carolina, and William Winans, delegate from Mississippi, gave notice to the conference that they intended to offer a resolution to amend the Sixth Restrictive Rule of 1808. It began, as did the one passed by the previous General Conference, by allowing the bishops three days to respond to any legislation of the General Conference that they thought was unconstitutional. A modification of the procedure was recommended, which reads:

96

The conference shall reconsider such rule or rules, and if, upon reconsideration, they shall pass a majority of two-thirds of the members present, they shall be considered as rules, and go into immediate effect; but
in case a less majority shall differ from the opinion of the bishops, and
they continue to sustain their objections, the rule or rules objected to
shall be laid before the annual conferences, in which case the decision
of a majority of all the members of the annual conference present when
the vote shall be taken shall be final.[31]

The motion was adopted by a majority of 64 to 58.[32] Tigert
reports: "Thus was the proper tribunal for an appeal at least partial-
ly recognized. Two-thirds of the General Conference, or a majority in
the Annual Conferences, could thus overrule the Bishops."[33]

A resolution offered by David Young, of Ohio, declaring the resolutions concerning the election of presiding elders "not of authority"
and not to be carried into effect, was brought to the floor on 22 May
and passed two days later by a vote of 63 to 61.[34] The *Journal of General
Conference* reports: "The Senior Bishop had prosecuted to a successful
conclusion his issue from the action of a General Conference to the
tribunal of the Annual Conferences; and the Delegated General
Conference, acting under a constitution, formally recognized the
supremacy of the primary bodies which had called it into existence."[35]

Emerging Regional Differences

On Wednesday (26 May), the conference elected two general
superintendents. Joshua Soule was chosen on the second ballot with
sixty-five votes and Elijah Hedding on the third with sixty-four.[36]
Each was widely and correctly understood to represent one of the
two parties—Soule a "constitutionalist," and Hedding a "revisionist." After the second ballot, John Emory, another "revisionist" candidate, withdrew to ensure the election of Hedding. Had he not
withdrawn, it is likely that the other "constitutional" candidate—
William Beauchamp—would have been elected. Each party had successfully elected a champion.

The action taken earlier with respect to the suspended presiding
elder resolutions was then challenged on the basis that not all of the
annual conferences had voted on the measure and so, theoretically, it
could still pass. William Winans wanted them to be considered as
"unfinished business." Eventually, a motion introduced by Robert

Payne and William Capers passed: "It is the sense of this General Conference that the suspended resolutions, making the presiding elder elective, &c., are considered as unfinished business, and are neither to be inserted in the revised form of the Discipline nor to be carried into operation before the next General Conference."[37]

Through the use of this parliamentary strategy, the matter was effectively put on hold for another four years, and a significant milestone was passed. The conference had finally agreed with the principle stated by Joshua Soule during the debates and earlier by McKendree that "the General Conference is not the proper judge of the constitutionality of its own acts. . . . If the General Conference be the sole judge in such questions, then there are no bounds to its power."[38] The limitations contained in the Restrictive Rules imposed by the adoption of a constitution had also been protected.

This action foretold an ominous future in ways not obvious to most. The conferences had divided on the constitutional issue and emerged with the South and West aligned against the North and East. The differences between them were both sectional and political. "In our Church, as in our nation, the division was along the line of strict construction of the powers delegated by the constitution, on the one hand, and a loose and broad interpretation of those powers, on the other."[39] American Methodism, leading the nation, was now on the road to division. McKendree, for one, grasped the seriousness of the situation. "The course I took relative to the suspended resolutions was not to defeat them, but to bring them into operation conformably to the constitution, and thereby confirm the 'peace-measure' and to harmonize the preachers. To this the preachers who prefer the old system are willing to submit for the sake of peace."[40] That is why, in spite of his firm conviction that the resolutions authorizing the election of presiding elders were unconstitutional, he was willing to urge their passage in the interest of unity. But the reformers wanted more, and Soule had warned McKendree they would. Soule wrote to McKendree from New York in May 1821:

> If I had any sufficient security, that the adoption of those resolutions, *in constitutional order*, would be the means of reconciliation, and lay the foundation for a permanent peace, I would cordially recommend them for such adoption. But it is impossible for me to conceive that those brethren who, for so many years, have contested the radical principles of the government, will rest satisfied while the essential features of Episcopacy remain.[41]

Soule's fears were well grounded. Some of these "radical" brethren in fact wanted even to introduce laypersons into the councils of the church, and that effort would divide the church in another decade, creating the Methodist Protestants. But Emory's biography makes it clear that the advocates of lay representation were not united with those who desired to elect presiding elders. Emory himself favored electing presiding elders but was opposed to lay representation.[42] The outspoken advocates of lay representation, associated with the Wesleyan Repository, saw themselves as a third party. "As we courted neither party [those for or against the election of presiding elders], so *have we not identified ourselves with either party: we have spoken of you both, on all occasions, as an independent or a third party would speak.*"[43] The reasons for this were interesting. H. D. Sellers, who favored lay delegates in the General Conference, wrote:

> The advocates of a lay delegation, however, were not all favourable to the election of presiding elders. Some of us held very firmly to the opinion, that the power of the episcopacy was conservative against the body of preachers, and were disposed to believe that any accession of power to them would obstruct the introduction of a lay delegation.[44]

Subsequent events indicate that he was right. It is interesting, however, that the MPC, which was begun in November 1830 after separating from the MEC, featured lay representation and abandoned the episcopacy altogether.

CHAPTER 8

Modifying the General Superintendency

From the beginning of its separate and independent life in America in 1784, the MEC faced controversies that had the potential to divide it at regular intervals, yet the MEC managed to remain largely intact. It avoided division when Strawbridge and the Virginia Methodists decided to forgo the administration of the sacraments and affirm Asbury's leadership. O'Kelly's personal animosity toward Asbury, and his protest of episcopal power and practice resulted in schism in 1792, but he failed to win widespread support for his republican Methodists. Richard Allen's response to racism in St. George's Church in Philadelphia in 1787 also produced a new denomination, the African Methodist Episcopal Church. None of these, however, seriously hindered the growth and spread of episcopal Methodism. But by 1824, currents were running that would converge into the torrent leading to division in 1844.

At the end of the General Conference of 1824, the church had five bishops, one of whom, McKendree, was in poor health and able to give only limited service. Joshua Soule and forty-four-year-old Elijah Hedding had just been elected. Hedding, from the New England Conference, was born in New York but grew up in Vermont. He joined the New York Conference in 1803 and was ordained a deacon by Whatcoat and an elder by Asbury. When the conference boundaries were redrawn in 1805, Hedding became part of the New

England Conference, serving mostly in Vermont and New Hampshire. At the time of his election to the episcopacy, he was the presiding elder of the Boston District. Hedding's antislavery sentiments later caused him considerable personal distress as he found himself caught after 1836 between these convictions and his duty to obey the directives of the General Conference. He was active until 1848, when ill health forced him to limit his work.

There were seventeen annual conferences in 1824. Following the pattern first established in 1816, the bishops divided the work between them rather than itinerate through every conference. The General Conference of 1824 gave formal encouragement to their practice in the form of a resolution that asked the bishops to constitute themselves into a council "to form their plan of travelling through their charge."[1] Although the General Conference did not require the creation of such a council, and the bishops had already been doing what the conference asked, they met immediately following the close of the sessions and agreed how to divide the work. It was determined that Roberts and Soule would oversee the southern and western conferences, while Bishops George and Hedding would attend those in the North and East. McKendree would itinerate, as he was able, through as many as possible. After two years, the plan called for them to exchange conferences so that each bishop would have the experience of being in every annual conference before the next meeting of the General Conference.[2] They were not together again until April 1826, when they met in Philadelphia where George and Hedding were holding the Philadelphia Conference.[3] Roberts did not attend. At this meeting (reported only in McKendree's unpublished notebook but reproduced by Tigert in his *Constitutional History*), there were two major items of business: (1) to appoint a fraternal delegate to the English Conference, and (2) to arrange the details related to the exchange and oversight of the annual conferences. They sought first to name the fraternal delegate. William Capers of South Carolina was nominated by Bishop McKendree and supported by Bishops Soule and Roberts. Bishops George and Hedding were opposed to Capers because he was known to be a slave owner. They were fearful he would be offensive as a delegate both to the English and to the northern conferences in the United States. George suggested the names of Ezekiel Cooper and Wilbur Fisk.

Methodism and Slavery

The Methodists were by this time involved in the escalating conflict over the institution of slavery. Prior to 1800 there could be no question of their opposition to the institution. The Conference of 1780, a majority of whose delegates lived south of Maryland, said, "Slavery is contrary to the laws of God, man and nature, and hurtful to the society; contrary to the dictates of conscience and pure religion and doing that which we would not others should do to us and ours."[4] When the church was organized in 1784, the Christmas Conference legislated that any slaves owned by preachers should be freed in any state in which the law allowed it, and excluded slaveholders or sellers of slaves from membership. Opposition in the South, however, made it increasingly hard to enforce the second provision. It was a cotton economy heavily dependent on slave labor. Eli Whitney invented the cotton gin in 1793, and the textile industry in England shifted from wool to cotton, increasing the demand for the product. By 1860, three-fourths of the almost four million slaves in the United States were directly engaged in the production of cotton.

By 1800 the Methodist position on slavery was changed to favor gradual emancipation, already accomplished legally in several states in the years immediately following the American Revolution (Pennsylvania, 1780; Rhode Island, 1784; Connecticut, 1784; and Ohio, 1802). In theory they were still committed to the principle that the institution of slavery per se was contrary to both the civil and political views of justice and the "spirit of Christian religion." Where "practicable," preachers who became slave owners by any means were to legally emancipate their slaves "agreeably to the laws of the state wherein they live."[5] However, the section urging conferences to petition their state legislatures to enact laws allowing gradual emancipation was stricken, and the following was added in 1804: "Let our preachers from time to time, as occasion serves, admonish and exhort all slaves to render due respect and obedience to the commands and interests of their respective masters."[6]

The next step in this sad story shifted the responsibility from central to local authority. Each annual conference was authorized by the General Conference of 1808 "to form their own regulations relative to buying and selling slaves."[7] Southern church leaders were later to cite this action as exemplary in its implications for preserving the unity of the denomination, while antislavery forces saw it as the moment when a clear and definite position was fatally compromised. The real compromise, however, came in 1816. "Under the present existing circumstances in relation to slavery," they said, "little can be done to abolish a practice so contrary to the principles of moral justice." They concluded "that the evil appears to be past remedy."[8] No significant new legislation on slavery was enacted between 1820 and 1836.

William Lloyd Garrison published the first issue of *The Public Liberator and Journal of the Times* on 1 January 1831. In August of the same year, Nat Turner led a slave rebellion in Virginia. The American Antislavery Society was founded in 1832. In 1836 a gag order was imposed on the church by the General Conference. In their "Pastoral Address to the Church" the bishops declared, "The only safe, Scriptural and prudent way for us, both as ministers and people, to take is wholly to refrain from this agitating subject, which is now convulsing the country." This echoed the report of the Committee on Slavery, which resolved "that it is inexpedient to make any change in our book of Discipline respecting slavery, and that we deem it improper further to agitate the subject in the General Conference at present."[9] At the same time, the Methodists in the South were arguing that slavery was a political, not a religious issue, and beginning to defend it from Scripture. For them, slavery was more than just an economic issue, it was the way to control a large population. The populations of both Mississippi and Georgia in 1860 had a majority of African Americans. Missionary efforts directed at the conversion of African Americans, led by preachers like William Capers, had by that time produced two hundred thousand African American Methodists.

Although the law of the church did not prohibit either preachers or laypersons from owning slaves, the practical issue was how the slaves could be freed by those who desired to do it. The American Colonization Society was organized in 1817, but in the first ten years of its existence it managed to free and transport only about two hundred former slaves to Liberia. Opponents of slavery were vocal in their determination to abolish the institution. A delegate to the General Conference of 1820 from Mississippi, Thomas Griffin, was not pleased with comments he heard from his northern brethren against slavery nor with the attitude of those who made the comments. Reflecting his frustration, he observed, "It appears that some of our Northern brethren are willing to see us all damned and double-damned, rammed, jammed, and crammed into a forty-six pounder, and touched off into eternity."[10]

Sectionalism and the Bishops

Given the spirit of the times, maybe it is not surprising that the bishops were unsuccessful in completing the simple task of naming a delegate to the English Conference. When the deadlock could not be broken, Bishop George expressed his opinion that the language of the General Conference resolution did not actually require them to send anyone. Bishop Soule produced a copy of the legislation that both "authorized and requested" the superintendents to appoint a delegate. While it is possible to interpret this action as Bishop George had done, the force of the resolution made it clear a delegate was expected. But after more discussion, they were still unable to reach agreement. McKendree, who as the senior bishop was presiding, postponed the decision in order to move on to the subject of exchanging the conference assignments. Bishop George protested that he was in a hurry and asked to schedule another meeting to finish their work. The others agreed to the postponement. McKendree's account says they were together about "three quarters of an hour."

They met again five days later, on 18 May 1824 at 6:00 A.M. in McKendree's rooms—hardly the hour at which such meetings of bishops are generally held today. The second meeting was a copy of the first. They failed again to nominate a delegate to the English Conference, with Hedding now agreeing with George that it would be better not to send a delegate than to send a slaveholder. Hedding is quoted in the biography written by D. W. Clark as remembering that "[t]he two bishops . . . who had nominated Rev. W. Capers [McKendree and Soule], refused to yield their nomination, or to concur in ours, alleging that slaveholding should not be a bar to any office in the appointment of the Church." Since nobody would compromise, they agreed to postpone the matter until the following year and took up the plan to assign the conferences.[11] It should be noted that the General Conference of 1828 did not exhibit the sensitivities of Bishops George and Hedding to slaveholders, and elected Capers the fraternal delegate to the English Conference. The bishops were never able to agree on a nominee.[12]

Bishop George was also opposed to exchanging conferences,

pronouncing it "inadmissible."[13] Claiming a pressing need to get back to business, he summarily ended the second episcopal conclave. Despite further attempts on the part of McKendree to arrange the exchange, it never happened. For more than twenty years George and Hedding continued to serve in the North and East, with Roberts and Soule caring for the conferences in the South and West. Between 1824 and 1844, Bishop Hedding made but a single tour of the southern conferences, and that in 1831, seven years after he became a bishop. In the same year, Bishop Soule made his first episcopal visitation in the North.[14] The Asbury-McKendree model of itinerant general superintendency now no longer existed. Localized episcopacy in various forms effectively became the norm in the church.

It is often the case that significant change comes in the guise of simple and seemingly inconsequential modifications of practice. McKendree tried valiantly to keep the concept of general superintendency alive, but the divisions were already too pronounced to allow it. Following the bishops' meeting, McKendree wrote George and Hedding, "I have advised you and the other Bishops to change, in order for each to visit all the Annual Conferences before the next General Conference." But he then went on to say that he could "claim no authority over my colleagues" and "if, therefore, the change involves insurmountable difficulties, on your part, it is your right to decline such a course."[15] Hedding and George responded a week later: "We have received yours of yesterday, and are of opinion that the plan will be impracticable."[16] They cited reasons of health for not being able to cooperate—ironic in view of the fact that McKendree continued to itinerate throughout the connection in spite of ill health, and sought without success to maintain the bonds between the various sections of the church.[17] It may truly be said that McKendree was American Methodism's last real itinerant general superintendent. Despite his best efforts, as Tigert says,

> The work of division was accomplished in the years 1820-1828. During that period it came to pass, perhaps before many of the active participants were awake to it, that the line of division, constitutional and sectional, had been run through the Church, separating it, in all but name, into two sharply contrasted Episcopal Methodisms.[18]

By the end of the 1824–28 quadrennium the church had been divided North and South by the practice of the bishops and among the bishops themselves. This is not surprising, since two of them,

Soule and Hedding, had been elected by well-organized party and sectional interests representing the divisions. Tigert's advice to those looking at Methodist history in America is both astute and correct: "He who hangs his theory of the division of the Church upon the slender thread of the accidents of an episcopal matrimonial alliance, or even upon the difference of civil institutions, North and South, alone, may satisfy himself. But his proceeding is unhistorical."[19]

Bishop James O. Andrew recalled three decades later that the delegates to the General Conferences of 1820 and 1824 "did little else for much of the time than listen to the most violent denunciations of the tyranny and oppression of the episcopacy." He remembered his confusion upon hearing these charges at the first General Conference he attended in 1820: "As we in South Carolina had neither felt nor heard of these awful and crushing evils belonging to our system, I was perfectly astounded to hear Methodist preachers talk after such a fashion."[20] The only hope, they said, was to *republicanize* the system by electing presiding elders, admitting laypersons to the conferences, and limiting the power of bishops.

The General Conference of 1828

The situation was different eight years later when McKendree opened the sessions of the General Conference of 1828, meeting for the first time in Pittsburgh. A conservative backlash had taken place. The suggestion of electing presiding elders and the effort to seat laypersons in the General Conference had galvanized those who wanted to protect the old system. Joining with the other opponents, they laid the presiding-elder question to its final rest and made it clear they were unwilling to include laypersons as members of the various conferences. The bishops and their administration were also vindicated and the old system of strong episcopal power was reaffirmed. Those determined to have lay representation realized what had happened, accepted defeat, and began the process of separating from the denomination to form the Methodist Protestant Church.

The most fundamental area of disagreement between those who united to become Methodist Protestants and episcopal Methodists was the practice of vesting legislative, executive, and judicial power in the body of preachers. At the heart of the new movement was a commitment to representative government in which both laypersons and clergy played an equal role. They created a scheme with a one-order ministry (elders) in which "governing pastors" had no place, and eliminated both bishops and presiding elders. Their conference was led by a president. Representative Methodists held "that to the ministry is given divine authority to preach the Gospel, but that authority to rule can only come from those who are ruled."[21] From the beginning, laypersons were included in equal numbers in their general, annual, and quarterly conferences. The membership of the quarterly conference was constituted by election in the church; and in all levels of government, laypersons had an equal right to vote on any question affecting the whole. Property was held by elected trustees who were directed by the will of a majority. "Representative Methodism originated with the people, and naturally secured to members of the church the right, by virtue of their membership to vote directly or by representative on all questions affecting the church. Episcopal Methodism originated with the preachers, and naturally makes no place for lay suffrage."[22]

Midway through the General Conference of 1828, the presiding-elder question was finally decided. Working together, as they often did, William Winans of Mississippi and William Capers of South Carolina moved and seconded as follows:

> That the resolutions commonly called the suspended resolutions, rendering the presiding elders elective, &c., and which were referred to this conference by the last General Conference as unfinished business, and reported to us at this conference, be, and the same are hereby rescinded and made void.[23]

This motion carried and, although it was unsuccessfully appealed the next day, the matter was finally closed. The conference enjoyed little peace, however, for other significant issues had taken its place.

Since making the office of presiding elder elective required amending the Restrictive Rules of the constitution, the conference belatedly got around to enacting legislation to provide for an orderly process for such amendment. The experience in 1821 of submitting questions regarding the constitutionality of legislation enacted in General Conference to the separate annual conferences had demonstrated the ineffectiveness of that practice. Although seven conferences judged the legislation authorizing the election of presiding elders to be unconstitutional, six of them had recommended its adoption by the next General Conference anyway. The New England, New York, Genesee, Philadelphia, and Baltimore Conferences refused to act, thereby blocking it entirely. Wilbur Fisk was the author of the change in 1828, which provided

> that upon the concurrent recommendation of three-fourths of all the members of the several annual conferences who shall be present and vote on such recommendation, then a majority of two-thirds of the General Conference succeeding shall suffice to alter any of such regulations excepting the first article. And, also, whenever such alteration or alterations shall have first been recommended by two-thirds of the General Conference, so soon as three-fourths of the members of the annual conferences shall have concurred, as aforesaid, with such recommendation, such alteration or alterations shall take effect.[24]

With the passage of this measure and its subsequent ratification in the annual and General Conferences during the 1828–32 quadrennium, Tigert correctly concludes that "the Annual Conference rightfully ceased to be in any sense a constitutional unit."[25]

The General Conference of 1832

With nineteen annual conferences represented by about two hundred twenty-five delegates, the General Conference of 1832 was the largest ever held. Although small by today's standards, there was concern about it becoming too large. The newly enacted process to amend the constitution was put into operation to change the Second Restrictive Rule to modify the ratio of delegates in the General Conference to members of the annual conferences. It was amended again in 1836. This was the last General Conference attended by William McKendree, and was judged in Bishop Paine's account of his life to have been "the most harmonious and conservative session held since the organization of the delegated body in 1808."[26] McKendree had led the church through deep and troubled waters, and his courage and influence had doubtless been important in preserving the system of original Methodism. But even his good leadership would have been unable to protect it from the difficult days immediately ahead.

The conference in 1832 elected two new bishops on the first ballot, James O. Andrew and John Emory. Once again sectional interests were balanced and accommodated. Before the conference opened, William Capers was the leading candidate from the South and the favorite to be elected. But he declined to be considered because he owned slaves. "Billy Sugar," as Capers was affectionately named by Asbury (a frequent visitor in Caper's boyhood home), would later be the first bishop elected in the newly created MECS.

Ironically, James O. Andrew, the compromise candidate, had been recommended and supported by Capers because he was also from the South but did not own slaves. His situation changed shortly after the election, and Andrew's status as a slaveholder became the focus of the controversy in 1844.

Andrew was born in Georgia but spent the major portion of his ministerial career in the South Carolina Conference, which he joined in 1812. He too came from old Methodist stock, his father being the first Georgian ever to enter the itinerant ministry of the Methodist Church. Before his election, Andrew had served with distinction as a preacher in Charleston, Columbia, Augusta, and Savannah, and as presiding elder.

John Emory, who was elected with Andrew on the first ballot, was born in Maryland. A scholarly individual, he studied and practiced law in Centerville, Maryland, before joining the Philadelphia Conference in 1810. Later he transferred to the Baltimore Conference and served churches in Washington, D.C., Annapolis, and Baltimore. From 1818 to 1824 he was assistant book editor for the connection. He became book editor and editor of the *Methodist Magazine* in the next quadrennium. John McClintock, the first president of Drew Theological Seminary, who knew Emory well, characterized him as "a man of great talent. But he was not a man of genius." Nevertheless, Emory gained recognition through his writing and sermons, especially on controversial issues. He is probably best known for his book *Defence of Our Fathers and of the Original Organization of The Methodist Episcopal Church*, a carefully reasoned and well-written apology for the episcopal organization of Methodism. He was also the founder of the *Methodist Quarterly Review*, successor to the *Methodist Magazine*. Emory presided at the closing session of the General Conference at which he was elected, the only time he was ever to fill that role. His episcopal service was cut short in 1835 when he was killed in a carriage accident while on his way to Baltimore, thus becoming the first bishop to die in the exercise of his duties.

When the Committee on Episcopacy, in its report to the delegates, noted that it was "inexpedient to require each of our bishops to travel throughout the whole of their extensive charges," the bishops asked for a clarification from the conference, without debate.[27] They asked the delegates to respond whether it was their intention "simply to relieve the bishops from the influence of the resolutions passed at the last General Conference on the same subject, and to leave them now at liberty on their joint and several responsibility to make such arrangements among themselves . . . as they shall judge most conducive to the general good."[28] They also asked in the same communication whether the delegates sought to give them "direction or advice whether it be or be not expedient for each of the bishops, in the course of the four years, to visit each of the annual conferences, should they themselves find it convenient and practicable, and judge it for the general good so to do?"[29] The committee replied that the bishops had correctly understood their intention was to give them freedom to make whatever arrangements seemed best for serving the needs of the connection.

In the light of now well-established episcopal practice, it is interesting that the bishops should have raised the question at all, for they made no changes in what they were doing. They appeared to regard the affirmation of the delegates merely as a vote of approval of that practice. It is nevertheless significant that the bishops clearly assumed their work to be under the direction of the General Conference. The nature of that relationship was soon to be questioned and sorely tested.

CHAPTER 9

The Road to Division

Episcopal Methodism approached the General Conference of 1836 in a weakened condition. McKendree's long tenure as bishop had come to a close with his death on 5 March 1835, marking the end of the second era of the episcopacy in the history of Methodism. Then the tenure of recently elected Bishop John Emory was unexpectedly cut short by his death from injuries suffered in a carriage accident in December 1835.[1] This left four bishops to share the responsibility for overseeing twenty-eight annual conferences plus a mission conference in Liberia. It was far more than they could manage. Perhaps coincidentally 1836 was one of the few years in Methodism's early history when the church as a whole showed a decrease in membership. Although the decline in its numbers may not be linked directly to the inadequacy of episcopal oversight, the church realized the need for additional superintendents.

The General Conference of 1836

There were one hundred fifty-four delegates who gathered in Cincinnati for the General Conference of 1836. Their first order of business was to elect bishops. The process of electing bishops remained essentially the same as had been established at the creation of the delegated General Conference. After a determination of how many bishops to elect had been made by the Committee on Episcopacy, the delegates were instructed to write names of the proper number of persons (in the case of 1836, three) on a ballot without nomination. The number of preachers present and voting on each ballot determined the number of votes needed for a majority. Balloting continued until the proper number to be elected had been chosen by the majority of delegates.

Seniority among the bishops, then and now, is determined by the order of election. If more than one bishop is elected on the same ballot, the one receiving the largest number of votes will be considered senior.[2] The 1836 Conference chose Beverly Waugh, Wilbur Fisk, and Thomas Asbury Morris.[3] Waugh and Fisk were elected on the first ballot with eighty-five and seventy-eight votes, respectively. Fisk, who was not present, declined to be ordained when notified of his election. Morris was not elected until the sixth ballot, when he received eighty-six of the votes cast. Fisk, the first president of Wesleyan University, was in Europe to represent the denomination at the British Methodist Conference, and in hopes of improving his health.

Fisk is a unique figure in Methodist history. He was the first person elected by a General Conference at which he was not present, the second after Joshua Soule to refuse ordination after being elected, and the only man ever to be elected and decline the office in two countries. (The second person ever to be elected by a General Conference when not present was Edmund S. Janes in 1844.) Fisk had been elected a bishop by the Canadian Methodist Episcopal Church when it was organized in 1828, but refused to be ordained there as well. He declined in both instances because of his health and because of his conviction he could render more useful and effective service to the denomination as a college president. He had told his friends in 1836 before the General Conference opened that he did not wish to serve, but they disregarded his wishes and elected him anyway. Fisk's health continued to fail and he died before the General Conference met again.

Beverly Waugh was born in Fairfax County, Virginia, in 1789, and joined the Baltimore Conference in 1809. After serving a number of appointments, he became assistant book agent under John Emory, and book agent in 1832 when Emory was elected to the episcopacy. During his years as book agent, he was a member of the New York

114

Annual Conference. He served for twenty-two years in the episcopacy and died in 1858. From 1852 until his death he was the senior bishop in the MEC.

Thomas Asbury Morris was the editor of the *Western Christian Advocate*, published in Cincinnati, when he joined the ranks of the episcopacy. A native of West Virginia, his appointments were mainly in the Ohio Annual Conference, except for 1821–28 when he served in the Kentucky Conference while struggling with bad health. In 1833 he was presiding elder of the Cincinnati District. He became editor of the *Western Christian Advocate* in April of the following year. Morris had been a delegate to every General Conference since 1824. He died in 1874 after a short illness.

Bishop Roberts, in poor health and impaired in his ability to continue in active service, submitted his resignation from the episcopacy to the 1836 Conference. The delegates, however, refused to accept it and passed a resolution similar to the one voted earlier in the cases of Asbury and McKendree. The conference gave Roberts permission to "pursue such a course as he may think best during the ensuing four years, for the improvement of his health, and to prolong his useful life, affording, in the mean time, all the service he can, as a joint superintendent or bishop in our Church."[4] The same resolution had also to be voted for Hedding.[5] The action was well intended but somewhat premature; Roberts died in 1843, and Hedding in 1852.

Slavery Issues

In addition to these changes in personnel, the episcopacy was affected by the growing unrest in Methodism and the nation generated by sectional interests, particularly the tensions around the overwhelming presence of slavery in the South and the rising opposition to slavery in other parts of the country. From 1820 until 1836, General Conferences found it easier to ignore than to address the complex issues related to slavery and slaveholders who were Methodists. No significant new legislation on the subject was enacted at any of these conferences. By 1836, however, the level of agitation had risen sufficiently to cause the church to adopt the principle of silence on the subject of slavery, and to condemn "modern abolitionism." There were good reasons for this action. It was now obvious to everyone that the controversy swirling around the institution of slavery had the power to divide the church. Methodists, who cherished their tightly knit organization, were determined to preserve its unity if at all possible. However, many of those opposed to slavery believed that the position of the church (which they regarded as essentially "pro slavery") was a direct result of the form of its government and the power of its episcopal leaders. The question increasingly confronting both church and nation was whether the moral imperative to resist the evil of slavery was powerful enough to overshadow the need to conserve and protect unions long in place. In 1836 the church affirmed its decision that unity was a higher good. Jesse T. Peck, writing about it later, said, "The Church came into harmony with a great dominant political idea, Union first, principle afterward."[6] The Episcopal Address to the General Conference of 1844 summarized the position taken in 1840, which was itself reflective of the view of the General Conference of 1836:

> At the last session of the General Conference [1840] the subject of slavery and its abolition was extensively discussed, and vigorous exertions made to effect new legislation upon it. But after a careful examination of the whole ground, aided by the light of past experience, it was the solemn conviction of the Conference that the interests of religion would not be advanced by any additional enactments in regard to it.
>
> In your Pastoral Address . . . you solemnly advised the whole body to abstain from all abolition movements, and from agitating the exciting subject in the Church. This advice was in perfect agreement with the individual as well as associated views of your Superintendents. But, had we differed from you in opinion, in consideration of the age, wisdom, experience, and official authority of the General Conference, we should have felt ourselves under a solemn obligation to be governed by your counsel. We have endeavoured, both in our official administration, and in our private intercourse with the preachers and members, to inculcate the sound policy and Christian spirit of your Pastoral Address.[7]

In 1836, the Pastoral Address disavowed support for any form of radicalism:

> From every view of the subject which we have been able to take, and from the most calm and dispassionate survey of the whole ground, we have come to the solemn conviction, that the only safe, Scriptural, and prudent way for us, both as ministers and people, to take, is wholly to refrain from this agitating subject, which is now convulsing the coun-

try, and consequently the Church, from end to end, by calling forth inflammatory speeches, papers and pamphlets.[8]

The committee appointed to draft this address had been given explicit instructions "to take notice of the subject of modern abolition" and "let our preachers, members, and friends know that the General Conference are [sic] opposed to the agitation of that subject, and will use all prudent means to put it down."[9]

Reflecting the sentiment expressed in the Pastoral Address, the delegates in 1836 refused even to print the address of the English fraternal delegate, who counseled "opposition to slavery on the ground of its repugnance to the law of Christ."[10] After a heated discussion, the General Conference also voted to censure two delegates from New England who addressed a meeting of the Cincinnati antislavery society during the time the General Conference was in session. Antislavery memorials were not considered by the conference, since "it was 'improper further to agitate the subject in the General Conference at present.'"[11] Orange Scott, who led the abolitionist delegates, responded to the censure resolution with a pamphlet, "An Address to the General Conference of The Methodist Episcopal Church, 1836."

Enforcing the Gag Rule

After the General Conference adjourned on 27 May 1836, the responsibility for following its mandate to guard the denomination from anything that might agitate the connection on the subject of slavery fell largely on the bishops. The battlefield on which they fought was the annual conference. Each conference was different. Some had already taken action on their own: antislavery societies had been formed in the New England and New Hampshire Conferences in 1835; Ohio, Baltimore, New York, Philadelphia, Pittsburgh, Michigan, and some other conferences passed resolutions expressing confidence in the antislavery position of the church and condemned the actions of the abolitionists. The Philadelphia Conference refused to ordain L. C. Matlack, despite his having been recommended for ordination by his quarterly conference, because he had a role in organizing a Wesleyan antislavery society.

The requirement of the General Conference for silence on the subject of slavery put the bishops squarely in the middle of the strug-

117

gles. Not infrequently these encounters raised related questions of power and authority—such as, who controlled the agenda of the annual conference, the body of preachers, or their presiding officer? Although setting the agenda, which was mandated in large measure by the historic disciplinary questions, was a prerogative traditionally granted to the bishops, they could no longer assume it would be honored. Conferences finding themselves silenced by the bishops on the question of slavery sought to claim the agenda for themselves in order to debate the issue. In spite of the protests, the bishops proved to be an effective tool in resisting both the radical abolitionists and conservative antislavery forces.

The hotbed of abolitionist sentiment was in the New England, New Hampshire, and Maine Conferences, and the sharpest challenges confronted the bishops presiding in their sessions. Hedding was unfortunate enough to hold both the New England and New Hampshire Conferences. To make matters worse, they met only a month after the adjournment of the General Conference of 1836. The New England Conference came first. During the sessions of the General Conference, Orange Scott, who led the abolitionist movement in New England, had convinced most of his colleagues to support his position. Hedding, though personally sympathetic to the antislavery cause, believed himself obligated to follow the directive of the General Conference to restrict debate. "To form a just estimate of his course, we must bear in mind that he cordially and fully approved of, and felt himself ecclesiastically, morally, and religiously bound, as an officer of the Church, to obey the behests of its highest judicatory."[12] It was a difficult decision for Hedding, for not only were his sympathies with those who would oppose him, but virtually all of his episcopal service had been in these antislavery conferences. He had even been elected president of the first Methodist antislavery society organized in 1834 but declined to accept the position.

Now Hedding's obedience to the law of the church forced him to discipline Orange Scott. Because of Scott's constant agitation on the subject of slavery, and refusal to heed the mandate of the General Conference, Hedding removed Scott from his appointment as presiding elder of the Providence District, despite his having completed only two years of a four-year term.[13] During the annual conference, the bishop also refused to allow consideration of a report from the "Committee on Slavery."[14] In Hedding's dealing with Scott there is evidence of both his loyalty to the General Conference and a reaffirmation of the traditional role of the presiding elder as an extension of episcopal power. (Presiding elders who for any reason cannot support their bishop, or who ignore the law of the church, cannot serve.) Scott responded to being removed by taking his case to the public and assailing Hedding in bitter terms. Because of his role as presiding officer, the bishop was in a poor position to respond to the criticism that was heaped upon him.

Scott began his agitation against slavery in 1834, utilizing church gatherings and the pages of *Zion's Herald* to discuss the issue with preachers or anyone else who would listen. He once personally subscribed to and paid for one hundred copies of the *Liberator* to be sent to members of the New England Conference. He was successful in enlisting persons to his cause, and by 1835 a majority of the members of the conference were abolitionists.[15] The election of its delegates to the General Conference of 1836 was so political and controversial that the conference was only barely able to elect the required number and went to Cincinnati without reserve delegates. When Scott was himself elected to the delegation, there were concerns that he might not be allowed to take his seat in the General Conference.

The New Hampshire Conference met immediately after the New England Conference, and once again Hedding found himself in trouble. George Storrs was the Orange Scott of the New Hampshire Conference, leading the effort there to elect abolitionist delegates. This time Hedding was pressed to appoint Storrs a presiding elder. While he was not opposed to this appointment in general, Hedding refused to make it without receiving "some assurance that Storrs would cease to distract the Church by active participation in the ultra measures of the day." Storrs replied that he felt himself under "no such obligation," read a paper to the conference expressing his conviction "that he could not take an appointment under an officer of the General Conference in view of the action of that body on the subject of slavery," and asked to be located.[16]

Early in the conference the usual motion was made to elect a Committee on Slavery. Hedding agreed to allow the formation of the committee if (1) all conference business necessary to make the appointments was completed first, and (2) the contents of the report were subject to review and veto by the president of the conference if, in his judgment, they contained resolutions contrary to the position of the General Conference as expressed in the Pastoral Address of 26 May 1836. The preachers rejected Hedding's conditions, and he in

119

turn refused to allow them to elect the committee. He also overruled a motion to condemn an action taken in the Baltimore Conference interpreting the church's General Rule on slavery. Hedding's ruling was based on the premise that it was not in keeping with the Methodist economy for one annual conference to pass judgment upon the acts of another, each annual conference being amenable to the General Conference alone for its individual action.[17] Hedding argued that if this were allowed, the church would be thrown into a state of anarchy and confusion. He was immediately charged with exceeding his authority.

Hedding defended his position to the conference by discussing the rights of the body of preachers in the annual conference and the duties of their president and presiding officer.[18] It was a speech that he was to give several times in a variety of places. Citing the provisions in the *Discipline* that gave the bishops responsibility to set the day for ordinations and required them to meet the conference for at least a week, Hedding argued that these provisions conveyed both the right and responsibility to arrange the business in such a manner that each could be done. As a presiding officer, he said, the bishop is under no obligation "to put to vote every resolution that is offered." The real issue was whether he had an obligation to put before them every question he knew they wished to adopt. The answer for Hedding was to be found in the nature of the annual conference itself. "An annual conference," he told them, "is not a primary, independent body. Though it was so originally, when there was but one annual conference . . . consisting of all the travelling preachers in full connexion, [it is not so now]." He refuted the claim of the preachers to conference "rights" by saying:

> An annual conference is constituted by the General Conference; it is dependent on, and responsible to it. And the General Conference has told the annual conference what to do; its duty and rights are laid down in the Discipline. That is its charter, and it has no other rights as a conference, only those which are granted either by statute or by fair inference in that charter.[19]

Hedding freely acknowledged that members of annual conference had "other rights as men, and as Christians, and as Methodist preachers, but not as an annual conference." Its president was appointed by the General Conference, could not be removed from the chair, nor could the conference do business without him, "and you and he are obliged by law to do just what the Discipline tells you, and no more." Then he speculated that in annual conferences where there were slaves and slave owners, a discussion of the subject might be in order and allowed. But in places where slavery did not exist, "where you have no jurisdiction over slaves or slave owners, it is impossible to make it appear that you have any authority in the case." Therefore, the *Discipline* did not require the president of an annual conference to conduct this order of business. Moreover, he told them, they had no right as an annual conference to determine what business they would do. That was the right of the General Conference alone; if it were allowed to an annual conference, it would usurp General Conference's control over the president. One cannot help but note that if Hedding's logic were followed, the General Conference rather than the president of an annual conference would seem to have ultimate power over the annual conference's agenda. The inescapable conclusion would be that the bishop has only those powers granted by the General Conference.

Although he and the other bishops had the full backing of their brethren in the General Conference, Hedding suffered personally at home because of the stand he took. "I have been unjustly and cruelly held up to public view," he said, "as one who infringed on the 'rights' of my brethren, merely because I did not consent to do what I was under no obligation to do, what I was bound by no law to do, and what I have never promised to do."[20] Later he confessed, "I was oppressed with the business of the conference. That business has affected my nerves for the few past years, so that sometimes I have been unable to speak or stand without trembling."[21] Hedding eventually became so alienated from his New England colleagues that he moved his home from Lynn, Massachusetts, where he had lived for a number of years, to Lansingburgh, New York.[22]

In an attempt to answer his critics and exonerate himself, Bishop Hedding filed charges in 1838 against Orange Scott and La Roy Sunderland, editor of *Zion's Watchman*, but both were acquitted when they were brought to trial in their annual conferences.[23] He then appealed this decision to the General Conference of 1840, but withdrew the complaint before it could be considered.

Other bishops took a similar and consistent line and suffered criticism because of it. Bishop Beverly Waugh had experiences similar to Hedding's when he presided in the New Hampshire Conference in 1837. It was indeed unfortunate that during those years there was no arena in which the whole church, through the mechanism of its annual conferences, could discuss and debate a moral issue of such magnitude and significance for the entire connection. During the time in which the gag rule was being applied to antislavery conferences in the North, southern conferences were adopting pro-slavery resolutions affirming the moral good of slavery and defending their relation to it. The action of the Baltimore Conference, which prompted the attempt to vote censure in the New Hampshire Conference, is a good illustration of what was being done. The resolution interpreted the General Rule on Slavery to make the morality of buying or selling slaves dependent on the circumstances of "cruelty, injustice, or inhumanity." Slaveholding could take place, they resolved, with "kindness and good intentions." When it did, that changed its moral status.[24]

In response to the restraints imposed on them by the General Conference and the bishops, Methodist abolitionists went outside the system and held a number of "unofficial" conventions at which the subject of slavery was debated openly. The first of these, held in Lynn, Massachusetts, in October 1837, discussed thoroughly the subject of conference rights as well. Eventually, the abolitionists managed to take action in their annual conferences.

In 1838, the New England Conference proposed to change the Rule on Slavery to forbid "the buying or selling; or holding men, women or children as slaves under any circumstances, or giving them away unless on purpose to free them."[25] The bishops were asked to submit the resolution to other conferences for concurrence. When they did, only New Hampshire agreed. The sentiment in the denomination as a whole favored the preservation of union above everything else, and it was clear that changes such as this would drive the South away.

The General Conference and the Annual Conferences

When the General Conference of 1840 opened in Baltimore, it was presented with a flood of memorials, many of which were designed specifically to limit episcopal power, while others raised questions concerning the rights of annual conferences. The bishops led off in the Episcopal Address, delivered by Bishop Waugh, by condemning the northern and eastern conferences because they were "in contravention of your Christian and pastoral counsel," and the subject of slavery "has been agitated in such forms, and in such a spirit, as to disturb the peace of the Church."[26] They reaffirmed that the General Rule on Slavery, which was in the constitution, had "stood from the beginning unchanged, as testamentary of our sentiments on the principle of slavery, and the slave trade." As a result of this, Waugh declared, "the solemn conviction of our minds, that no new ecclesiastical legislation on the subject of slavery, at this time," would be conducive to peace and harmony. But due to the variety of interpretations to which the General Rule on Slavery had been subject, the bishops thought it well to request "that a body, having legitimate jurisdiction, should express a clear and definite opinion [on the meaning of the Rule], as a uniform guide to those to whom the administration of the Discipline is committed." Battered by their encounters in the various annual conferences during the previous quadrennium, the bishops requested a clarification of "the Constitutional powers of the General Superintendents, in their relations to the Annual Conferences, and in their general executive administration of the government; and the rights of Annual and Quarterly Conferences, in their official capacities."

Having described the problem in general, they asked more specific questions on the subject of episcopal power in relation to that of the body of preachers. When there are questions of law, for example, does the constitutional power to decide the question belong to the president or the conference? Does the conference have a constitutional right to do business other than that which is mandated by the *Discipline*? Does the president, by virtue of his office, have the right to decide whether such questions should be submitted to a vote? With these questions before the delegates, they proceeded to outline their understanding of the law of the church with respect to their authority.

"The General Conference is the only legislative body recognized in our ecclesiastical system, and from it originates the authority of the entire executive administration." As the bishops understood it, the exclusive power to create annual conferences belonged to the General Conference, the bishops had the authority to set the time of their meeting, no annual conference could make any rule for the entire church, and none could elect its president. All annual conferences were organized and governed by the same laws, and all had "identically the same *rights*, and *powers*, and *privileges*" from the

General Conference. The same principle applied to the superintendents. They were elected by, amenable to, and constituted presidents of annual conferences by the General Conference. Their primary responsibility to the church was to preserve its itinerant ministry, maintain uniformity in their administration, and preserve unity.

The bishops also officially acknowledged what all the delegates already knew well: there were now six general superintendents, three of whom were "enfeebled by labour, age and infirmity," trying to serve twenty-eight annual conferences in the connection. The bishops urged the conference to add to their numbers since an itinerant superintendency, which is *"effective*, not imbecile; *general*, not sectional; *itinerant*, not local," is essential to the functioning of the itinerant system.[27]

The General Conference of 1840 responded by upholding the rights of bishops to set agendas and to control annual conference discussions. They even allowed, in opposition to the long-standing rule that bishops must allow annual conferences to sit for at least a week, that a bishop had the power to adjourn an annual conference when, "in his judgment, all the business prescribed by the Discipline . . . shall have been transacted." By vote they declared the bishop in an annual conference and the presiding elder in a quarterly conference to have the power to decide all questions of law. The application of that law, however, was left to the annual conference.[28]

Everyone attending the conference in Cincinnati was acutely aware that the threat of division hung over the denomination as never before. Ignoring the plea in the Episcopal Address to add additional persons to the episcopacy, the delegates declined to elect any new bishops. The original recommendation from the Committee on Episcopacy to the conference was to elect two. But the conservatives, led by men like Peter Cartwright and William Winans, defeated the proposal, since they knew that any election, driven as surely it would be by sectional interests, would further divide the church. While they were successful in blocking the proposed elections, their action served only to delay rather than to prevent the inevitable division of the denomination.

The immediate result of the reaffirmation of episcopal power, in combination with sustaining the church's position on slavery, was a schism that led to the formation of the Wesleyan Methodist Connection in May 1843. John Nelson Norwood says that while it is obvious "the only real cause of the secession was dissatisfaction with the position of the church on slavery," there were other grievances incidental to it.[29] The Wesleyans rejected the general superintendency because bishops had been a major force in blocking the program of the abolitionists. The new denomination, which modeled its government after that of English Methodists, eliminated the office of bishop, prohibited slavery, provided for lay representation, and allowed conferences to elect their presidents. Appointments were made by a stationing committee. When first organized, the Wesleyan Methodist Church stretched from Maine to Michigan to the Mason-Dixon line and had about six thousand members. Orange Scott was among those who joined the new denomination.

As members began to leave the MEC, many of those remaining became convinced of the necessity to foster the antislavery spirit in order to stop the exodus. Spellman correctly observes:

> Whereas before the secession of the Wesleyan Connection the moderates had vigorously sought to silence the abolitionists for fear they would divide the church and drive the southern conferences into secession; after the Wesleyan break the moderates worked just as vigorously to hold the abolitionists, even at the expense of losing the south.[30]

Prelude to Division

The issues now before the church and soon to be before the country were immensely complicated. Despite the rhetoric on both sides, there were no easy answers, just dilemmas—greater and lesser choices of evils in many cases. Timothy Smith has given a fine summary of these issues in *Revivalism and Social Reform*. In the 1840s, the Methodists would be called upon to decide:

> (a) Whether churchmen might any more than politicians jeopardize the unity of the nation in pursuit of freedom for the slave. (b) At what point the solidarity of national religious and benevolent societies became less important than a clear witness against human bondage. (c) Whether the proper role of the churches in a democratic society was to regulate individual conduct or to impose Christian principles upon social and legal institutions. (d) Whether in disciplining individual conduct the central or the local governing bodies of the sects should act, and by what procedures. And, (e), whether Christians might do violence for loving ends.[31]

The General Conference of 1840 made one other decision that set the church on a fateful course. A petition from the Westmoreland Circuit in the Baltimore Conference, submitted unsuccessfully to the General Conference of 1836, protested the long-standing practice of the Baltimore Conference to refuse ordination to persons who were slaveholders. The petitioners, although within the bounds of the Baltimore Conference, lived in the state of Virginia, where the law prohibited the emancipation of slaves. The petitioners could not be ordained because they owned slaves who, they contended, could not be freed because of the laws of Virginia. Their original petition four years earlier had sought relief by asking to be transferred to the Virginia Annual Conference. They now sought an exception on the basis of the long-standing provision in the General Rule on Slavery that exempted persons in their circumstances from having to free their slaves. The practice of the Baltimore Conference, they argued, was an abridgement of their rights under the *Discipline*. Therefore they called upon General Conference to endorse the following resolution:

> Resolved, by the delegates of the several Annual Conferences in General Conference assembled, That, under the provisional exception of the general rule of the church on the subject of slavery, the simple holding of slaves, or mere ownership of slave property, in states or territories where the laws do not admit of emancipation, and permit the liberated slave to enjoy freedom, constitutes no legal barrier to the election or ordination of ministers to the various grades of office known in the ministry of The Methodist Episcopal Church.[32]

The resolution was endorsed, setting the stage for a debate about the suitability of a slaveholding bishop for service in the Methodist connection—a debate that would lead to the division of American episcopal Methodism into northern and southern branches.

CHAPTER 10

Division, 1844

Meeting in New York City from 1 May until 11 June, the General Conference of 1844 provided the stage for the final act in the drama of separation. There were one hundred forty-nine delegates from thirty-three annual conferences who gathered at the opening session. The New York Conference was the largest present, with eleven delegates; the Texas Conference was the smallest, with two delegates. Prior to the General Conference, northern abolitionists, southern radicals, and a new brand of conservatives had all been active and outspoken on the subject of slavery. The quadrennium following 1840 saw a removal of the gag rule imposed by two previous general conferences, and the bishops did not attempt to hinder a full discussion of slavery. Conservatives, who had previously given their support to the South, became increasingly antagonistic toward it. Mathews's chapter subtitle on this period summarizes this change well: "The conservatives discover antislavery without abolitionism."[1]

The Few Resolution

The rallying cry for the abolitionists and the symbol to them of the church's unwillingness to take a stand was the "Few Resolution," introduced by Ignatius A. Few of the Georgia Conference and passed by the General Conference of 1840. It stated that "it is inexpedient and unjustifiable for any preacher among us to permit coloured persons to give testimony [in church trials] against white persons, in any state where they are denied that privilege in trials at law."[2] The measure highlighted not only the injustice and unfairness of the social system, but clearly put the church on a par with civic morality when its very nature committed it to a higher standard.

Between 1840 and 1844 condemnations of the Few Resolution were passed in one annual conference after another. The church press was pressured to open its pages to discussions of slavery and abolition. New editors like Thomas Bond Sr. of the *Christian Advocate and Journal*, Abel Stevens of *Zion's Herald* in Boston, and Charles Elliott of the *Western Christian Advocate* in Cincinnati spoke for the emerging new brand of moderate who made a distinction between the institution of slavery and the persons who held slaves. They were committed to stand firmly against slavery but had no desire to expel persons from the membership of the church simply because they were slaveholders. Despite the fact that antislavery societies now sprang up even in the West, in places like Indiana, Michigan, and Ohio (where a convention was held in 1841), the old-style radical abolitionists were losing their influence. In June 1842, before he left the MEC in November, Orange Scott, a tired champion of abolition, wrote of his disappointment in *Zion's Herald*: "I have now no expectation that the M. E. Church will ever take action against slavery, so long as it exists in the country—or that a majority of the general conference, or of the church, will ever be abolitionized 'till slavery ceases in the land."[3] The issue was bigger than the church could handle. Scott even admitted, on reflection, that he would have been more successful on behalf of his cause if during the early years he had been less strident in his condemnations of those who did not agree with him. George Storrs left the MEC after the General Conference of 1840; La Roy Sunderland went out with Scott in 1842. William Wightman, editor of the *Southern Christian Advocate*, and John B. McFerrin, editor of the *Southwestern Christian Advocate* in Nashville, prophetically predicted that the General Conference of 1844 would see the end of the Methodist fellowship in America as it had existed from the beginning. They were not saddened by the prospect that they judged to be inevitable.

The Appeal of Francis A. Harding

Hamby Barton correctly observed, "There is no question that the real issue of the Conference of 1844 was slavery. But the point of attack was one of the bishops of the church."[4] The bishop was James O. Andrew. Although he was not a slaveholder when elected to the episcopacy in 1832, he became involved with slavery through inheritance and marriage not long afterward. Andrew's relation to slavery was almost identical to that of Francis A. Harding, who had been "suspended from his ministerial standing" in the Baltimore Conference "for refusing to manumit certain slaves which came into his possession by his marriage."[5] Harding had married a "Miss Swan" of St. Mary's County, Maryland. She was the owner of five slaves. According to the Baltimore Conference's "well known usage" not to tolerate "slavery in any of its members," Harding was required to record a deed of manumission for three of the five during the current conference year. He protested that he could not make such a pledge because the laws of his state forbade this action, and was suspended until the conditions imposed by the Baltimore Conference were met. In response, Harding appealed his suspension to the General Conference.

The circumstances in Harding's case were similar to those Bishop Andrew presented, although Harding and Andrew lived in different states. There were two basic questions in the Harding case: according to the laws of Maryland, did he become a slaveholder by his marriage, and was it possible for a slaveholder in the state of Maryland to free his slaves? In an article printed in the *New York Advocate* on 23 October 1844, there is a careful analysis of the statute in question.[6] The author, who is biased, signs himself "Maryland," and the style and the character of the essay strongly suggest the writer was a lawyer.

The author first points out that the law governing such cases in Maryland was passed in 1796. It provided for slaves to be freed either by provisions in a will or by a deed. There was no limit to this power of manumission except that it could not be used in the case of slaves who were unable to support themselves or those over the age of forty-five. And there is a limit imposed on insolvent debtors.

Then the author notes another statute passed in 1831 that he says is "the basis of the false notion which extensively prevails, that a separation from a personal relation to slavery is legally impossible." The purpose of the act was to ensure the removal of all free people of color from the state. The third section, which is the crucial one, recognized the right of emancipation by will and deed according to the act of 1796, but required that the names of such persons be reported to a board of managers charged with the responsibility of removing them from the state. The board of managers in turn would propose "to the American or Maryland Colonization Society, that at the expense of such society, they shall remove such emancipated slaves to Africa, if they are willing to go there." If the freed persons were unwilling to relocate voluntarily, they would nevertheless be removed from the state. The law provided even for them to be arrested and removed by the sheriff. The sole reason for doing it was because the former slaves were free.

With regard to the question of whether Harding had become a slaveholder by his marriage to a woman owning slaves, the relevant general law declared that slaves were personal property and all such property belonging to a single woman vests in her husband by marriage. However, an 1840 statute had secured slaves owned either before marriage or acquired afterward to the woman as her separate and distinct property. But this statute allowed that the "control and management of such slaves, the direction of their labor, and the receipts of the production of it are vested in the husband." During the husband's lifetime, no other person had any right whatever in the management of these slaves. In addition, the husband was "the contingent owner of the remainder." As such, in the event of his wife's death the slaves descended to her children, if she had any, but remained subject to the use and management of her husband for life. If she had no children, her husband became the absolute owner. At his death, it was possible that for a number of reasons the freed slaves might be returned to the status of a slave. Based on this fact, the argument was made that "being still contingently liable to a state of slavery on the death of his master, the slave is incapable of being the subject of freedom."

During the marriage, if the slaves were sold by a joint deed from husband and wife, the money from the sale belonged to the husband. But the law is clear that so long as the wife was alive the husband had no absolute right to own the slaves and the slaves could not be freed, either by deed or will, without the consent of the wife. "Maryland" argues in the article, however, that the concern of both the conference and the *Discipline* was not about property but about morality, and

130

they did not expect Harding to relinquish the rights of his wife, only his own. "He cannot of course affect the rights of other parties, but he can legally relinquish his own rights." "Maryland" concluded that nothing in the law would prohibit Harding from acceding to the directive of the conference and, in refusing to comply with its demands, Harding had forfeited his ministry.

The Case of Bishop Andrew

Although the states involved are different, both the circumstances and legal implications of Bishop Andrew's case are similar, if not identical, to Harding's case. After days of debate in the General Conference, Harding's appeal was denied by a majority of 2 to 1. This vote, which took place before any resolutions were offered in the case of Bishop Andrew, was significant for two reasons. In the first place, it marked the first time the South had lost an important vote in a General Conference. The Baltimore Conference voted as a block in support of its own decision, but all the rest of the southern conferences voted against it. The border conferences divided; John Clark from Texas and James M. Jamieson from Missouri were the only southern delegates who broke ranks and voted "no" with the northern conferences.[7] The level of sentiment present in that act is revealed in a letter to the other Texas delegate, Littleton Fowler. After the General Conference, R. Alexander wrote Fowler about Clark's conduct: "Clark is held in the highest degree of disrespect in the west and a large part of the community indulge in feelings of an indignant character. I do not think he could travel through the west without being mobbed."[8] The vote in the Harding case was also a reliable preview of the outcome in Bishop Andrew's case. Conference lines were clearly drawn and the final outcome determined even before the debate started.

The Committee on Episcopacy, assigned to review the case of the bishop, first interviewed Andrew and asked him for a statement of the facts pertinent to his situation. Andrew explained then, and later in writing, that after his election to the episcopacy in 1832 he had inherited in trust a young female slave, who, upon reaching the age of nineteen, provided she gave her consent, was to be freed and sent to Liberia. When she became nineteen, however, she refused to leave the bishop's home, and under state law he was prohibited from setting her free. Five years after receiving the female slave, Andrew's mother-in-law left her daughter a Negro boy, who, at the mother-in-law's death, became the property of the bishop's wife. Then, as would have been the case in Maryland, this boy passed to the bishop upon the death of his wife. Moreover, the bishop's wife died without a will, leaving the distribution of her property to be determined by state law. The boy, said the bishop, "shall be at liberty to leave the state whenever I shall be satisfied that he is prepared to provide for himself, or I can have sufficient security that he will be protected and provided for in the place to which he may go."[9]

Since Andrew received the young woman shortly after his election to the episcopacy in 1832, his decade-long connection with slavery had either escaped the attention of the church—there were literally hundreds of persons among the preachers in slaveholding states whose circumstances were similar—or was simply ignored until the agitation from abolitionists became so heated that it could no longer be overlooked. Besides, under the legislation of the General Conference of 1840, Andrew could not legally be kept from his office simply for owning slaves.

To complicate matters further, Andrew remarried in January 1844. His new wife, a widow, owned slaves inherited from her deceased husband. His biographer says Andrew did not expect trouble from this new association with slavery, but it is clear that he was concerned enough about it to take legal measures to distance himself from her slaves. He did this by means of a deed of trust that secured the slaves to her.[10] If "Maryland's" interpretation is correct, by this act Andrew had done what he was morally obligated to do under the *Discipline*— that is, he had relinquished his interest in her property. Although he did not "own" her slaves in the strict sense of that term, there was no denying that he was and had been involved with the institution of slavery for a considerable length of time, and had benefited from his connection with slaves.

Preliminary Debates and Resolutions on Andrew and Harding

Andrew knew his status as a bishop would be challenged in New York. There had been calls in the South for the election of a slaveholding bishop in order to give them full representation in the church. That such an election could never happen was obvious if bishops were expected ever to serve as general superintendents and preside in conferences opposed to slavery. There were places in the connection in which a slaveholding bishop would not be welcome, just as there were places where involvement with slavery would be no impediment to effective leadership.

Traveling to New York, Andrew learned there would be trouble. Having no special love for the episcopal office, he announced his willingness to resign in a meeting of the southern caucus of delegates before the conference actually convened. They refused to allow him even to consider giving up his office because they were convinced it would be a "fatal concession" to their northern adversaries. After they discussed it thoroughly, the following resolution was passed:[11]

> Whereas, Bishop Andrew has signified to the delegates of the Conference in the slave-holding States a purpose to yield to the present distressing urgency of the brethren from the Northern States, and resign his office of Bishop, and whereas in a meeting of said delegates to consider this matter, after solemn prayer and much deliberation, it appears to us that his resignation would inflict an incurable wound on the whole South and inevitably lead to division in the Church, therefore we do unanimously concur in requesting the Bishop . . . not to allow himself for any consideration to resign.[12]

Andrew's case did not come before the conference until Monday, 20 May. That day, John A. Collins, a member of the Baltimore Conference delegation, offered a resolution asking the Committee on Episcopacy to "ascertain the facts" in the case of Bishop Andrew and "report the results of their investigation to this body tomorrow morning."[13] This request for the facts was only a device to put a larger question on the floor. Most, if not all, of the delegates already knew Andrew's situation well, and the bishop's prompt, candid reply two days later informed the rest.

The Committee on Episcopacy reported to the conference as requested in the morning session, 22 May, that it "had ascertained, previous to the reference of the resolution, that Bishop Andrew is connected with slavery, and had obtained an interview with him on the subject."[14] They also submitted a copy of Andrew's written statement and had it printed in the record.

In response, a resolution was promptly offered by Alfred Griffith and John Davis, delegates from the Baltimore Conference, "that the

Rev. James O. Andrew be, and he is hereby affectionately requested to resign his office as one of the Bishops of the Methodist Episcopal Church."[15] Speaking in support of the motion, Griffith said, "We are here concerned exclusively with an officer of the General Conference," and the issue is "whether the General Conference . . . has power to regulate her own officers—that is the question."[16] In actuality this was not the real issue, but whether the denomination was willing to have a slaveholding bishop. Even so, the debate quickly shifted to consider the relation of the General Conference to its bishops. Andrew had violated no rule of the *Discipline* and no charges had been filed against him. The very difficult practical question was whether a majority of the General Conference had the power to force the resignation or remove a bishop without formal charges and a trial.

The next morning, a substitute motion was offered by James B. Finley of Ohio. It changed the substance of the Griffith motion:

> Whereas, the Discipline of our Church forbids the doing of anything calculated to destroy our itinerant general superintendency, and whereas, Bishop Andrew has become connected with slavery by marriage and otherwise, and this act having drawn after it circumstances which, in the estimation of the General Conference, will greatly embarrass the exercise of his office as an itinerant general superintendent, if not in some places entirely prevent it; therefore, Resolved, That it is the sense of this General Conference that he desist from the exercise of this office so long as this impediment remains.[17]

This substitute offered cause why the bishop should voluntarily "desist from the exercise of his office"—it would "embarrass" or "prevent" his work as an itinerant general superintendent, and thereby invalidate the chief function of the episcopacy to protect and promote the itinerant system. It was the Finley motion that was actually debated. The substitute was manifestly accepted by the northern and antislavery delegates "as expressing the firm purpose of the General Conference not to be responsible for 'the enormous evil of slavery,' in connection with the sacred office, but to relieve itself from this responsibility with the least possible injury to the Bishop and to our brethren in the South."[18]

Needless to say, the South saw it differently, and their position had its merits. Even Jesse Peck, the antislavery delegate from the Troy Conference in upstate New York, in speaking for the Finley substitute, could understand why delegates from the South could support a slaveholder in the episcopal office: "Coming up to the question of right from one direction, what was more natural than that men who knew no other effective method of service or social system but what rested on the basis of slavery, should pronounce it no more wrong in a Bishop than in any other minister of the Gospel."[19]

Bishop Soule, who was at the conference when the Finley substitute was offered, asked for the privilege of the floor, then reminded the delegates that many persons would be following their discussion and urged calmness and charity during their debates.[20] "I beseech you," he said, "by a voice from the tomb of a Wesley and a beloved Asbury . . . to let your spirits on this occasion be perfectly calm and self-possessed, and perfectly deliberate." Soule continued:

> So far as I know, there is not a sister (Protestant) Church in these United States . . . having any legislation on the subject of slavery. I say in this we are unique, we are alone. We therefore stand in our action on this subject before the tribunal of all the Christian Churches of our land, and our actions will certainly be judged of by that tribunal.

He concluded by saying he was not without anxiety and deep concern "for the perpetual union, and undivided interest of this great body," and urged decorum in the debates. "I myself love to hear hard arguments, but I love to hear them in soft words," he said. Soule spoke several more times during the debate.

The question before the conference was larger than the matter of the church's relation to slavery, or even of how a particular bishop was related to it. It was a basic dispute about polity and particularly about how the powers of the delegated General Conference and its episcopacy were balanced. Reflecting their general conservatism, the southern conferences defended the traditional Asburian structure of church government, which saw conference and episcopacy as two equal components. The church's moderate and liberal elements, on the other hand, had sought over the years to create a more democratic organization by electing presiding elders, admitting laypersons, enhancing the power of the General Conference, and thereby limiting the episcopacy. Spellman says:

> Refusing to debate slavery, the Southerners took issue with their northern brethren at their weakest point—on polity. Here the North seemed most vulnerable, for they had deviated considerably from the

135

Asburian tradition. Although polity was not the main issue, it was nevertheless a real and vitally involved issue with a long history of disagreement between the North and South.[21]

Ancillary Issues

The debate swirling around a slaveholding bishop was as much about other issues as it was about Andrew. First, did a General Conference have the power to demand the resignation of a bishop without charges and a trial? Nobody, including the bishops, disputed the fact that bishops were amenable to the General Conference for their administration and conduct, but Andrew was not accused of wrongdoing or maladministration. He had served twelve years without complaint. He was now accused only of being associated with slavery and benefiting from the labor of slaves. For years the *Discipline* of the church had been clear that slaveholding did not bar membership in the church, its ministry, or in its episcopacy when civil law made it impossible to free them. The General Conference of 1840 had reiterated, as the delegates were reminded

> that the simple holding of slaves, or mere ownership of slave property, in States or Territories, where laws do not admit of emancipation, and permit the liberated slave to enjoy freedom, constitutes no legal barrier to the election or ordination of ministers, to the various grades of office known in the ministry of the Methodist Episcopal Church, and cannot, therefore, be considered as operating any forfeiture of right, in view of such election and ordination.[22]

At no time during the debates was Andrew's character questioned. In the language of the church, he had been "blameless" in his life and administration. Moreover, his treatment of his slaves was humane. As a matter of fact, he maintained in his statement to the delegates that it was because of his Christian commitment to them that he kept the slaves belonging to his first wife. He described himself as a "slaveholder for conscience' sake." Addressing the conference he said:

> I might have avoided this difficulty by resorting to a trick—by making over these slaves to my wife before marriage, or by doing as a friend who has taken ground in favour of the resolution before you suggested: "Why," said he, "did you not let your wife make over these

negroes to her children, securing to herself an annuity from them?" Sir, my conscience would not allow me to do this thing. If I had done so, and those negroes had passed into the hands of those who would have treated them unkindly, I should have been unhappy. Strange as it may seem to brethren, I am a slaveholder for conscience' sake.[23]

The debate went on for days and touched a variety of issues. For example, it was alleged that Andrew had been elected in 1832, when others better qualified were passed over, simply because he was a southerner who did not own slaves. That case was difficult to sustain.[24] Others accused him of acting in bad faith to have accepted the office at all. "I was never asked if I was a slaveholder," said Andrew in response to the charges. "No man asked me what were my principles on the subject—no one dared to ask of me a pledge in this matter, or it would have been met as it deserved."[25] Obviously frustrated, no doubt angry, and speaking out of those strong feelings, Andrew put the matter squarely before the delegates: "The conference can take its course," he said, "but I protest against the proposed action as a violation of the laws of the Discipline, and an invasion of the rights secured to me by that book." But he went on to urge the conference to "act forthwith": "I wish you to act cool and deliberately, and in the fear of God; but I would rather that the conference would change the issue, and make the resolution to depose the bishop, and take the question at once, for I am tired of it."[26]

The maker of the substitute motion, James B. Finley, rose immediately to reply to Andrew. He declared:

> There are two great principles to be determined in this resolution which have not been decided in the Methodist Episcopal Church. One is this: Has the General Conference a right, or has it the power, to remove from office one, or all of the bishops, if they, under any circumstances, become disqualified to carry out the great principles of our itinerant general superintendency? The second is: Will the Methodist Church admit the great evil of slavery into the itinerant general superintendency?[27]

In their Episcopal Address at the opening of conference, the bishops had collectively conceded their accountability to the General Conference. That was never in dispute. They accepted the fact that a bishop was, as Jesse T. Peck declared, "an officer of the whole Church, responsible to the General Conference."[28] The bishops declared:

The office of a Bishop or Superintendent, according to our ecclesiastical system is almost exclusively executive; wisely limited in its powers, and guarded by such checks and responsibilities as can scarcely fail to secure the ministry and membership against any oppressive measures. . . . So far from being irresponsible in their office, they are amenable to the General Conference, not only for their moral conduct, and for the doctrines they teach, but also for the faithful administration of the government of the Church, according to the provisions of the Discipline, and for all decisions which they make on questions of ecclesiastical law. In all these cases this body has original jurisdiction, and may prosecute to final issue in expulsion, from which decision there is no appeal.[29]

The bishops even somewhat surprisingly acknowledged that their power to ordain persons for the ministry did not belong to their office alone, but was mutually shared with the body of preachers.

The Bishop can ordain neither a Deacon nor an Elder, without the election of the candidate by an Annual Conference: and in case of such election he has no discretional authority; but is under *obligation* to ordain the person elected, whatever may be his own judgment of his qualifications.[30]

Hamline's Response

But the bishops did not address the central issue: Did the General Conference have the power to depose them without formal charges or a trial? Specifically, in the case of Bishop Andrew the question was whether slaveholding, though not illegal, constituted a sufficient "impediment" to the exercise of episcopal functions to warrant removal. It was certainly disingenuous, if not hypocritical, to claim, as some of his opponents would, that Andrew would be unable to serve the whole church. Bishops had not itinerated throughout the connection for twenty years. He clearly could be fully occupied if he limited his work to conferences where he was acceptable. The conference had set itself up to determine whether expediency alone constituted sufficient ground to remove a bishop and if the General Conference had the right and power to do it. Bishop Soule thought the answer to both questions was "no" and addressed the delegates again to say so:

I wish to say, explicitly, that if the superintendents are only to be regarded as the officers of the General Conference of the Methodist Episcopal Church, and consequently as officers of the Methodist Episcopal Church liable to be deposed at will by a simple majority of this body without a form of a trial, no obligation existing growing out of the constitution and laws of the Church, even to assign cause, wherefore—I say, if this doctrine be a correct one, everything I have to say hereafter is powerless, and falls to the ground.[31]

Soule reminded the delegates that he had been present at the first delegated General Conference in 1808 but spared them the obvious additional fact that he was the author of the constitution it had adopted, and which they were now trying to interpret. He concluded his remarks by reaffirming that the provisions for the trial of a bishop were essential and must be followed, since, unlike any other minister in the church, the "bishop has no place to appeal."[32]

The definitive contrary position supported by delegates from the northern and western conferences was articulated by an Ohio Conference delegate, Leonidas L. Hamline, editor of the *Ladies' Repository*.[33] If Asbury had been present, he might have exclaimed again, as he did of McKendree's sermon, that Hamline's "Croton River" speech had the power to make him a bishop. It did, and with a touch of irony Hamline presided in the session in which the Finley substitute was offered for a vote. Hamline supported and enlarged the position affirmed earlier by Griffith and Davis's motion that the bishop was only an officer of the General Conference and the conference has "full authority to regulate their own officers, to provide for any exigency which may operate as a barrier in the way of the accomplishment of the objects and purposes for which the officers were chosen."[34]

Hamline's concept of the episcopacy and its relation to the General Conference informed the polity and practice of the MEC throughout its existence. Speaking in support of the Finley substitute motion, Hamline asked, "Has the General Conference constitutional authority to pass this resolution?" and "Is it proper or fitting that we should do it?" Arguing the first point, he declared that throughout its history "strict amenability in Church officers, subordinate and superior, is provided for in our Discipline." He illustrated the point by briefly examining a variety of relationships, such as pastor to class leader, presiding elder to pastor, or bishop to pastors, and claiming that in each of them there is the power to exercise summary

139

removals. In most instances in which it becomes necessary to make a change, "it is a ministerial, rather than a judicial act. . . . It is for no crime, and generally for no misdemeanor, but for being 'unacceptable.'" Moreover, it is normally made by one person, and the individual affected has no right of appeal. He argued that by analogy the power to "depose a bishop summarily for improprieties morally innocent, which embarrass the exercise of his functions" was derived from "*the relations of the General Conference to the Church, and to the episcopacy.*" He said, "The General Conference, adjunct in certain exigencies with the annual conferences, is the ultimate depository of power in our church." He argued that it is supreme in its legislative, judicial, and executive authority and "is the fountain of all official executive authority. It is the '*Croton River*' of that system of executive ministrations which flow in healthful streams throughout our Zion." (Meeting in New York City, the delegates knew that the source of the city's good water was the Croton River, which supplied its upstate reservoirs.)

The variety of powers held by the General Conference allowed it to make rules and regulations, and the latter included electing and empowering a bishop. If that is admitted, said Hamline, it follows that "all that this conference can confer, it can withhold." Although Hamline did not cite the reference, many years earlier, in a different context, McKendree said of the General Conference: "They made me, let them unmake me."

Hamline then moved to the crucial point in his argument, and one that held the key to the northern understanding of episcopacy. "Our Church constitution recognizes the episcopacy as an abstraction and leaves this body to work it into a concrete form in any hundred or more ways we may be able to invent."[35] The clear implication was that the conference had the power at any time to reinvent its episcopacy. Moreover, the extent of its powers did not limit the General Conference to what had been passed into legislation. "Whatever this conference can constitutionally do it can do without first resolving that it has the power to do it—without passing a rule into the Discipline declaring its authority." Hamline then asked a rhetorical question: "Is there anything in the restrictive articles which prohibits the removal or suspension of a bishop?"[36]

Drawing out his earlier analogy with other officers in the church, and making a distinction between the person and the office, Hamline agreed that while bishops cannot be removed from the ministry without trial, their office can be taken away without one.

140

We have seen that when clerical orders or membership in the Church is concerned, crime only, or obstinate impropriety, which is as crime, can expel. This is Methodism. We have seen, on the other hand, that *as to office, removals from it may be summary, and for anything unfitting that office, or that renders its exercise unwholesome to the Church. . . . the General Conference, under certain restrictions, is the depository of all power.*[37]

Reaching his conclusion, Hamline reminded the delegates they were only being asked to do something that bishops themselves do on a regular basis. "Does he not summarily remove, at discretion, all the four years round, two hundred presiding elders, and two thousand of his peers; and shall he complain that a General Conference, which is a delegated body . . . should do to him what he so uniformly does to them?" In a final admonition, Hamline urged the delegates never to lose sight of the fact that "the General Conference is '*the sun of our system.*'" From it, all parts of the body draw light and power, and "when the Church is about to suffer a detriment which we by constitutional power can avert, it is as much *treason in us not to exercise the power we have, as to usurp in other circumstances, that which we have not*" (his italics).

As interpreted by Hamline and those who agreed with him, the Finley motion called for the use of executive rather than legislative or judicial power, all of which were granted by the constitution to the General Conference. Their view prevailed on 1 June 1844, when the Finley substitute was adopted by a vote of 110 to 68.[38]

The Minority Response

At the morning session on 6 June, a minority protest from the southern delegates was read by H. B. Bascom of Kentucky. The conference delegates had been informed earlier that it would be coming. It decried the "insult" that had been given to Bishop Andrew and presented the southern Asburian view of episcopacy as a co-ordinate branch of Methodist church government, with power delegated to it by the body of preachers, just like that of the General Conference.

As The Methodist Episcopal Church is now organized, and according to its organization since 1784, the Episcopacy is a co-ordinate branch, the executive department proper of the government. A Bishop of The

141

Methodist Episcopal Church is not a mere creature—is in no prominent sense an officer of the General Conference. . . . In a sense by no
means unimportant the General Conference is as much the creature of
the Episcopacy, as the Bishops are the creatures of the General
Conference.[39]

The *Protest* illustrates this equality of powers by pointing out
that if bishops failed to exercise their authority, given them by the
General Conference, to call meetings of the annual conferences, there
would be no elections and no delegates to constitute a General
Conference. The practical result is the General Conference cannot
remove those who are co-ordinate with it. Drawing an analogy from
the relation of appointed government officials to legislative bodies,
the protesters argued that the power of removal does not follow the
power to appoint. Similar to the situation of judges, bishops,

instead of being the officers and creatures of the General Conference,
are *de facto* the officers and servants of the church, chosen by the
General Conference . . . and no right of removal accrues, except as they
fail to accomplish the *aims* of the church in their appointment, and then
only in accordance with the provisions of law.[40]

By the time Hamline spoke, division was being openly discussed
among the delegates. As a matter of fact, early in the session Thomas
Bond, editor of the *Christian Advocate* in New York, who was not a
delegate, asked for personal privilege to deny a widely circulated
report that he had been involved in "a plan . . . formed by northern
members of the conference, to force the south into secession."[41] But
there were also attempts on both sides to preserve the union.

On 14 May, William Capers and Stephen Olin successfully
passed a joint resolution to create a "Committee of Pacification,"
composed of three delegates from the North and three from the
South to confer with the bishops in order to formulate a compromise.
The committee met, and Bishop Soule reported four days later on
their behalf that "after a calm and deliberate investigation of the subject submitted to their consideration," they were unable to "agree
upon any plan of compromise to reconcile the views of the northern
and southern conferences."[42] As the crisis intensified the bishops
independently sought ways to buy time, but the hour had passed
when the union could be preserved. They, along with the delegates,
were powerless to influence the outcome. A peace measure they

drafted urging postponement of any action in the case of Bishop Andrew for four years was tabled; Bishop Hedding quickly dissociated himself from it after it was presented.[43] The position of the southern delegates was clear and firm. They believed any action taken against Bishop Andrew would leave them no choice but to leave the connection. William Winans of Mississippi said of the Finley substitute:

> By the vote contemplated by this body, and solicited by this resolution, you will render it expedient—nay, more, you render it indispensable—nay, more, you render it *uncontrollably necessary*, that as large a portion of the Church should—I dread to pronounce the word, but you understand me. . . . If you pass this action in the mildest form in which you can approach the bishop, you will throw every minister in the south *hors du combat*, and you will leave us no option—God is my witness that I speak with all sincerity of purpose toward you—but to be disconnected with your body. If such necessity exists on your part to drive this man from his office, we reassert that this must be the result of your action on this matter.[44]

Winans closed his remarks with a question: "Will you drive us from the connection, or will you hold back your hands and prevent the pernicious effects of such action as is at present sought at your hands?"[45] Benjamin Drake, also of Mississippi, said it even more forcefully: "Bishop Andrew must be continued in the episcopal office, or you certainly divide the Church."[46]

But divide it they did. On 3 June, two days after the Finley substitute had been passed, William Capers offered the resolutions that provided for two separate General Conferences within one church. They were referred to a committee, which was unable to agree on a report favorable to the conference. Two days later, John B. McFerrin of Tennessee proposed that the conference "devise, if possible, a constitutional plan for a mutual and friendly division of the Church."[47] The Plan of Separation would be the result.

Bishop Andrew left the conference immediately after the vote on the Finley substitute was lost. Therefore, he did not know until later all that transpired in his case, nor was he certain what his status might be. In response to a request from the bishops for a ruling on some practical implications of the action taken in Bishop Andrew's case, the conference agreed that Andrew's name would continue to stand in the *Minutes*, the *Hymn Book*, and the *Discipline*; his salary and family support would be continued; and he would be free to determine in what work he would engage.[48]

Not knowing what Andrew might decide to do, since the choice was his, the bishops did not include him in their published plan of episcopal visitation. After learning he was not assigned any work, Andrew wrote to his friend William Wightman: "I see the bishops have interpreted the action of the Genl. Conference and I presume have acted out the true intent and will of their masters in giving me *no work*."[49]

The matter quickly became moot when Andrew was invited by Bishop Soule to attend the southern conferences with him. This later resulted in charges being filed against Soule that he, by not waiting for a written request from Andrew, had abused his authority and defied the will of the conference.

This charge against Soule reflects the diverging models of the episcopacy that were rapidly solidifying within Methodism. J. Hamby Barton nicely summarizes the mature form these differences would take: "In the South, the episcopacy was an aristocracy providing independent leadership for the church. In the North, the republican sentiments of a great middle class church culminated in the General Conference which employed the episcopacy as the chief administrative instrument."[50] These differences, germinating in a climate of social unrest and sectionalism, were about to separate the Methodist family again.

CHAPTER 11

The Methodist Episcopal Church, South

After the vote on Bishop Andrew's case was taken on 1 June 1844, fifty-one delegates from the fourteen annual conferences in slaveholding areas signed and issued a declaration to the General Conference. A. B. Longstreet of Georgia read the *Declaration* on 5 June:

> The delegates of the conference in the slaveholding states take leave to *declare* to the General Conference of The Methodist Episcopal Church, that the continued agitation on the subject of slavery and abolition in a portion of the Church,—the frequent action on that subject in the General Conference,—and especially the extra-judicial proceedings against Bishop Andrew, which resulted, on Saturday last, in the virtual suspension of him from his office as superintendent,—must produce a state of things in the south which renders a continuance of the jurisdiction of that General Conference over these conferences inconsistent with the success of the ministry in the slaveholding states.[1]

On 6 June, one day after the *Declaration* was read, H. B. Bascom of the Kentucky Conference added the formal *Protest* of the minority with regard to the decision taken in the case of Bishop Andrew. Speaking, he said, for five thousand ministers and half a million members, he rose to

145

protest against the recent act of a majority of this General Conference, in an attempt . . . to degrade and punish the Rev. James O. Andrew . . . by declaring . . . that he desist from the exercise of his episcopal functions without the exhibition of any alleged offense against the laws or discipline of the Church, without form of trial, or legal conviction . . . and in the absence of any charge of want of qualification or faithfulness in the performance of the duties pertaining to his office.[2]

The *Protest* sounded a note that would be repeated over and over. The southern delegates were united in their conviction that the continuing agitation in the MEC on the subject of slavery would make it impossible to carry on their ministry in the South successfully if they remained joined to it. And among the members of the majority, the abolitionists and their supporters were pleased with the possibility of division since, as they said, "schism was preferable to continued association with sin."[3]

The Plan of Separation

In response to the *Declaration*, the conference named a Committee of Nine, composed of three delegates each from the northern, middle, and southern conferences, chaired by Robert Paine of the Tennessee Conference, to draw up articles "to meet the emergency with Christian kindness and the strictest equity."[4] It presented the conference with a Plan of Separation in which (1) a guarantee was given that all the "societies, stations and conferences" going with the church in the South "shall remain under the unmolested pastoral care of the Southern Church," and the MEC would not attempt to organize congregations among them; (2) ministers were provided the choice to remain in the MEC or go "without blame" into the southern church; (3) a recommendation was made that the Sixth Restrictive Rule be amended by the various annual conferences to provide, after amendment, for a fair share of the property, and assets of the Book Concern and the printing establishments in Charleston, Richmond, and Nashville to be handed over to the MECS; (4) the division of these assets was to be based on the number of traveling preachers in churches North and South; (5) payments were to be made at the rate of $25,000 per year in cash and stock of the Book Concern until the southern church received "in the proportion that the amount due them, or in arrears, bears to all the property of the Concern"; (6) commissioners were to be named by the General Conference to determine the total amount due; (7) the agents appointed by each body were given full power to act on behalf of their respective organizations; (8) all other property, such as schools, colleges, churches and parsonages, were to be transferred free from any claim of the MEC; and (9) copyrights were to be held in common.

If the church was to be divided, the Plan offered a fair and equitable proposal that the southern delegates quickly accepted. Charles Elliott, editor of the *Western Christian Advocate* and delegate from the Ohio Conference, moved its adoption—something he would later regret. Elliott justified the idea of separation by affirming that dividing an already too large body into two parts would prove beneficial to both. "The measure contemplated," he said, "was not schism, but separation for their mutual convenience and prosperity."[5] The fundamental premise undergirding the Plan was the continuation of a united denomination operating in two General Conferences.

Alfred Griffith of the Baltimore Conference, the maker of the original motion regarding Bishop Andrew, quickly raised the obvious and complex issue—who had the power to divide the church? He denied that anyone had a right to divide the MEC. During the debate that the question sparked, Peter Cartwright, who said he thought the Plan of Separation "a wicked one which would rob both the north and the south of their rights," predicted (correctly) that the proposed "arrangements would create war and strife in the border conferences," and agreed with Griffith that the delegates did not have either a mandate or the power to divide the church.

Nathan Bangs, a member of the Committee of Nine, cautioned the conference against the use of the word *division*, which, he said, had been carefully avoided by the committee in their report. The charge to the committee had been to search for an acceptable solution, and "if they could not adjust the difficulties amicably, they were to provide for separation if they could do it constitutionally."[6] The Plan was presented, he continued, "in the event of separation taking place," thereby removing the onus from the General Conference and placing it squarely on those who might make a decision to separate. The fundamental choice before the conference, he argued, was between the lesser of two evils: If separation were to take place, would it be a peaceable parting or a violent disruption? If Methodism was bound to divide, he would not be party to denying the minority their rights. James Finley said the situation was analogous to the "liberty" given the Canadian conferences to establish themselves as a separate church. On that occasion the General Conference did not exercise any power to create the new body, since it did not possess it.[7]

Cartwright was not alone in recognizing the potential for conflict in the so-called "border" conferences. Thomas Bond, editor of the *Christian Advocate and Journal*, spoke at some length and quite specifically about it in reference to conferences like Baltimore, Philadelphia, Pittsburgh, and Ohio, all of which contained within their bounds both free and slaveholding areas. He urged strict adherence to the existing conference lines, saying, "And then we shall have peace"; but such was not to be the case.

Since the Plan called for an amendment of the Sixth Restrictive Rule to divide the property of the Book Concern, it had to be passed as a separate item by the various annual conferences in order for the Plan itself to take effect. Several speakers rose to clarify that the Plan of Separation itself was not being submitted to the conferences for ratification. Only the single portion that modified the Sixth Restrictive Rule required their affirmation. This too was to become a major area of disagreement, and eventually a legal battle.

The Process Leading to Division

The General Conference finally adjourned on 11 June 1844, and the process leading to division began immediately following adjournment. While still in New York, the delegates from thirteen conferences in slaveholding states met in caucus and determined to recommend to their respective annual conferences the calling of a convention to determine their relation to the MEC. In the Address sent to the ministers and members of their conferences, they stated their conviction that the "action of the General Conference, as now organized, will always be extremely hurtful, if not finally ruinous, to the interests of the Southern portion of the Church." Moreover, they declared the views of the church in the North on the subject of slavery to be "in direct conflict" with those of the South, and without capitulation to them "there is no hope of any thing like union or harmony."[8]

The Plan of Separation provided for the creation of a separate southern General Conference if the various annual conferences in the region found such a division necessary. It was, therefore, essential to have some formal declaration of their intent, and the caucus made the following recommendations for their "calm and collected" consideration: to call a convention in Louisville, Kentucky, to open 1 May 1845; for delegates to the convention to be appointed by the annual conferences; for these persons to be instructed by their conferences how to vote on the issues, as far as possible, in conformity with the wishes of their constituents.[9] It was signed by fifty-one delegates.

The Kentucky Conference was the first to meet and act. Establishing a pattern that would be repeated in the resolutions eventually passed by all the conferences, it condemned the action of the General Conference of 1844 in the cases of Francis Harding and Bishop Andrew but expressed regret at the prospects ahead: "We deeply regret the prospect of division growing out of these proceedings, and that we do most sincerely hope and pray that some effectual means, not inconsistent with the interests and honor of all concerned, may be suggested and devised by which so great a calamity may be averted."[10]

The Louisville Convention, 1845

Despite their protests of distress over the possibility of division in the church, each of the southern and western conferences passed the necessary resolutions to call the convention in Louisville, elected delegates to attend, and most created committees on "division" or "separation." One hundred delegates from fifteen annual conferences—including the Indian Mission and Florida Conferences, which were not among the original thirteen—gathered in Louisville on 1 May 1845. William Capers called the meeting to order and Lovick Pierce of Georgia was elected president *pro tem*. After the certification and seating of delegates was completed, a resolution was passed inviting the bishops in attendance to assume the chair and preside over the meeting. Bishops Soule and Andrew responded positively. Bishop Thomas A. Morris, who was also in attendance at various times during the convention, took part in leading worship but declined the invitation to preside.

The following day, William M. Wightman, Leroy M. Lee, and John B. McFerrin were named a committee to "prepare a full and correct synopsis of the proceedings of the Convention."[11] Rules of procedure were duly adopted, and Bishop Soule addressed the convention. He revealed his conviction that since the last General Conference he had considered division "inevitable" and, in the light of that conclusion, had worked "not to prevent it, but rather that it might be attended with the least injury, and the greatest amount of good which the case would admit."[12] As he had to the delegates of the final General Conference in 1844, Soule urged the convention to conduct its business in "the spirit of Christian moderation and forbearance," and assumed the chair.

Late in the day on 6 May, William A. Smith and Lovick Pierce introduced the following resolution to be laid on the table for discussion the next morning:

> *Resolved* . . . That we cannot sanction the action of the late General Conference of the Methodist Episcopal Church, on the subject of slavery, by remaining under the ecclesiastical jurisdiction of that body . . . we, therefore, hereby instruct the committee on organization, that if upon a careful examination of the whole subject, they find that there is no reasonable ground to hope that the Northern majority will recede from their position and give some safe guaranty for the future security of our civil and ecclesiastical rights, that they report in favor of a separation from the ecclesiastical jurisdiction of the said General Conference.[13]

When the vote on the motion was finally taken a week later, on 14 May, it passed with but a single dissenting voice. Three days later, ironically with Bishop Andrew presiding, the formal resolution to separate from the MEC and to create the Methodist Episcopal Church, South, was passed. William Gunn, George W. Taylor, and John C. Harrison cast the only negative votes on the decision to divide the church. The date was set in 1846 for the first General Conference of the new church to meet in Petersburg, Virginia.

In the Pastoral Address to their constituents, the delegates were clear that, at least in their minds, they had not withdrawn from "the true Christian and Catholic pale of The Methodist Episcopal Church." Their complaint was against the majority in the General Conference, and not against the church in itself. "The General Conference, or a majority thereof, is not the Church."[14] They urged a peaceful settlement according to the provisions of the Plan of Separation. James O. Andrew signed the address as president on 16 May 1845.

Orange Scott, the organizer of Methodist abolitionists in New England, celebrated the news of the division when it came. "A division of the ME Church," he wrote, "will hasten the abolition of slavery in our country, it cannot be otherwise."[15] Other antislavery advocates, especially in the annual conferences of New England, also weighed in with their praise, but thought the General Conference had not gone far enough in the case of Bishop Andrew. And, as Mathews noted, the South became the enemy because it had "decided to repudiate the Methodist heritage."[16]

It is essential to understand that the conferences organizing into the MECS believed themselves, as the Report of their Committee on Organization declared, empowered to act with the full and legal authority of the General Conference of 1844 "to judge of the propriety, and decide upon the necessity of organizing a 'separate ecclesiastical connexion,' in the South."[17] Furthermore, they had acted according to the expressed mandate of sixteen annual conferences in forming the new church. In the Pastoral Address presented by the first General Conference, which met a year later, this point was central.

> The new organization in which we find ourselves re-embodied and united, and with a unanimity as unexpected and surprising to ourselves as it can be to others, was originally authorized . . . by the direct provision and approval of the General Conference of the whole church, in 1844, as shown in the Plan of Separation adopted by that body.[18]

This affirmation was significant because, in the North, they were immediately cast into the role of schismatics, willfully breaking from mother church in support of a moral evil and acting in accord with a General Conference that did not have the power to divide the church. In its Report on the State of the Church, the MEC General Conference of 1848 told its members: "We claim that The Methodist Episcopal Church, South, exists as a distinct and separate ecclesiastical communion solely by the act and deed of the individual ministers and members constituting said church."[19] They further declared, "We affirm it to be impossible to point to any act of the General Conference of The Methodist Episcopal Church erecting or authorizing said church."[20] It was three decades before agreement could be reached that the southern church was a legitimate branch of one Methodist family, and not schismatic. And only then was it possible for the two episcopal Methodisms to began the journey on the long road to reunion.[21]

Beginning immediately after the end of the General Conference in June 1844, a fierce war of words was initiated in the church press, both North and South. Especially active was the editor of the New York *Christian Advocate*, Thomas Bond. He was a special target of southern ire because it was widely believed, and had been alleged at the General Conference of 1844, that Bond was a leader in an organized effort to divide the church and force the South into isolation. Capers wrote to William Wightman to comment on an editorial written by Bond and published on 7 August 1844 in which Bond claimed that "the Bonds," "the Bangses," and "the Durbins" had given a pledge to spare no effort "to accomplish the blessed work of reconciliation and Church union." Capers told his friend: "That Dr. Bangs, indeed, may desire reconciliation and Church union, I am ready to believe; and I would not deny it of Dr. Durbin; but for Dr. Bond to pretend it of himself is absolutely unsufferable."[22]

Bishop Andrew became quickly involved, and Bond was forced to defend himself from the charge that he was "the main prosecutor in the whole business" of forcing Andrew from his episcopal duties.[23] Bond protested innocence of any knowledge in advance of the action of the General Conference. He told Andrew in an editorial: "I never saw the resolution calling upon the Committee on the Episcopacy to report on your case; nor the resolution offered to the conference requesting you to resign; nor the substitute for it which finally passed the conference, before they came under the action of the body." He called for an apology from Andrew and chided him for accepting the advice of the southern delegation not to resign, a move that Bond thought could have left the door open to other ways of addressing the problem without producing the results now sure to divide the connection. "Everybody knew the resolution in your case would pass," Bond told Andrew and his readers, "if it were not arrested by some terms of compromise. . . . Was it then unkind to suggest that you could effect this compromise by the slightest intimation, that if further proceedings were stayed, you would in some way relieve the difficulty?" Ominously, he warned him, "Henceforth the Church and the world must consider the Bishop—and the Bishop alone—as accountable for the consequences which may follow his connection with slavery."

By and large the arguments on both sides remained the same.

152

The South continued to affirm that the General Conference had acted unlawfully and recklessly by forcing Bishop Andrew to cease from his episcopal duties. So far as they were concerned, the General Conference did not have the power to remove bishops because of "necessity." Charges of wrongdoing leading to conviction in a formal trial were the only grounds for removal recognized by the church. The northern position was built on the premise that bishops were officers of the General Conference and could be removed by it at any time for any reason. The analogy drawn to support this claim was the power of the executive branch in civil government to appoint and remove its officers. "But from the first, the General Conference has provided against the abuse of Episcopal prerogative by holding the Bishops immediately responsible to the body which appoints them, and subjecting them to removal from office by a vote of the majority of the body."[24] Both positions, in the final analysis, were extreme, but there was genuine disagreement between the parties on the nature of episcopacy and its relation to the General Conference.

The First General Conference of the Methodist Episcopal Church, South—1846

The first General Conference, authorized by the Louisville Convention delegates in 1845, met on 1 May 1846, at the Union Street Church in Petersburg, Virginia. Since Bishop Andrew had not arrived and Bishop Soule had yet formally to give his notice of adherence to the new denomination, William Winans of Mississippi called the delegates to order. John Early of Virginia was elected president *pro tem*. Delegates from fourteen conferences took their seats. The Alabama and Georgia delegations arrived the next day, as did Bishop Andrew, who then assumed the chair. Bishop Soule addressed the conference, formally declared his allegiance to the MECS, and was welcomed by a standing vote of the delegates. Committees were organized, among them a Committee on Episcopacy, whose charge was to determine the number of new bishops necessary to serve the church. A hymnal was authorized for publication.

The Committee on Episcopacy presented its first report on 7 May and recommended the election of two additional bishops. The conference moved immediately to the election, and on the second ballot, William Capers of South Carolina and Robert Paine of the

Tennessee Conference were chosen. They were the first of sixty persons to be elected to the episcopal office in the southern church.

Capers had been a strong candidate for election in the MEC in 1832 but had characterized himself at that time as "inextricably a slaveholder" and nominated another southerner who was not—James O. Andrew. It seems likely that if the church ever had determined it permissible to elect a slaveholder to the episcopacy, Capers would have been the one. A native of South Carolina, he attended South Carolina College and for a time studied law. But in time he decided to preach, was admitted to the South Carolina Conference, and became one of the premier preachers in the South. He was also a great missionary leader of the denomination, having been appointed by Bishop McKendree to serve in a mission to the Creek Indians, and later heading the mission to the slaves, serving ten thousand adults. In 1836 he was elected the first editor of what became the *Southern Christian Advocate*. Capers served in the episcopacy of the MECS until his death in 1855.

Bishop Paine was born in North Carolina but moved to Tennessee early in his life. He joined the Tennessee Conference in 1818 and was ordained both deacon and elder by William McKendree. Paine is the author of McKendree's two-volume biography, written at the request of the General Conference. In 1830 he was elected president of La Grange College in Georgia and was in that office when he was elected to the episcopacy. He worked closely with the Colored Methodist Episcopal Church when it was organized in 1870 and (with Bishop Holland McTyeire) ordained its first bishops.

Division of Assets of the Book Concern

The new branch of episcopal Methodism faced a variety of difficult problems. Most were issues related to the provisions of the Plan of Separation, and a significant one involved the equitable distribution of the assets and proceeds from the Book Concern. Its agents, Lane and Tippett, who were located in New York, withheld payment to the MECS because the changes in the Sixth Restrictive Rule authorized by the General Conference of 1844 were not approved in the requisite number of annual conferences. The annual conferences that had opposed abolition found it hard to vote to divide the church, and many of them refused to ratify the changes required to do it, thus denying the South its fair share of the money. "When the final vote on separation was tabulated, 2,135 ministers favored division and 1,070 opposed it." Of the votes in opposition, 1,067 were cast in northern conferences. Only 1,164 in the North favored a peaceful schism.[25]

The annual conferences in the North also rejected the proposed amendments to the Sixth Restrictive Rule. As a result, the assumption of the majority of delegates in the MEC General Conference of 1848, and its bishops, was that since the essential portion of the Plan of Separation failed to pass, the entire proposal was null and void and could not go into effect.[26] The withholding of funds from their share of the Book Concern assets was protested by the first General Conference of the MECS in 1846, but to no avail. The only recourse finally available to them was to seek remedy in the civil courts. A suit was filed in July 1849 to recover a fair share of the assets and profits of the Book Concern. After a lengthy legal battle, which went all the way to the Supreme Court of the United States, they won a favorable decision. The Court ruled that the MECS had acted in accord with the provisions of the Plan of Separation, and that the General Conference had the power to divide the denomination. Speaking of the General Conference, the Court wrote:

> It cannot, therefore, be denied—indeed, it has scarcely been denied—that this body, while composed of all the traveling preachers, possessed the power to divide it, and authorize the organization and establishment of the two separate independent churches. The power must necessarily be regarded as inherent in the General Conference.[27]

Responding to the Plan of Separation

The action of the General Conference of 1848 declaring the Plan of Separation "null and void" placed the southern church in the position of schismatics. They, for their part, did not regard the formation of the MECS as secession. It was rather an exercise of their free choice to accept the wisdom of the General Conference in providing for two separate governing bodies in light of what they deemed to be inevitable circumstances that, if not addressed, would impair the effectiveness of Methodist work in the southern United States. "We do nothing but what we are *expressly authorized to do* by the supreme, or rather highest legislative power of the Church."[28]

Moreover, this authorization provided, and they expected, that preachers at all levels would be given a choice of affiliation, and that all property such as churches, parsonages, and schools in the area designated for the southern church would belong to them, plus a fair share of the assets and proceeds of the Book Concern to which they had contributed through the years. When it came to the actual process of determining the allegiance of preachers and congregations, especially in the border conferences, there were conflicts and hard feelings on both sides, as Peter Cartwright and others had predicted. Incidents were so numerous that the Committee on Episcopacy of the newly formed MECS, at their first General Conference in 1846, was instructed

> to institute special inquiry into the character and grounds of the charge, so repeatedly preferred by the Editors and correspondents of the Western Christian Advocate and the Christian Advocate and Journal, against Bishops Soule and Andrew, to the effect, that they have in numerous instances, not only constructively infracted, but gross violated, both the spirit and the letter of the General Conference Plan of Separation, in appointing ministers to border charges, stations, or societies, where the people, or members of the church, had not adhered South. . . .[29]

Formal charges were filed in the MEC against Bishop Soule, and he was prohibited by the members from holding one of his scheduled annual conferences in Ohio.

Preachers in the northern annual conferences also indirectly expressed their displeasure with their own preachers and the Plan of Separation when electing delegates to the General Conference of 1848. They chose only a few former delegates who had expressed reluctance to support the Plan in 1844—not an easy thing to do, since all the resolutions related to the Plan of Separation passed the General Conference by large margins. But by and large they cleaned the slate and elected persons who were not delegates to the previous General Conference. In contrast to the usual pattern of reelecting delegates, the Baltimore Conference selected only one of eleven who had attended in 1844; Providence, not any; New England, one; New Hampshire, none; New York, five of thirteen; and so on. Some of the casualties were acknowledged leaders in prominent positions, such as Nathan Bangs and Abel Stevens. Charles Elliott, editor of the *Western Christian Advocate*, who had made the motion to adopt the

156

Plan of Separation and praised it on the floor of the conference, was not elected by the Ohio Conference.

The negative results of a well-meaning attempt by both North and South to provide for a peaceful and amicable separation were lasting—bitterness created by the division, heightened by the war of words in the church press, and intensified by the civil conflict that later swept the country kept the two episcopal Methodisms apart for almost a century. This separation allowed the two churches to develop their own understanding of church government, including the practice and style of episcopacy. Since the southern church accepted the *Discipline*, Articles of Religion, and doctrinal standards without modification, the dispute leading to separation certainly was not theological in nature. Perhaps the supreme irony is that the southern church also accepted the provisions on slavery without modification. What was at stake had little to do with the formal provisions of church law.

CHAPTER 12

The Methodist Episcopal Church, South: Defending the Asburian Ark

From its organization, the MECS adopted the Asburian notion of episcopacy as a separate and co-equal branch of church government. This understanding influenced both the role assigned to the General Conference in southern Methodism and also the practice and author-ity vested in its bishops. The debates in the General Conferences of 1844 had made the delegates from the fourteen slaveholding confer-ences acutely aware of the differences between that concept of epis-copacy and the one articulated by Leonidas Hamline and others in the MEC. Moreover, the disposition of the case of Bishop Andrew would forever stand as a beacon to warn of the dangers present in a General Conference whose powers were unchecked. It was not a mis-take they would make in the new organization.

The Shape and Form of Asburian Episcopacy

Asburian episcopacy was worked out and given form in the life and long episcopal service of Francis Asbury. Asbury had no models for episcopal leadership when he was ordained to the office in 1784. With the possible exception of what he might have learned from the example of John Wesley and whatever experience he might have had of the prelates in the Church of England, Asbury had, so far as we know, never known a bishop when he became one. There were none in the United States. Even if he had the opportunity to observe them, most would not have provided a positive role model for the Methodists in America, nor have been compatible with America's unique form of itinerant ministry. It was something that Asbury created and that became uniquely identified with him as a person. Much of it was done by trial and error. It has already been noted that shortly after Asbury's ordination in Baltimore, Jesse Lee saw him wearing the gown and bands of a bishop. Lee's surprise and obvious disapproval of such trappings, probably echoed by other preachers as well, caused Asbury to swiftly lay the gown and bands aside. The experience taught Asbury that, as he was later to say, in America "a bishop among us is a plain man." We have no way of knowing what he and Coke discussed about the work of a bishop, but it is hard to imagine they did not consider it, especially in the early years when they changed the name from "general superintendent." The failed experiment of the Council in 1789–90 is but another example of an instance in which Asbury overstepped the bounds of his authority, and he was forced to abandon it too. Even when operating within the limits imposed by General Conference, as he was when the Genesee Conference was created, Asbury did not hesitate to seek the support of the preachers when challenged, and in so doing he established a precedence upon which others would call.

Despite the evolving nature of the office, Asbury's authority was personal and unique and could not be duplicated by others. He was a strong individual whose charisma and exercise of power lent authority to whatever he did or said. Strawbridge and O'Kelly were powerful antagonists, and each had a following, but they could not prevail over Asbury. Although his appointment originally came from Wesley, Asbury quickly became an independent authority among the Methodists. What he did in his role as a leader required ego strength and singleness of purpose, traits that Asbury had in abundance from the beginning. Rankin came to America in 1773 with Wesley's mandate to lead the Methodists. Asbury, like all the preachers connected with Wesley in America, was subordinate to him, but it was not easy. His "judgment was stubbornly opposed," Asbury said, and he complained in his journal of "the overbearing spirit of a certain person."[1] A large number of other preachers simply left the connection rather than submit, and Asbury was tempted to leave too. But he stayed, demanded to be heard, and when he did not receive the appointment to Baltimore that he expected, he appealed directly to Wesley.

Although William McKendree never held the power that Asbury held, he too was a strong individual with sufficient confidence to contest Asbury's practice and even to face him down on the conference floor in 1812 after McKendree delivered the first Episcopal Address. Whatcoat, on the other hand, lacked this confidence. Yet both individuals were regarded by Asbury as junior to him and as "assistant bishops." Richey properly described Asbury as having "personalized authority, both in the sense of having it focused upon his person and in the sense of exercising it in personal fashion."[2] By the end of Asbury's life, his authority in American Methodism could not be separated from his person. This pattern was to be repeated many times over in Methodism, especially in the South where strong individuals were chosen to fill the office of bishop.

With ego strength there is always the potential for autocratic behavior. O'Kelly's protest in 1792 was as much motivated by his personal dislike for Asbury and his monarchal tendencies as it was a commitment to democratic practice in the appointment of preachers. More than a few persons would feel the same way about Bishops Warren A. Candler, U. V. W. Darlington, and Collins Denny.

Asbury's episcopacy was characterized primarily by his devotion to the enhancement, promotion, and defense of the itinerant form of ministry. Episcopacy in the Asburian mode can never be understood apart from its role in the itinerancy. In the annotated *Discipline* of 1798, Asbury and Coke outlined the duties of a bishop. Although the statement is modest in this early form, it grew in importance over time. They assigned to the bishop the responsibility to preside in the conferences, fix the appointments of the preachers, discipline them as required between sessions of the conference, oversee the spiritual and temporal business of the societies, and to ordain bishops, deacons, and elders.[3] Although traditional roles associated with the episcopal office in the church in the West were present, the clear priority and focus was on the relation to the body of preachers and their ministry. The locus of this power finally was the authority to fix the appointments of the preachers. This was a task Asbury reserved for himself for the better part of thirty-two years, and on the occasions when for any reason he was not able to do it, he delegated it to persons of his choice. Methodist preachers were sent into their places of service, and for most of the three decades after 1784 they

161

were sent by Asbury. The bishop determined who went where, and they obeyed.

There is no denying that Asbury enhanced his authority by doing himself what he expected those under him to do. He led by example. He was the epitome of an itinerant preacher, sharing the same experiences, hardships, joys, and sorrows, and scorned any-thing—from marriage to a preference for life in the cities—that had the potential to limit his effectiveness in spreading scriptural holiness in the land. From the beginning it was clear that bishops who for any reason ceased to travel in the episcopal office "without the consent of the General Conference" were ineligible to exercise any ministerial office within the church.[4] Apart from the traveling ministry, a bishop had no place in the connection. Asbury himself had to receive a dis-pensation allowing less than full-time service when he became too ill to continue his duties, but he was prepared to resign his office had it not been given, and he did not ask for it.

Asbury was an "overseer" in the New Testament meaning of the word. That understanding of the office of bishop included both the temporal and spiritual aspects of its practice. By 1800, Asbury's authority was so well established that before others could be elected to the episcopal office their status in relation to Asbury had to be determined. And despite the fact that the General Conference affirmed that all Methodist bishops were equal in their power and authority, so long as Asbury lived they never were. He was *the* bish-op of the people called Methodists.

Despite the unique power that he exercised and the role he played, both literally and symbolically, in the life of the Methodists, it is interesting that it was Asbury who lodged authority within the body of preachers assembled in conference by demanding to be elected to the office of a general superintendent. In so doing he cre-ated the basis for the alternative view of central authority in the denomination. As Richey notes, in 1784 "American Methodists stood poised between two principles of authority, one [conference] fairly broadly shared, the other highly focused and personalized."[5] Because ambiguity prevailed at the organizing conference, the door was left open to the disagreement that divided the church North and South.

But while Asbury was willing to subject himself to the confer-ence and to the body of preachers, neither he nor his successors in the Asburian tradition hesitated to challenge that power when they thought it abused. The Asburian form assumed that it was the bishop's responsibility to provide the checks and balances necessary to offset the power of the General Conference. Second only to their role as defenders of the itinerant system, bishops who understood themselves to follow in the tradition of Asbury were watchful of excesses in the General Conference.

McKendree supported Asbury's interpretation of episcopal government and acted on the premise that "from the preachers *collectively* both the General Conference and the General Superintendents derive their powers."[6] At the same time, in the face of the decision to elect presiding elders, which he judged unconstitutional, McKendree exercised a veto and—following the earlier example of Asbury in the controversy over the Genesee Conference—appealed to the wider body of preachers.

By 1844 the practice of the Asburian form was sufficiently clear that Bishop Horace DuBose correctly understood that Joshua Soule, the author of the Third Restrictive Rule, entered the MECS when it was organized because "as he saw it, the Asburian ark, with the scroll of the law and the staff that budded, went with the minority rather than with the majority."[7]

Episcopacy North and South

In a sense, the story of the episcopacy in American Methodism can be understood as an ellipse with two foci, each embodying one side of the ambiguity that had been present in its polity since 1784. The first was Asbury himself, and the second was the General Conference of 1844, in which the concept of an episcopacy created, directed by, and responsible to a strong General Conference was articulated and affirmed. The Asburian idea of a co-equal conference and episcopacy found expression in the MECS, while the MEC defended the concept of a strong conference with ultimate authority. The discussion of those differences in 1844 (in some sense mirroring the conflict over states' rights in the nation) demonstrated that while the disagreement over polity was not the sufficient cause for the split, it was a major source of conflict leading to it. The fundamental issue between North and South was the denomination's relation to slavery, but the debate over slavery was focused on a bishop of the church and his relation to the powers exercised by the body of preachers through their delegated General Conference. Bishop Andrew was both the subject of those deliberations and a symbol of the fundamental difference in the two positions. The MEC favored a strong General Conference whose officers, the bishops, were entirely subject to it. The South feared it, and their worst fears were confirmed by their experience of its disposition of the cases of Bishop Andrew and Francis Harding. Southern Methodism was born with a commitment to establish and defend the ideal of episcopacy as a co-equal branch of church government sharing power with the General Conference.

The more emotional side of the controversy was revealed in the half true, but often expressed, conviction that to remain in a united Methodism subject to the powers of a General Conference biased against slavery would end any possibility of effective ministry in the South, especially among the slaves. William Capers wrote to the *New York Christian Advocate and Journal* in response to the anonymous "A. C.'s" appeals for union: "We can never again belong to the jurisdiction of the same General Conference. It would destroy us to attempt it."[8]

So far as the MECS was concerned, its Asburian episcopacy was essential to its mission and the sentinel forever guarding the church from the abuse of power by the General Conference. The debates of 1844 were about the constitution of the church too. The leaders of the MEC, as described by the southern Committee on Organization, regarded the constitution of the church as limited to the six Restrictive Rules. The General Conference, like the national government in its Constitution, could do anything that was not expressly prohibited by restrictions. In the judgment of the southern church that view was flawed since "very few indeed of the more fundamental and distinguishing elements of Methodism, deeply and imperishably imbedded in the affection and veneration of the Church, and vital to its very existence, are even alluded to in the Restrictive Articles." An even more startling assumption, they said, was "that a Bishop of The Methodist Episcopal Church, instead of holding office under the constitution, and by tenure of law, and the faithful performance of duty, is nothing in his character of Bishop, but a mere officer at will, of the General Conference, and may accordingly be deposed at any time, with or without cause, accusation, proof, or form of trial. . . ."[9]

If the General Conference can create a bishop, Leonidas Hamline argued in New York, it can depose one too for the good of the church. In summary, the conferences sympathetic to the northern interpretation of the government of the church believed the General Conference could do with its officers anything not specifically prohibited by the Restrictive Rules. Although episcopacy could not be eliminated because the office was protected by the constitution, individual bishops could be set aside by the General Conference.

As understood and explained by the Committee on Organization in the MECS, the original jurisdiction of the MEC was in the hands of the body of preachers, under the direction of a preacher appointed by John Wesley—for example, Thomas Rankin or Thomas Coke. The power later exercised by the delegated General Conference was at that time in the hands of the separate annual conferences, which acted individually on measures proposed to them. Any single conference had the power to veto proposed legislation. All had to agree for any proposal to become law in the church as a whole. The separate conferences were bound only by the measures they had approved. It was this unworkable arrangement that led to the brief unsuccessful experiment of Asbury's Council, and then to the creation of a General Conference composed for a few years of all traveling elders with at least four years of service in the connection. Practical concerns for fairness and experience persuaded them finally to delegate power to elected representatives from the various annual conferences. This delegated body in 1808 was made subject to constitutional restrictions and limitations.

The uniting of the sixteen slaveholding conferences to form the MECS, according to the Committee on Organization, changed "no principle in the existing theory of General Conference jurisdiction." In this "simple division of jurisdiction," done with "the full consent" and "official sanction of the Church as represented in the General Conference," the new MECS received all the authority that the MEC had to convey.[10] There could therefore be no legitimate talk of secession or schism since there was none. One episcopal Methodism now existed in two equal General Conferences, whereas it had been in one. The sole reason for creating a new separate jurisdiction known as the MECS was "to restore and perpetuate the peace and unity of the church."[11]

The primary purpose of the episcopacy as conceived in the MECS, as they declared it had been from the beginning, was to strengthen and protect the itinerant system. They reaffirmed Asbury's conviction that no spiritual reformation was possible without a well-directed itinerancy, and that it was the lack of one that prevented Asbury from being more enthusiastic about a possible union with the United Brethren—not, as is sometimes thought, their unwillingness to give up the use of the German language. In his eulogy for Martin Boehm on 5 April 1812, Asbury asked a rhetorical question: "Why was the German reformation in the middle States that sprang up with Boehm, Otterbein, and their helpers not more perfect?" He answered: "There was no master-spirit to rise up and organize and lead them."

"Some of the ministers," he continued, "located, and only added to their charge partial traveling labors; and all were independent."

"It remains to be proved," Asbury concluded, "whether a reformation in any country, or under any circumstances, can be perpetuated without a well-directed itinerancy."[12]

In terms of their duties in the episcopal office, the powers given to southern bishops by the *Discipline* were those that had been present from the beginning. During the life of the MECS, however, these were enhanced and embellished until its bishops became the most powerful in the history of episcopal Methodism in America. T. B. Neely, a bishop in the MEC, summarized these early powers when, with obvious nostalgia and no little regret, he reviewed the changes that had limited or reduced episcopal authority in the MEC since Coke and Asbury first described duties of a bishop in the *Discipline* of 1798. He wrote:

> In the early days the bishop acted as a superior court and decided appeal cases;
> The bishop could receive a preacher into the ministry, and, on the other hand, could suspend a preacher from the ministry;
> The bishop could prevent a preacher putting anything into print and circulating the same;
> The bishop could veto the election of any preacher to clerical orders and refuse to ordain any one so elected by a Conference;
> And the bishop could also veto the election of a minister to the bishopric, and refuse to consecrate him to that office. But all these powers have disappeared from the episcopacy.[13]

Neely could also have listed the power to speak, make motions, and debate in the General Conference. The MECS was more successful in preserving some of these powers because of its commitment to the concept of equal powers in the government of the church. The chief distinction between the two branches of episcopal Methodists remained their understanding of the relation of the episcopacy to the General Conference.[14]

Because of the deep and bitter disillusionment the southern delegates experienced in the General Conference of 1844, they were determined to limit the conference's authority. In an address to the Kentucky Annual Conference, discussing the General Conference's resolving the case of Bishop Andrew, a speaker declared, "The episcopal office is degraded, beyond all precedent of friend or foe, and the powers of the General Conference magnified in equal ratio."[15] According to Stotts, "It came to be accepted as the doctrine of the Methodist Episcopal Church, South, that the formal establishment of the constitution in 1808 did in fact establish the episcopacy as a co-ordinate office."[16] The MEC was never able to support this interpretation.

Exercising Co-ordinate Power: The Veto

Building on its determination to limit the power of the General Conference, the third General Conference of the MECS in 1854 gave its bishops power to object to any action of the General Conference that they deemed unconstitutional. The question of who could determine the constitutionality of the acts of the General Conference had been present from the time of its creation. The decision of the MECS to vest this power in its bishops was consistent with its concept of church government with co-ordinate branches. But the General Conference of 1854 also established a procedure that checked the authority of the bishops by giving the General Conference a means to override an episcopal veto. "If after hearing the objections and reasons of the Bishops, two-thirds of the members of the Conference present shall still vote in favor of the rule or regulation so objected to, it shall have the force of law—otherwise it shall be null and void."[17] Norman Spellman regarded giving veto power to the bishops in the MECS as "the historic act which marked the peak of episcopal power in The Methodist Episcopal Church, South—indeed, in any branch of Methodism."[18]

The 1854 act proved to be flawed and was replaced by new legislation passed in 1870. The basic concept remained in place, and the revisions introduced had the same practical effect. The change did not remove the traditional authority of the bishops to pass on the constitutionality of the acts of the General Conference but based it on stronger historical and theoretical grounds.

The occasion for the review of the legislation passed in 1854 was the reorganization of the church, which took place in New Orleans at the end of the Civil War. At the General Conference of 1866 a special committee, chaired by the venerable Leroy M. Lee, was created to study existing legislation on the episcopacy. Lee's committee found that "the veto power does not inhere in the Episcopal office, and does not belong to it by any legitimate act or authorization of the church."[19] In other words, the veto power was not given to the bishops by the constitution in 1808. The action taken in 1854 they judged to be defective "in authority as a law, and that it is not, and of right cannot be either received or maintained as a part of the Constitution of the Church."[20] The committee's recommendation proposed a substitute, adopted by the delegates, which provided

> that when any rule or regulation is adopted by the General Conference, which, in the opinion of the Bishops is unconstitutional, the Bishops may present to the Conference which passed said rule or regulation, their objections thereto, with their reasons; and if then the General Conference shall, by a two-thirds vote, adhere to its action on said rule or regulations, it shall then take the course prescribed for altering a restrictive rule [be sent to the various annual conferences for ratification], and if thus passed upon affirmatively, the Bishops shall announce that such rule or regulation takes effect from that time.[21]

The basic principal reaffirmed by this action was that final authority in the church resided, as in fact it always had, in the body of preachers. They modified the legislation in order to define and limit both the General Conference and the bishops on the basis of this principle. If they had allowed either to determine the constitutionality of the acts of a delegated body, they would have compromised that final authority, something they refused to do.[22]

Episcopacy, Southern Style

The enhancement of the role of bishops in the South called from the preachers certain types of men prepared to fill a powerful office. The practice of episcopal authority in the daily life of the church resulted in a southern "style" of leadership that gave to them, as it had with Asbury, power based on individual charisma and authority that sometimes went far beyond anything bestowed formally by the *Discipline*. It is the considered opinion of historians such as Bishop Nolan B. Harmon that the power that inhered in the southern bishops from the time of the Civil War to unification came not so much because of the nature of the office and its construction but because of the character of the men who were elected.[23]

While not disputing Bishop Harmon, it is likely that it was also the definition of the office that called out such powerful men. Persons were elected to the episcopacy in the South whose character was compatible with the demands of the office; and because they tended to be strong individuals, they shaped it in turn. Bishops such as Candler, Denny, Darlington, McTyeire, Cannon, Mouzon, and Arthur Moore illustrate these traits.

The first bishops of the MECS were Joshua Soule and James O. Andrew, who responded to the invitation from the Louisville Convention in 1845 to join the new denomination on its formation. Although both quickly accepted, Bishop Soule expressed his sense of obligation "in good faith, to carry out the official plan of Episcopal Visitations as settled by the Bishops in New York, and published in the official papers of the Church, until the session of the first General Conference of the Methodist Episcopal Church, South."[24] Although he attempted to hold the conferences assigned to him, his decision to leave the MEC was well known and he was not warmly received in some and refused entirely in others. Andrew, who had been given no work under this plan, accepted the invitation immediately.

In the first decade after its organization, the bishops of the MECS came almost exclusively from the ranks of college presidents and editors of the church papers, with William Capers, H. H. Kavanaugh, and Enoch Marvin being the notable exceptions. Bishops Paine, Bascom, and Pierce were or had been college presidents. Bascom was serving as editor of the *Southern Quarterly Review* at the time he was elected. David Doggett was a professor at Randolph Macon College. Bishop John Early was the book agent of the church when he was elected in 1854. Wightman, McTyeire, John C. Keener, and Linus Parker were all editors of church papers. Alpheus Wilson was the first of a number of Missionary Secretaries to be elected. Others were Henry Clay Morrison, Seth Ward, Walter Lambeth, John M. Moore, and William Beauchamp.

Emory College in Oxford, Georgia, produced an exceptional

number of bishops, including Atticus Haygood, R. G. Waterhouse, James Dickey, and Warren A. Candler. Candler was the epitome of a southern bishop. Short and round, the brother of Asa Candler (who owned the Coca-Cola Company), Warren A. Candler served the church for a number of years in various capacities, including the faculty and presidency of Emory College. His students described in the yearbook what they had learned from their teacher and in so doing told more about him than about their own accomplishments. They said they had learned "that what Shorty [Candler] does not know has not been found out. Shorty did not make the earth, but was put there to run it. . . . Shorty is sorry for those that [sic] disagree with him, for they are wrong."[25]

Several bishops were elected out of administrative roles in educational institutions. Eugene Hendrix was president of Central College in Missouri. J. C. Kilgo was president of what is now Duke University. W. B. Murrah was president of Millsaps College in Jackson, Mississippi. James H. McCoy was president of Birmingham College. U. V. W. Darlington was president of Morris Harvey College. Bishop Ainsworth was a pastor in Macon, Georgia, when elected, but prior to that appointment he had been president of Wesleyan College in the same city. H. A. Boaz was president of Southern Methodist University when he was elected, as was his successor, Charles C. Selecman. Bishop Hoyt Dobbs and Paul Kern were former deans of the theological school at Southern Methodist. Ivan Lee Holt was its dean of faculty, and the first member of the School of Theology faculty to hold a Ph.D. degree. Edwin Mouzon, formerly a professor at Southwestern University, was its founding dean. Alex C. Smith and Collins Denny taught at Vanderbilt.

It was not until almost the time of unification in 1939 that a significant number of pastors began to appear in the ranks of southern bishops. Arthur Moore, Paul Kern (previously a faculty member and dean at Southern Methodist University), and A. Frank Smith, all elected in 1930, were pastors in Birmingham, San Antonio, and Houston, respectively, at the time. A. Frank Smith never moved from Houston during his long episcopal service. In the class of 1938, Ivan Lee Holt, Walter Peele, Clare Purcell, and William C. Martin were all pastors of large churches.

Strong, sometimes autocratic, personalities were welcomed into the southern ranks of episcopacy and well suited to its practice. Collins Denny, perhaps the best legal mind ever to occupy the episcopacy in either Methodist denomination, opposed unification up until the time the Plan of Union was passed in 1939 and was the only bishop who refused to sign the documents at the Uniting Conference in Kansas City. Bishop Warren Candler also strongly opposed unification. James Cannon Jr., a fanatic advocate of the cause of temperance and leader of the national anti-saloon league, was eventually forced by his opponents into a legal struggle that finally was resolved in the United States Supreme Court. Atticus G. Haygood, a troubled but vastly gifted man, displayed wisdom well beyond his time in his understanding of racial issues in the United States following the Civil War. His report on Negro education in the South, published in 1885, was a milestone, as was his earlier work entitled *Our Brother in Black, His Freedom and His Future*.

Due at least in part to the nature of the episcopal leadership, democracy made slow progress in the southern church, and some of the reforms that came after 1918 can only be seen as a form of "backlash" against the power of formidable, autocratic bishops.[26] Bishops like Candler and Denny did not hesitate to use the episcopal veto power as a tool to squash "progressive" reforms or other movements in the church with which they were not in agreement. For example, it was used three times at one General Conference to stop legislation on the rights of laywomen and to defeat a proposal to substitute "Christ's Holy Church" for the "Holy Catholic Church" in the Apostles' Creed. Writing in the *Christian Advocate*, Rembert G. Smith of Marietta, Georgia, described the veto as "a tool of the episcopacy to exercise power over the General Conference, rather than a tool to protect the Annual Conference from General Conference excesses, as the bishops insisted." Bishop Mouzon later admitted in a letter that Bishop Denny was largely responsible for this liberal use of the veto. In that correspondence he said he cautioned Denny "that the man who insists on using all the authority he has will soon not be permitted to use the authority he ought to have."[27]

Supervising Overseas Missions

Both branches of Methodism faced the problem of providing episcopal supervision for missionary conferences overseas, and solved it in different ways. The southern church stationed its general superintendents overseas, while the MEC, consistent with its understanding of a limited episcopacy, met the need by creating an entirely new form of the office, called the "missionary bishop." Although the southern practice of appointing bishops overseas created considerable hardship for them and their families, it also provided a unique opportunity for service in which several of them flourished. Bishop John M. Moore declared the best years of his entire episcopal tenure were the four spent in Brazil. Bishop Arthur Moore was heavily involved with missions throughout his long episcopal service. Several with missionary backgrounds—for example, Bishop Lambeth, the child of missionary parents and a medical doctor—spent most of their careers posted overseas. From 1934 until union in 1939, Bishop Arthur Moore had responsibility for all the overseas work of the MECS except for Cuba. He is properly remembered today as a great missionary leader. After the MC was organized, Moore continued his work in the Board of Missions.

Despite the hardships and inconvenience of requiring service from its bishops both in the United States and overseas, the MECS preserved the distinct features of an itinerant general superintendency and did not confuse its commitment to the Asburian understanding of the office by creating a new class of bishops who were limited in power and jurisdiction.

CHAPTER 13

The Methodist Episcopal Church: Evolving the Form of Episcopacy

The Third Restrictive Rule of the Constitution of 1808 requires that "the General Conference shall not change nor alter any part or rule of our government so as to do away episcopacy, nor destroy the plan of our itinerant General Superintendency." Both branches of American Methodism honored the restriction by retaining it in their respective *Disciplines*, but nevertheless felt free to change and modify its form and practice to meet their needs. This liberty was more consistent with the understanding of episcopacy in the MEC than in the MECS. As a result, the office of bishop in the MEC changed dramatically from the Asburian model on which historically it was based.

Forces for Change

The forces motivating this change were strong enough to prevail, even if it required amending the Third Restrictive Rule. This was particularly the case with the move to create an entirely new form of the episcopal office intended exclusively for service in missionary outreach overseas. Gerald Moede has argued persuasively that this change coincided with the acceptance of localized episcopacy. Episcopal service overseas in the MEC was limited to one missionary area. Language requirements and other circumstances made it easier to station bishops and leave them in one place. The difficulty and hardships of travel in the United States inevitably raised the same question there. Would the conferences be better served by episcopal leaders who had more frequent contact with them? The strain on family life of those in the office also suggested the value of a more limited assignment. In both branches of the church, the forces that successfully produced change often appeared to have little concern for the theological and constitutional implications of the innovations being made.[1] Methodists in America have always been, and remain today, a practical people, and they seldom allow theory or theology to overrule changes that they deem essential to progress. An understanding of the episcopacy in its modern form requires us to know what has changed, how these changes were accomplished, and their implications for theory as well as practice.

Episcopacy, Northern Style

The MEC emerged from the General Conference of 1844 having successfully articulated and defended the concept of a strong general conference, and of an episcopacy dependent on it. The leading spokesperson for this understanding of the office of bishop in the MEC was Leonidas L. Hamline, who in 1852 became the first bishop ever to resign his office. Although ill health motivated him to take the step, he certainly felt free—as an officer of the General Conference—to resign the office he had been given. In a real sense, a more concrete demonstration of his understanding of episcopacy as an office given by the General Conference cannot be imagined than his resignation. Although Hamline was the first person to actually leave the office, he was certainly not the first to contemplate doing it. The first was none other than Francis Asbury, who decided to resign in 1800 because of poor health. McKendree faced a similar situation. Both he and Asbury would have had no option but to leave the ministry entirely had they not been given permission by the General Conference to undertake only as much work as their health would permit. If a bishop could not travel, he could not serve. The same offer was made by the General Conference to Hamline, but he insisted on resigning. Bishop Roberts offered his resignation in 1836 because his health would not allow him to fulfill his duties, but it was not accepted.

Thomas A. Morris indicated his intention to resign because he said he was not suited to the office and was uncomfortable presiding in the annual conferences, but he did not actually resign.[2] No bishop in the MECS resigned during its ninety-four years of existence, perhaps reflecting the difference in the understanding of the nature of the episcopal office.

Bishop Edmund S. Janes, one of the youngest persons ever elected a bishop, decided to leave the office in 1855 because of the difficulties his service created for his family. "Painfully as I regret this," he said, "I know of but one way to relieve the affliction, namely to resign my office."[3] It is clear that the bishops of the MEC believed they had the power to resign the office, and Hamline's action proved they could.

The families of bishops have always been forced to cope with the added inconvenience and stress created by a spouse or parent in the office. That was exacerbated when the available modes of transportation necessitated being away for long periods of time in order to fulfill the assignments, but extensive travel is still required of bishops today. Matthew Simpson estimated that in the many years of his long episcopal service (1852–84), he traveled twenty-five thousand miles. This was especially true during the first decade after his election, when he lived in Evanston, Illinois, a remote and difficult place to reach. It was not even readily accessible from nearby Chicago. During the first quadrennium of his service, he was assigned to hold the California and Oregon Conferences, which entailed being away from home for almost six months in 1854. Travel was especially difficult during the 1860s because of disruptions caused by the Civil War and because there were so few bishops to oversee the entire work. Simpson moved to Philadelphia in 1863 to be more conveniently located.

Simpson's first episcopal tour was made shortly after his wife had given birth to a daughter: "I was very glad to learn from Charles' [their son] short letter that you were better, and I hope the disease has passed away. I shall be obliged to fulfill the appointment at Middletown on Sabbath and, as soon as I can with propriety leave, thereafter I will turn my face homeward but probably shall not get home before Friday." With some obvious guilt as well as a heavy burden of responsibility, he continued, "My duties are pressing. . . . Yet these duties call me from home, and you feel the burden imposed upon you."[4] Simpson held nine annual conferences during 1863, scattered from Maine to Michigan. Writing from Detroit, he said, "I arrived here this morning very fatigued. I closed conference last evening—rode all night, changing routes twice, and had no sleeping car. I do not feel very well today." He finished his brief note with a perennial complaint: "I hope to hear from you. I did not receive any letter at Upper Sandusky."[5]

His letters to Ellen and his children, often written during sessions of an annual conference, especially when trials were the order of business, are replete with accounts of experiences familiar to all travelers: loneliness, bad food, missed connections, poor accommodations, lost luggage, and boring companions. When Simpson traveled by sea from New York to San Francisco in 1854 (crossing the Isthmus of Panama) in order to preside at the California and Oregon Conferences, he added shipwreck to his list of unpleasant travel experiences. Despite almost superhuman efforts to reach his destination on time, he arrived at the site of the Oregon Conference just as the final hymn was being sung. Their first question was "Where have you been?" They were gracious enough to reconvene long enough to hear him preach.

Always there were the thoughts of home and family far away. From New Hampshire in the spring of 1860, he wrote his wife, Ellen:

> Today is bright and beautiful after the rain. How I wish you were here, or that I could look on our home on Lake Michigan. How are you? Is your health improving? Are all well? Did you buy that new bonnet Charlie [his son] spoke of when he wrote, and does it please you? Are the ribbons "greenish-blue or bluish green"? Is it the "coal scuttle" pattern, or is it of the old "Kiss-me-quick" shape? I think the last is my preference. It certainly must be most popular with gentlemen. How is the garden making coming in? Get the boys to put plenty in the ground, and in the summer I can attend to the dressing.[6]

It is little wonder that election to the episcopacy was viewed by families as, at best, a mixed blessing. When the word of his election reached the wife of Eugene Russell Hendrix in 1886, she wrote: "The telegram bearing the sad tidings of your election to the office of a bishop reached me about an hour ago. How can I give you up, my husband? I hope I appreciate the honor the church has bestowed upon you, but what a lonely life my future will be."[7]

While it seems always to have been understood, at least by the bishops themselves, that one could resign the episcopal office, there has been pressure not to do it, and few persons have actually left the office for any reason. After Hamline's resignation in 1852, the next to leave office was a missionary bishop, William F. Oldham, in 1904. The next itinerant general superintendent to resign was a bishop in The UMC, A. James Armstrong, in 1983. Rumors abounded that Bishop Gerald Kennedy, who was young when he was elected, became bored with the office and wanted to resign and return to the pastorate. He was reported to have been given some "fatherly advice" by older members of the Council of Bishops and eventually found a way to appoint himself as pastor of a church in Pasadena, California, while continuing to serve as a bishop. The theoretical ability of any bishop to resign and the practical implications related to doing it are quite different. Methodist bishops were and are expected to serve for life. But the pressures felt by them and their families added to sentiments favoring a more localized form of episcopacy.

Custom and Practice

The missionary outreach of both episcopal Methodisms during the nineteenth century also affected the practice of itinerant general superintendency. Along with the emphasis on missions came the organization of various boards and agencies designed for the supervision of special interests in the church, such as missions, education, temperance, publishing (The Book Concern), and Sunday schools. As their power and influence grew, these boards (whose members included powerful laypersons) and their leaders came to challenge, if not rival, the bishops in power and influence.

The addition of laypersons to the boards in order to take advantage of their expertise, interest, and financial resources further strengthened their power in the church. Eventually, both branches of episcopal Methodism came to allow lay representation in the various conferences. This too had a limiting effect on the general superintendents.

A 1964 study of the episcopacy commented: "The role of the bishop in The Methodist Church has historically been shaped more by the acts of the men after election than by formal legislation."[8] Bishop N. B. Harmon's observation about the role of strong men in the episcopacy of the MECS was noted earlier. We also observed that at first there were no models for bishops to follow, since the office and its operation were new to Methodism. Bishops learned, then and now, "on the job." But a pattern of practice and custom evolved that through long use assumed the force of law. The Committee on Judiciary of the MEC in 1928 based one of its decisions on "custom and practice." "A custom," they said, "is a usage which has obtained the force of law. In other words, it is a law established by long usage."[9] Custom became a powerful force in the hands of strong, aristocratic leaders in a climate favoring local autonomy in the MECS. Methodists of all sorts, however, have tended to favor change in response to need. They are most comfortable when legislation follows practice.

Missionary Bishops

An illustration of this evolution in the episcopacy is the way in which the MEC responded to the appeal for episcopal supervision from its overseas missions, utilizing its commitment to an episcopacy that is "an abstraction" to be worked "into a concrete form in any hundred or more ways we may be able to invent."[10] Although Methodists had been involved in missions since 1784, it was not until the nineteenth century that they extensively operated them in foreign countries. Through the leadership of Nathan Bangs and Joshua Soule, the Missionary Society was organized in 1819 and officially sanctioned by the General Conference of 1820. Its constitution called for it "to assist in the support and promotion of missionary schools and missions in our own and foreign countries."[11]

The Liberia mission was launched in October 1832 by Melville Cox, who was in Liberia only a few months before he became ill and died in July 1833. The missions in South America were begun two years later. The questions of their supervision and relation to the General Conference were present from the beginning. The Liberia Annual Conference was organized in 1834, and became a full mission annual conference with the rights of any annual conference except that of naming delegates to the General Conference and electing its own bishop. Beginning with the General Conference of 1836, it memorialized every General Conference with an appeal to be provided episcopal supervision.[12] The General Conference of 1836 properly judged it inexpedient to undertake it; but at their meeting later in the year, the bishops adopted a recommendation "to select one of their number to visit our work in Western Africa, in the course of the ensuing four years."[13] Nobody went. The Episcopal Address to the General Conference of 1840 urged the creation of an autonomous Liberia Annual Conference, but the delegates refused to elect a bishop for it, and again declared it inexpedient to require one of the general superintendents to visit Africa.[14]

Their position is understandable, logical, and likely correct. There were only six bishops in the church at the time, and none were readily available to undertake such an assignment. It was obvious that older members of the Board of Bishops could never successfully make such a journey even if one of them could have been spared. At its best the trip was long, dangerous, and expensive. Moreover, it was doubtful that an American bishop could have any lasting impact on the situation in Africa by making a brief visit. Another solution was needed. In 1852, the Liberia Conference made yet another formal request to be furnished with a bishop.[15] In response, the Committee on Missions recommended to the delegates that rather than try to solve the problem, it would be better to wait until the Liberia Conference became an autonomous church and could elect its own bishops. It also recommended that when it gained its autonomy, Francis Burns, superintendent of the Liberia Mission, should be elected a bishop by the General Conference. The creation of a missionary episcopate eventually made that possible.

Amending the Third Restrictive Rule

Setting aside the difficulties of providing episcopal supervision from the United States, there was an interesting precedent dating from the days of Thomas Coke that mitigated against any general superintendent serving overseas. Coke was forbidden by the General Conference in 1787 to exercise any power as a general superintendent when he was absent from the United States, and in 1808 he was denied the right to act as a bishop at all unless invited back to America specifically for that purpose. Beginning with Asbury, general superintendents were understood to be elected for service in the United States, and in 1852 it was affirmed that "no bishop of The Methodist Episcopal Church could be placed in the foreign field as a permanent resident."[16]

Even so, the appeals from Liberia for episcopal supervision continued and were joined by others as the church extended its work overseas. The MEC was determined to respond and did so by amending the Third Restrictive Rule in order to create an entirely new form of the episcopal office. The proposal, presented first at the General Conference of 1852, was to create a new order of bishops whose work would be "exclusively devoted to our missions in foreign countries." The authority to direct the work of these bishops and to establish limits to their power was retained by General Conference. Although this initial attempt failed, the delegates were fully convinced of the need to make some provision for episcopal leadership in their overseas missions. Legislation, which was approved, provided that in the absence of "missionary bishops" for service in Liberia, one of the regular bishops should visit at least twice during the quadrennium.[17] Following this mandate, newly elected Bishop Levi Scott drew the short straw and made the first episcopal visit by a Methodist to Africa. His report to the General Conference of 1856 spurred the conference to further action.

Upon his return, Scott convinced his episcopal colleagues of the necessity for episcopal supervision on the mission field, and they used the Episcopal Address in 1856 to describe the situation in Liberia and affirm Scott's recommendation that an episcopal presence "on the spot is very desirable." They conceded, however, that "it cannot be regularly furnished from this country without embarrassing our home work." Three alternative solutions were proposed: first, to send a bishop to organize the Liberia mission into the Methodist Episcopal Church of Africa; second, to let them organize themselves into a church and elect a bishop who would come to America for ordination; and, third, to appoint a missionary bishop to take charge of that work, the General Conference in North America retaining jurisdiction over it.[18] The Committee on Missions once again recommended amending the Third Restrictive Rule to allow for the appointment of "a Missionary Bishop or Superintendent for any of our foreign missions, limiting his episcopal jurisdiction to the same respectively."[19] This time it passed by a large margin, 159-27.

This legislative action (as opposed to a constitutional change) established a precedent by which the form of episcopacy could be modified by amending the Third Restrictive Rule. The position taken in the MEC was built on its conclusion that the Constitution of 1808 mandates no specific form of episcopacy and gives the General Conference power continually to reshape it to meet the needs of the church. The episcopacy is protected in the constitution only by the stipulation that it cannot be eliminated.

The amendment of the Third Restrictive Rule was submitted to the annual conferences for ratification. The enabling legislation that went with it also authorized the Liberia Conference to "elect an elder in good standing in The Methodist Episcopal Church" and present him for ordination as a bishop at any time after the amendment had received the necessary number of votes for ratification.[20]

The legislation creating the missionary episcopate was quickly ratified by a majority of the annual conferences and became law in the MEC. Francis Burns, an African American, was elected by the Liberia Conference and subsequently ordained as a missionary bishop by Bishops Janes and Baker at the session of the Genesee Annual Conference in October 1858. He was both the first member of the new office in the episcopacy and the first African American ever to be elected a bishop in the MEC.[21] Burns had gone with John Seys to Liberia in 1834 as a missionary teacher. He served there in various capacities, including presiding elder and president of the conference, until his election and return as a bishop. He died in 1863.

A second African American, John Wright Roberts, was consecrated in New York City, 20 June 1866. Roberts had immigrated to Liberia early in his life and joined the Liberia Annual Conference. In 1841, he was elected to elder's orders in that conference and came to America to be ordained. After election as a missionary bishop, he served the Liberia mission until his death in 1875.

The first Anglo ever to be elected a missionary bishop was William Taylor in 1884. He was also assigned to work in Africa.

Defining the New Episcopal Office

When the legislation was proposed to create missionary bishops, regulations defining its status and duties were drafted by Missionary Secretary J. P. Durbin and presented to the conference for approval. They required the bishop to live "in the particular mission field assigned him," and gave missionary bishops power to perform all the duties of a bishop so long as they were in their area. Should a missionary bishop, however, cease to "reside in said mission field, he shall exercise no episcopal powers, and shall become a member of the annual conference from which he was elected."

The fact that missionary bishops were not allowed to exercise any episcopal functions outside of their areas established a practice that was the analogue of the strictures applied first to Thomas Coke, who had no episcopal authority when out of the United States. The final provision was that financial support for the new bishops was to "be furnished in the same manner as in the case of other missionaries." The intent of these provisions was clear—not all Methodist bishops were equal, and missionary bishops were not itinerant general superintendents. They were in reality diocesan bishops with limited powers. The only way in which missionary bishops were fully comparable to general superintendents was that both were amenable for their conduct to the Investigating Committee of the General Conference.[22]

With his usual attention to matters related to the polity of the church, Bishop T. B. Neely, years later, discovered that the amended version of the Third Restrictive Rule had been inadvertently omitted from the *Discipline* until 1872. The omission was discovered by William Harris, a newly elected bishop who was assigned to edit the 1872 *Discipline*. Harris inserted the amendment, but stated it incorrectly. The original motion had read "limiting his episcopal jurisdiction." Harris left out the word *episcopal*, and printed it as "limiting his jurisdiction." Neely suggested that "if through all those long years 'episcopal' had been in, it might have prevented much confused controversy as to the status of the missionary bishopric."[23] Harris's mistake was not corrected until 1892.

Harris's omission highlighted the need to define the power and authority of missionary bishops in relation to itinerant general superintendents. In what sense were they equal to them? Had the word *episcopal* been included, it would have clarified their status as being co-equal with general superintendents while serving as bishops in the areas to which they had been assigned. The omission of the word *episcopal* left open the question of what they could do, although it made it clear where they were empowered to do it—only in the area to which assigned.

It fell to Bishop Neely to play the central role in finally defining the power and jurisdiction of missionary bishops. At the General Conference of 1888, Neely chaired the subcommittee and wrote the report presented to the delegates that finally established the historical and legal analysis for the missionary episcopacy. The report answered eight questions that had been posed to the committee about the office of missionary bishop: (1) Is a missionary bishop a "true" bishop? (2) Is a missionary bishop a "general superintendent"? (3) What are their powers as compared with those of a general superintendent? (4) Is a missionary bishop subordinate to a general superintendent? (5) Can a missionary bishop be made a general superintendent? (6) Should missionary bishops be supported from the Episcopal Fund as general superintendents are? (7) Does paying a missionary bishop from the Missionary Fund have any impact on his status as a bishop? (8) How is the missionary bishop related to the Missionary Society?[24]

The Neely report, which was adopted by the General Conference, declared that missionary bishops were true bishops but elected for service in a specific foreign mission field. While there they enjoyed full episcopal powers but limited jurisdiction; a missionary bishop could function only in the area in which he was elected to serve. Although not general superintendents, missionary bishops were co-ordinate with them in authority while serving in their assigned areas. A missionary bishop could not become a general superintendent unless elected to that office, but they, like the general superintendents, received their support from the Episcopal Fund. They also had a co-operative relation with the Missionary Society. Upon the death of a missionary bishop, a general superintendent assumed responsibility for the bishop's work. Transfer of preachers from the supervision of a missionary bishop to a general superintendent or vice versa was permitted by mutual consent. The same was true when the move was from the area of one missionary bishop to that of another. If a complaint concerning administration or conduct was made against a missionary bishop, the procedure was the same as for a general superintendent. However, a missionary bishop might be tried before a Judicial Conference in the United States. Once again it was made clear that the United States, and not an overseas conference, was the locus of authority for the episcopacy. The only time at which a change was made in this understanding was in 1892, when the General Conference placed the support of missionary bishops back in the Missionary Fund.[25]

As it turned out, Neely became even better qualified to speak on the subject. He was elected a general superintendent in 1904 but assigned to Buenos Aires as the MEC's first bishop in South America. After having had the experience of serving overseas, he argued that the restrictions placed on missionary bishops were not limits at all, but rather a means of empowerment and liberty to do their work.

183

They had, he said, "liberty to stay and learn the customs and characteristics of a peculiar land and people, and liberty to stay and apply the knowledge of language, of race, and of usage, that he has learned."[26]

The MEC, responding to the need to provide episcopal supervision for its work overseas, not only created a new form of episcopacy, but opened a Pandora's box of questions about the nature of the episcopal office itself. Although the MEC had been consistent in creating the new form of episcopacy, it had not foreseen the consequences of its action. For example, it could not escape the question of whether missionary bishops violated at least the spirit of the constitution's Third Restrictive Rule, which had been intended to preserve and protect an "itinerant general superintendency." The MEC was quickly forced to define the power and jurisdiction of the new bishops, and to explain their relation to the general superintendents who also served the church. Although the issue was not raised directly, there was clearly an uncertainty as to whether the General Conference in the United States had the right to elect persons exclusively for service outside its boundaries. It had not done so before. Nor could anyone escape the obvious implications of the presence of a limited missionary episcopate for the office of general superintendents. If the church could elect and appoint a missionary bishop and limit episcopal service to a particular area, could the same be done with a general superintendent?

From the beginning of the episcopacy in American Methodism there had been a determination to protect it from becoming localized. Speaking in their Episcopal Address in 1844, the bishops reiterated: "Having noticed in what the superintendency chiefly consists, it is proper to observe that the plan of its operation is *general[,] embracing the whole work in connectional order, and not diocesan, or sectional.*"[27] Either they did not know, or simply chose to disregard the fact that the practice of episcopacy had become sectional long before 1844. In 1852, they addressed the subject again:

> We call your attention particularly to this subject, and admonish you of the necessity of guarding against any such modification of the General Superintendency as would be likely to result in the introduction of Diocesan Episcopacy, and thus infract the constitutional restriction here brought to view. We cannot but fear that any such modification of the plan of our itinerant General Superintendency as would be involved in restricting Episcopal labours to a definite and limited sphere, would,

at no distinct period, lead to the introduction of Diocesan Episcopacy, than which, in our judgment, nothing would be more likely to destroy the itinerant General Superintendency, and in this way change the essential character of our economy.[28]

Powerful forces were already at work, however, which would (as the bishops feared) essentially reduce the itinerant general superintendency to a localized episcopacy. Creating a new form of the office by the introduction of missionary bishops was a clear step in that direction. Ten missionary bishops were elected between 1884 and 1916—William Taylor, James Thoburn, Edwin Wallace Parker, Francis Wesley Warne, John E. Robinson, William Fitzjames Oldham, John Wesley Robinson, Joseph Crane Hartzell, Merriman Colbert Harris, and Eben Samuel Johnson. Oldham and John W. Robinson were eventually elected general superintendents.

Implications for the Itinerant General Superintendency

The already complicated situation in the MEC with respect to the episcopacy was made even more complex at the General Conference of 1920, when yet another innovation moved the denomination even closer to limited and localized episcopacy. In response to repeated calls from their African American members and conferences, Matthew Wesley Clair Sr. and Robert Elijah Jones were elected that year as general superintendents. Both were African Americans who were clearly understood by all to have been elected for service exclusively in the African American annual conferences of the United States. There was never any intention for them to act as "general superintendents" who were eligible for assignment anywhere in the connection, nor were they missionary bishops. Their limited status was specifically highlighted by Bishop James Cannon Jr., a member of the MECS:

So two Negro bishops were elected by the Northern General Conference of 1920. When assignments were made for episcopal supervision, the colored bishops were given only colored Conferences, although some of the colored Conferences were put under the supervision of white bishops as heretofore. Although these colored bishops were in office for nineteen years before the Plan of Unification was finally adopted, never were they given supervision over any white Conference.[29]

By electing Clair and Jones, the MEC introduced yet a third variation on the episcopal office—African Americans, elected as general superintendents exclusively for service in African American annual conferences within the United States. Because of the limitations on their place of service, they were clearly a new category of general superintendent. At the same time, the church continued to have missionary bishops; and to complicate matters further, the General Conference of 1920 also elected fourteen new general superintendents and promptly assigned several of them overseas. Assigning general superintendents overseas was not a new practice, but no new missionary bishops were elected. The church now simultaneously had an episcopacy that contained (1) missionary bishops with full episcopal powers but limited jurisdiction, elected exclusively for service in foreign mission fields; (2) two African American general superintendents with their jurisdiction limited to African American conferences in the United States; and (3) general superintendents with unlimited jurisdiction assigned overseas and in the United States. Truly the office had been shaped in a variety of ways. In only two aspects were all the bishops comparable: they were all amenable to the General Conference for their administration and conduct, and they all had full episcopal powers when serving where assigned. Bishop Neely, who believed the stationing of general superintendents in missionary conferences to be unconstitutional, argued that the elections in 1920 "transformed all the effective missionary bishops into general superintendents and left them in their foreign mission fields."[30]

The almost unlimited possibility for confusion was forestalled only when every mission field in the MEC was organized into a "central conference." This was completed by 1924. The General Conference of 1928 proposed to amend the Third Restrictive Rule again in order to enable the central conferences to elect their own bishops, thereby creating still another form of the episcopal office—the bishop elected in the mission field for limited service there. The General Conference of 1932 finally brought the era of missionary bishops to a close when it formally accepted Bishop Neely's conclusion about the 1920 elections (probably most delegates without knowledge of it) and elected all the remaining missionary bishops general superintendents.

It is ironic that the desire in the northern conferences to protect the church from local autonomy and sectionalism, which had been one of the major causes of conflict in 1844, now was actively supported by both branches of Methodism. This joining of minds assisted the church in its movement toward reunion in 1939 but failed to answer many of the perplexing questions that the changes had created for the understanding of episcopacy.

The experience in the MEC with regard to its bishops is but a further illustration of how the favored strategy for effecting change in American Methodism has been to modify practice to meet a demonstrated need and then to respond by enacting legislation. On rare occasions the necessary legislation was enacted first—for example, the Third Restrictive Rule was amended by the annual conferences to allow for the creation of the office of missionary bishop—but without consideration of the full consequences of such actions, which must be worked out later. And on yet other occasions, Methodists have achieved their goals by structural reorganization. This too always affects practice. The best example of this strategy in operation was the long process leading to unification and the formation of the MC in 1939. The church was reunited by reorganizing.

CHAPTER 14

Localizing Episcopacy, North and South

The MECS, which sent its first missionaries to China in 1848 (Charles Taylor, M.D., and the Reverend Benjamin Jenkins), never created a missionary episcopate but provided supervision for its missions through its general superintendents. In this regard it anticipated the later practice of its northern brethren who first created the missionary episcopate and then began assigning its general superintendents abroad. Eventually both branches reorganized their missions into autonomous central conferences and gave them power to elect indigenous leadership.[1] This was a more satisfactory arrangement for all concerned.

The Central Conferences

By 1884 the burden of overseas travel related to episcopal visitations had created dissatisfaction in the General Conference of the MEC, and the delegates once again asked the general superintendents whether in their judgment they should be stationed overseas. The bishops responded that it would not be wise to attempt to make such a change and retain the heavy schedule of visitations to the overseas missions. It proved only a temporary solution, however, and in 1896 the first general superintendent of the MEC was assigned to China and

Japan. As a general superintendent, the bishop had full powers to itin-erate throughout the church but was actually given a limited jurisdic-tion overseas, large in area though it may have been. When the newly organized central conferences were authorized to elect their episcopal leaders, as could have been predicted, several chose former missionar-ies from North America. John William Tarboux was elected the first bishop of the Methodist Church in Brazil after forty-seven years of missionary service there. All of the missionary bishops elected in India were selected from former missionaries assigned to that field. This added yet another variation to the form of missionary episcopacy. Although since 1888 the MEC had made clear distinctions between general superintendents and missionary bishops, in practice these dis-tinctions were blurred. Even so, the existence of two distinct classes of bishops was clear, and as early as 1876 the general superintendents were voicing their criticism of the concept of missionary episcopacy. Their comment on the conference in Liberia reveals their concerns.

> The superintendency of the missionary bishops, though quite satisfac-tory to that Conference, failed to inspire the zeal and awaken and direct the enterprise of the Church in that country as largely as it was hoped would be the case when they were elected. Their reports to the Missionary Board and home Churches did not keep alive the interest which for many years was felt in that, our oldest, foreign mission.[2]

The overseas conferences were not satisfied with the arrange-ment, since the presence of a missionary bishop only delayed the time until they were able to elect indigenous persons, which was their ultimate goal. Nevertheless, the office of missionary bishops continued from 1858 until the General Conference of 1920 finally began the process of phasing them out by electing only general superintendents. The General Conference of 1932 finally brought the era of specialized episcopacy to an end, with the exception of the spe-cialized election of African Americans for service in (and only in) African American annual conferences in America. That practice was carried into the MC in 1939 through the organization of the Central Jurisdiction and was not finally ended until the years immediately prior to the formation of The UMC in 1968.

It is ironic that in seeking ways to provide episcopal supervision for its missions overseas the church took a giant step toward a local-ized episcopacy. During the talks leading to reunion and the creation of the MC in 1939, the commitment to local autonomy, which had

190

once been valued primarily in the MECS, was now affirmed also by their colleagues in the MEC. The conversion of itinerant general superintendency into localized or diocesan episcopacy, though slow in coming and often decried, became the shape of the superintendency in the reunited MC.

Central conferences, created out of former overseas missions, were first authorized by the General Conference of the MEC in 1884. The move was prompted by a proposal to unite the missions of the MEC in Japan with those of the Methodist Church of Canada, and by a request from the conferences in India to create a delegated conference (the second such appeal from India).[3] The empowering legislation that was passed by the General Conference provided that when any annual conference or mission was directed either by General Conference or by a majority vote of the conferences or missions to pursue uniting into a central conference, they could meet to create this new structure at the call of the presiding bishop.[4] This legislation was amended in 1892 to limit such unions to conferences or missions of the MEC.

In 1920 a Commission on Central Conferences was created. The first central conference was in India, but others soon followed; and many of them later became members of autonomous churches or parts of united churches such as the ones formed in South India, Japan, and Korea. Central conferences enjoy considerable freedom (although some of them even in recent years lack printed *Disciplines*[5]) in such matters as ritual, regulations governing ministerial qualifications and preparation, and management of church property. But they do not enjoy full legislative autonomy, since they are forbidden to enact any measures contrary to the constitution of The UMC, including the Restrictive Rules. This means that they cannot do away with episcopacy if they should decide it is in their best interest not to have it. For years their legislative actions were subject to veto by the presiding bishop. In situations like the Church of South India, where former Methodist bodies have become part of an autonomous church that stands only in an affiliate relationship to The UMC, the new body is limited only by its own constitutions.

Central Conference Bishops: Power, Term, Duties

In 1928, the Commission on Central Conferences of the MEC recommended that central conferences be allowed to elect their own bishops. The Committee on Judiciary quickly ruled that the General Conference did not have the power to authorize such elections. Its committee report stated, "To permit the central conferences to select their own Bishop would be giving unwarranted authority. Such action would be contrary to the restrictive rule."[6] However, the consensus of the members of the committee was that it could be done legally by amending the Third Restrictive Rule to provide for it, as was done to create the office of missionary bishop. They reached the same conclusion when the question of creating term limits for central conference bishops was also proposed.[7] Two amendments to the Third Restrictive Rule were passed, which (1) authorized the General Conference to organize annual conferences, mission conferences, and missions into central conferences; and (2) allowed the election of "Bishops or General Superintendents whose Episcopal supervision shall be within the territory included in the Central Conference by which they have been elected."[8]

Some African American leaders opposed the proposals, particularly those requiring both the organization of the conferences and election of bishops to be authorized by the General Conference. Nevertheless, the necessary changes in the Restrictive Rule were adopted in 1929 by the requisite majority in the annual conferences, and it was amended. In February 1930, the Central Conference of Southern Asia, China, elected Chih Ping Wang and John Gowdy to the episcopacy, and a few months later the Central Conference of Southern Asia (India) elected Jashwant Rao Chitambar.

The MECS also had made provisions for supervision in its overseas conferences by granting the necessary powers to mission conferences or annual conferences to become autonomous. Its 1934 *Discipline* carried provisions for the creation of central conferences. This legislation provided that "any Annual Conferences or Missions which may find joint deliberation desirable may organize a Central Conference based on race or language or territorial relationship."[9] After the MC was organized the central conferences assumed the same status as the jurisdictional conferences.

Central Conference Bishops and the Board of Bishops

Having created the central conference structure and authorized the election of their bishops, the Committee on Judiciary in the MEC was called upon to define the status of these new bishops in relation to other members of the episcopacy. In their ruling they declared that "two types of Episcopal Supervision are now recognized by the Constitution—General Superintendency and Limited Superintendency, the first class is protected by the Constitution from legislative interference in the prescribed functions. The other is subject to limitations imposed by legislation."[10] This ruling upheld the now well-established distinction in the MEC between constitutional and legislative definitions of episcopacy. General superintendents in the United States, excepting African Americans who were limited in jurisdiction by practice rather than by law, were protected by the provision of the constitution in the first portion of the Third Restrictive Rule that forbids their elimination. Missionary bishops and bishops in the central conferences (who could be called "general superintendents") were defined and limited by the amendments to that rule. This is what allowed bishops in central conferences to be subject to term limits and for their election to take place only when authorized by the General Conference in the United States. By contrast the powers of bishops in affiliated churches overseas were defined by their own constitutions. Their only limitation from the side of The UMC was that they were entitled to only two delegates to General Conference and these delegates had voice but no vote. Autonomous central conferences were represented by at least two delegates from each annual conference and equal numbers of lay and ministerial delegates.

One of the places where practical questions raised by these distinctions became complex was in the MEC Board of Bishops. Although their gathering has had a variety of names, the bishops had been meeting together since the early years of the nineteenth century. At first they were charged with creating a plan to ensure meeting the various annual conferences (to create a "plan of visitation" as it was sometimes called) and to devise and oversee the course of study. Through the years they have taken on added responsibilities as a group, such as making nominations and relating to the boards and agencies. The MECS also created an effective College of Bishops.

Questions inevitably arose in the MEC about what role and status the central conference and missionary bishops would have on the Board of Bishops. Although co-equal with the general superintendents in their duties and episcopal powers while serving in their areas, it was clear that they were not expected to exercise leadership in the denomination in the United States. Since they did not have the same jurisdiction as general superintendents, should they have been included in the meetings of the board made up of general superintendents? Their status in the General Conference was also an issue, as was the compatibility of their ordination with that of the general superintendents who enjoyed life tenure. To what exactly were they ordained if their service was subject to limited tenure?

Despite the agreement in principle that all Methodist bishops were co-equal when in their appointed areas, the rules governing their participation in the Board of Bishops makes it clear the central conference bishops were a separate category. Although central conference bishops were permitted to attend the meetings of the Board of Bishops, they were restricted to speak only on issues related to their episcopal areas and were without a vote.[11] Even after they were designated "full" members of the Council of Bishops of the MC when it was organized in 1939, and declared eligible to attend all its sessions, regular participation of central conference bishops was effectively limited since their expenses were paid only to the meetings, which took place every four years just prior to the regular session of the General Conference.[12]

In 1936 the Committee on Judiciary in the MEC, consistent with its previous rulings, once again declared that "Central Conference bishops have no authority to exercise any Episcopal office outside the Central Conference." The report stipulated

Bishops for Central Conferences are elected by a limited constituency; they are limited both as to the area in which their jurisdiction is to be exercised and are further limited by being subject to such other conditions as the General Conference shall prescribe. . . . We are, therefore of the opinion that the Central Conference Bishops have no authority to exercise any Episcopal office outside of Central Conferences.[13]

The larger question being addressed in this decision, once again, was the relation of central conference bishops to the General Conference, and the specific issue was whether they were eligible as bishops to preside in the sessions of the General Conference. The General Conference of 1912 had voted to amend Article VI, paragraph 42.2 of the *Discipline* to allow missionary bishops to preside.[14] The fact that a concession was made to them indicates that they too were a special class of bishop. The prohibition on central conference bishops presiding in the General Conference continued in the reunited MC until 1960. Perhaps in honor of the seniority of his conference, as well as his own seniority, Bishop Shot K. Mondol of India was the first to preside. Another historic moment came when more than twenty years later Ole Borgen, a bishop in the Northern European Central Conference, became president of the Council of Bishops. Since his term, Bishops Emilio J. M. de Carvalho and Emerito P. Nacpil of the central conference in the Philippines have served as presidents, and the central conferences now take their place in the rotation of the council presidency with the other jurisdictions.

Missionary bishops and central conference bishops were all local, diocesan officials; central conference bishops serve a limited term in the episcopal office. As Gerald Moede noted, this was but a part of the larger movement leading to the localizing of the general superintendency and the creation of a de facto form of diocesan episcopacy throughout the denomination. It is fair to say that despite these innovations, there was no conscious and deliberate attempt to void or negate the provision of the Third Restrictive Rule protecting itinerant general superintendency. Virtually everything that was done through legislation represented a sincere attempt on the part of the church to meet an identified and significant need. But it is also true that the wider implications of their acts were often either ignored or misunderstood.

Locating Itinerant General Superintendents

The movement toward localized episcopacy flourished in the United States as well as overseas, and it sometimes was a logical and obvious answer to a problem. For example, from the organization of the church at the Christmas Conference in 1784 until 1872, bishops in the MEC determined where they would live. The choice of residence was entirely their own. Thus Matthew Simpson was living in Cincinnati when he was elected in 1852 but decided to move to Evanston, Illinois, because his good friend John Evans, for whom the town is named, invited him to come and made it attractive for him to do so. A decade later, Simpson moved to Philadelphia, where he spent the remainder of his life. But in 1872, the General Conference designated specific cities in which a bishop was to reside. The purpose was to ensure that the bishops were not all clustered in one section of the country, making it difficult to serve the entire church. Those were not the days when all that was necessary was a fax machine and proximity to an airport. The General Conference did not direct the individual bishops where to live, but it did rule that beginning with those newly elected (Bishops Thomas Bowman, William L. Harris, Randolph Foster, Isaac Wiley, Stephen Merrill, Edward Andrews, Gilbert Haven, and Jesse Peck), a bishop would reside at or near San Francisco, St. Louis, Boston, Atlanta, Chicago, Cincinnati, Council Bluffs or Omaha, and St. Paul. The list conveniently omitted mention of the cities in which senior bishops like Simpson were already living, such as New York and Philadelphia. The city of residence was chosen, as is usually the case with bishops, "from the places named according to their seniority in official position."[15] The mandatory nature of the directive was the only truly new provision. Attempts had been made since 1824 to establish, through informal arrangements, that the bishops could serve the entire connection from their places of residence. This was a first step in the process that would eventually lead the General Conference to assign bishops to their places of service.

When the decision was made to designate cities for episcopal residence, subsequent General Conferences were inundated with memorials urging the consideration of other sites across the country. There were economic consequences as well. Episcopal residences had to be purchased or rented in the designated cities where previously the bishops had been responsible for providing their own.

The 1872 arrangement of designating cities was continued until 1900. Each bishop decided where he would live from the list of episcopal residences that were vacant. From 1900 to 1939, when the MC was organized with jurisdictions, the General Conference stationed the bishops. After 1939 the central conferences were equated with jurisdictions, and bishops were elected and assigned within them. Episcopal service was limited to the jurisdiction in which the bishops were elected, and the assignment to areas was no longer made by General Conference but by the Jurisdictional Committee on Episcopacy.

Although the MECS lagged by a decade behind their brothers and sisters in the North, they followed the same path. In 1882, its General Conference recommended that "the bishops should be distributed by the College of Bishops in such manner, if practicable, that every great section of our work may have a Bishop residing in some one of the Conferences embraced in said section."[16] Four years later it made the request again but determined that no official actions would be taken to organize the annual conferences into permanent episcopal districts. Such action, however, was not too far over the horizon.

At the General Conference of 1884 the MEC, following the logic of its earlier decisions, asserted its power to assign the bishops. Basing its action on the amendment of the Third Restrictive Rule, which permitted the appointment of a missionary bishop to a specific area, the Committee on Judiciary reasoned that if the General Conference had the power to assign one class of bishop to a place, thereby limiting their jurisdiction, it could also assign the general superintendents. Although this argument was flawed, since there was a clear distinction between the two categories of episcopal leaders (constitutional and legislative), they declared:

> All our Bishops, other than Missionary Bishops, . . . are equal in authority and jurisdiction, and subject to the same regulations of assignment of residence and work . . . and the residences of its Bishops are assigned by order of the General Conference. It is the opinion of the Committee that the General Conference has the power to fix the residence of any of its Bishops in any part of the territory occupied by The Methodist Church.[17]

Four years later, following the pattern long established in the MECS, the MEC appointed its first general superintendent to serve overseas. "Thus was the theory of general superintendency . . . for all practical purposes laid aside; there was no real distinction now between the work of a missionary bishop and a general superintendent. The general superintendent could still itinerate, but his assigned residence represented a serious restriction of his freedom."[18] It is interesting to note that Bishop Neely, who was strongly opposed to stationing general superintendents abroad, supported the theory that location per se does not threaten the itinerant episcopacy, since "a residence does not and never was understood to confine the bishop to the particular point or its precincts."[19] In theory he was correct. It would be possible for a bishop to serve conferences outside the geographic region of his residence. But convenience, if nothing else, would dictate that a bishop was more likely to remain close to home.

Toward a Diocesan Episcopacy

In logical sequence the next step was taken toward diocesan episcopacy when it was proposed that General Conference should not only assign the bishops to a specific place of residence but assign them for a determined length of time. At the request of T. B. Neely, the Committee on Judiciary was asked to rule whether the bishops could be assigned to "districts" for four years or more. The committee said "no," and declared, "In our opinion such a regulation would necessarily operate to 'destroy' the 'plan of our itinerant general superintendency,' whether the limit be for four years or for a longer period."[20] Neely proposed a substitute for this report in which he asserted, "The assignment of general Superintendents by the General Conference to special sections or districts in the United States for a quadrennium is not prohibited by the Constitution." His motion, however, lost and the committee report was adopted.[21]

They could not, however, escape the implications of the proposed change in relation to the already established practice of assigning bishops to cities of residence. If the General Conference could determine the place of residence, why could it not also mandate the length of service in that area? In the ruling the committee clearly expressed its determination to protect the plan of itinerant general superintendency.

From a modern perspective it is hard to read this justification as more than a self-serving argument that essentially declares, "If a localized episcopacy was not intended by what has been done, it does not exist." Although the proposal to establish limits on years of service in one area was defeated in 1904, it would pass later. Current legislation limits bishops to eight years in one area, with certain exceptions being allowed for an extension of one quadrennium if the jurisdictional Committee on Episcopacy by a two-thirds vote determines it to be "in the best interest of the jurisdiction."[22] Previously, the language specified the exception to be allowed in the interest of "missional priorities."

Despite the negative judgment of the Committee on Judiciary, in 1904 efforts continued to establish a limit on the time a bishop could live in an episcopal area. At the General Conference in 1908, a way was found around the letter, if not the spirit, of the prohibition. The Board of Bishops was asked by the General Conference to organize the annual conferences into districts and to assign bishops to them. This action removed the General Conference from the role of mandating the change and had the added advantage of reaffirming a practice followed since 1816 delegating to the bishops ultimate responsibility for determining who would attend each conference.

The Committee on Episcopacy acknowledged in its report the need to modify the plan of supervision currently in use and noted the 1904 ruling of the Committee on Judiciary against localized episcopacy. They also reaffirmed the right of the Board of Bishops under the constitution "to assign individual Bishops to preside over Conferences in contiguous territory for a period of several years." It was a shrewd move that was within the letter of the Third Restrictive Rule's protection of itinerant general superintendency.[23] The delegates did urge the bishops to plan their work to enable them to "make at least two visits during the year into each Annual Conference within the United States which is assigned to them respectively."[24]

Another piece of seemingly unrelated legislation allowing the Central Conference of Southern Asia to limit the residences of missionary bishops to designated cities was also passed by the General Conference of 1908. Four years later this authorization was extended to allow them "to assign the Missionary bishops to such residences."[25] It was in fact a preview of what was to happen in the United States.

In 1912, the General Conference took the crucial step, going beyond its "recommendation" to the bishops four years earlier and creating the area system of episcopal administration. At the next General Conference the bishops, in their Episcopal Address, told the delegates that they were pleased to report that "the plan of residential supervision and presidential administration has given general satisfaction."[26] The Committee on Episcopacy agreed with this judgment and wrote in its report: "We must insist . . . that the supreme requirement of the 'Itinerant General Superintendency,' to wit: 'He shall travel through the connection,' has never been so fully realized in recent times as under the area system."[27] Once again practice had become custom and was well on its way to becoming law. It was again being done without modifying the constitutional commitment to itinerant general superintendency, and under the long-established understanding of episcopacy as having the power to reinvent itself to meet the needs of the church.

The MECS took similar steps to reach its own form of localized episcopacy. It did so while maintaining its commitment to understanding episcopacy as a co-equal body with the General Conference, and with the same commitment as their northern counterparts to preserving the power of its bishops as itinerant general superintendents. However, their bishops did not so readily endorse the change. Bishop

Collins Denny, delivering the Episcopal Address in 1918, signaled their concern over the creation of the area system of episcopacy.

> To break up the Church by a cast-iron scheme into fixed fragments would spoil its essential unity, and we do not believe, moreover, that it would be either wise or lawful to adopt any plan which would even imply that a bishop, once elected and ordained, could be made less by any subsequent action of his colleagues or of the General Conference than a bishop of the whole Church with an intrinsic right to exercise his episcopal functions in any of the Conferences.[28]

Localized Episcopacy and the Appointment Process

Both branches of Methodism shared a commitment to protect the system of itinerant episcopacy from changing to a diocesan form. These concerns had been present at least since the middle of the nineteenth century. The bishops of the MEC expressed it in their address to the General Conference in 1852. Once again the issue was practical. It was not deemed a good thing by either bishops or preachers for the same bishop to make appointments in the same conference year after year. It might not be effective:

> Also at every conference, some worthy brethren are disappointed in their appointments. . . . In this state of disappointment it is a relieving consideration that another Bishop will preside at the next session of the conference and may more correctly understand their character and more fully meet their claims. But if it was understood by them that the same Bishop was to fix their appointments for several years successively, their hearts would sink.[29]

Many a brother and sister from that day to this can attest to the truth of that reservation. The same reservations were echoed seventy years later when the MECS bishops touched on the same subject at the General Conference of 1922:

> Our general superintendency grows out of our general itinerancy, and the very genius of it calls for an administration that is wholly impartial and therefore, to a large extent, impersonal. This feature is, so long as human nature remains the same, constantly liable to be negatived by this order [four years in the same area]. It is easy to believe that a Bishop may know too little; it is barely possible that he may know too much. . . . Bishop Asbury has truly said, "Local men have local views."[30]

The southern bishops were never altogether convinced that the plan of assigning them to an area was satisfactory. They still expressed their concern as late as 1930 at the General Conference meeting in Dallas. They said:

> With the experience of four quadrenniums to instruct us, we desire to give expression to our judgment touching the wisdom of continuous quadrennial service in a fixed episcopal district. Frankly, we do not believe that this plan has been entirely satisfactory to the Church, and we think that we should let you know that it has not been altogether satisfactory to the bishops themselves. We doubt if one and the same bishop should make the appointments of the preachers from year to year for a considerable term of years. We are convinced that it would be best both for the Church at large and for the bishops themselves if the present plan be given a measure of flexibility.[31]

Their reservations notwithstanding, the momentum pushing toward localized episcopacy was strong and unrelenting. Whether it was intended to reach that place is hard to determine. On the one hand there were doubts such as those expressed by the southern bishops, but on the other hand there were also affirmations of success. What is clear is that the current system of local area episcopal administration with limits on service came through a series of unrelated changes passed by General Conferences in response to practical concerns and in the attempt to do what was best for the church and its mission. Yet the practical implications are surely apparent—the church was in the process of abandoning itinerant general superintendency. The process began as early as 1826, when Hedding and George refused to exchange conferences as McKendree had requested, and reached full fruition when the jurisdictional system was created in order to form The Methodist Church in 1939. The effects of that organizational change on episcopacy were the most far-reaching and significant in the history of American Methodism.

CHAPTER 15

Limiting Episcopal Power

As should now be apparent, there have been persons throughout the history of Methodism in America who have thought that episcopal power should be limited, and who have sought by various means to put safeguards in place to protect against the abuse of power by individuals holding the office. The most common early strategy was to argue for the right to appeal the decision of the bishop, particularly in regard to the stationing of the preachers. We have noted such proposals since at least 1792, when O'Kelly contested Asbury's power and left the MEC when he lost. Continuing resistance to this type of appeal was central to the separation of those who formed the MPC in 1830. Elements of this strategy have continued to the present but are best understood in the context of two other strategies for limiting episcopal power, strategies that became more prominent in the continuing course of American Methodism.

District Superintendents—Presiding Elders

The second common strategy to place limits on the episcopal office has been somewhat indirect. It involves legislative proposals focusing on the presiding elders. In a study made in 1960, this office (under its modern designation of "district superintendent") was described as the "alter ego of the bishop."[1] It has been understood as an extension of episcopal power and presence since 1792. The legislative proposals have typically tried to limit episcopal power by making the office of presiding elder one elected by the preachers. There has also been concern to restrict their terms of office and limit their eligibility to serve in consecutive assignments.

It was described earlier how Joshua Soule thought the relation of the bishops to their presiding elders was so crucial and so integral to the structure of Methodist polity that he refused ordination to the episcopacy in 1820 until legislation mandating the election of presiding elders was rescinded. While Soule was successful at the time, interest in this type of revision has resurfaced frequently. As late as 1924 the Committee on the Judiciary of the MEC was asked to rule on the question "Has the General Conference power to order the Election of District Superintendents?" In the summary of its ruling, a majority of the committee declared:

> It is incontrovertible that during the entire period since the Constitution was adopted, and even prior thereto, with the exception of a few brief years immediately following the organization of the Church in 1784 when we really had as yet no "established plan of government," the power to appoint the Presiding Elders has been exercised solely by the Bishop residing in the Conference. This is a practical admission that the appointing power resides in the Bishop. . . . It is clear that under the Constitution the General Conference is without power to authorize the election of District Superintendents.[2]

With the rulings consistently supporting the right of bishops to choose those who work most directly with them as district superintendents, some people have turned attention to limiting the appointive powers of bishops by enhancing the authority of presiding elders. A popular version of this approach has been to propose that bishops be required to make appointments in consultation with district superintendents. The current practice of appointment-making in The UMC is built around the idea of consultation. This formal model was adopted in 1976, but its roots go back much further. The 1916 General Conference of the MEC required the bishop to "consult the district superintendent in the district where the charge being appointed was located."[3] A century earlier, Bishop McKendree began the practice of utilizing a cabinet composed of presiding elders to assist him in making appointments, but until this legislation was passed in 1916, bishops had not been required to follow McKendree's example. Even with the new stipulation regarding process, bishops still retained final authority to make the appointment.

Term Episcopacy

A third strategy for limiting the power of bishops, more common in recent years, has been to challenge the life tenure of bishops by proposing that they be elected to serve a fixed term of years. Although life tenure of bishops has been the rule since 1784, proposals to change it to term episcopacy have come before many General Conferences. The MEC debated a motion to limit episcopal terms to four years at the General Conference of 1856. It was finally laid on the table. The subject surfaced again in 1884, with the recommended term now increased to twelve years.[4] Although the proposal did not pass, the idea never seemed to go away. There were fifteen memorials proposing term episcopacy presented to the MEC General Conference of 1928.[5]

The idea of limiting a bishop's term in office was even more popular in the MECS. One could surmise that it was appealing because of the presence of a number of older strong bishops whose seniority extended their power and influence. Proposals to create term episcopacy were presented in the MECS as early as 1888. There were concerted attempts to get it passed in 1926, 1930, and in 1934, just prior to unification. The momentum generated by the effort was sufficient to cause Bishop John M. Moore to devote a substantial portion of the Episcopal Address opening the General Conference of 1934 to refute the idea as "a contradiction in words and ideas."[6]

The most recent discussions on the subject naturally came in the conversations leading to merger with the EUBC in 1968. One forerunner branch of the EUBC, the Evangelical Association, had an episcopacy limited to two four-year terms from the time of its organization in 1894. (The Free Methodists, organized in 1860, adopted the same structure for bishops and also elect their district superintendents.) Persons supporting term episcopacy seized the occasion of the impending merger in 1968 to place the matter on the table again, but failed to win wide support.

Unlike the regulations governing the district superintendents that tend immediately to raise difficult questions of constitutionality, and notwithstanding the objections of Joshua Soule, there is a con-

205

sensus that term episcopacy could be established simply by amending the Third Restrictive Rule, similar to the way in which it was modified to allow for missionary bishops. In 1928, the Committee on Judiciary of the MEC declared, "The election of Bishops for a limited term can be accomplished only by the adoption of a constitutional amendment in the manner provided by the Discipline—and this remedy is of easy application whenever desirable."[7] The proponents of the change were quick to see an analogy with the pattern of electing bishops in the central conferences for a term and to note it had been approved by General Conference. However, the majority considered bishops in the central conferences to be in a separate category from general superintendents elected for service in the United States, and they rejected the analogy. Despite having the doors opened for a legislative change, the supporters of term episcopacy have been unable to generate sufficient votes to pass an amendment. Methodists continue to elect their bishops for life.

This does not mean that those challenging life tenure have had no victories. They did successfully champion a variation on term episcopacy in the form of prescribing limits to the length of time a bishop may serve in an area. This modification predictably gained momentum following the decision to assign bishops to residences in specific cities and episcopal areas. There can be little doubt that the presence of strong and autocratic episcopal leaders, especially in the South, gave impetus to both term and residency limits. Bishops in general, and southern bishops in particular, have never favored the idea.

Speaking for himself and his colleagues in the MECS College of Bishops, Bishop John M. Moore defended the practice of life tenure in 1934 by arguing that episcopacy is an "order" that cannot be set aside. He defined *order* as

> a permanent ecclesiastical office into which induction is and has always been made by the religious ceremony of ordination. Ordination as understood and practiced by Methodism is not a bestowal of sacramentarian grace and authority . . . but it is the setting apart and investiture of the person ordained with such certain responsibilities, definite duties, and prescribed prerogatives and powers as may be determined and authorized by the Church.[8]

From this Moore concluded that episcopacy cannot be set aside, drawing an analogy from the ordination of clergy: "It has always taken ordination as well as election to create bishops, and ordination has never been given for a term of years. Ordination is an act to confirm permanency. . . . Term episcopacy is a contradiction in words and ideas."[9]

A story is told in the biography of Bishop A. Frank Smith, that he and fellow southern bishops Paul Kern and Arthur Moore were discussing their future at one General Conference where the sentiment to establish term episcopacy was especially strong. All agreed they would resign if the proposal passed, but were considering the more practical question of how each of them would occupy the remaining years if they were forced to leave the episcopacy. Bishop Kern, a former faculty member and dean, said he would return to teaching. Bishop Moore, the great missionary leader and preacher, proposed to return to the evangelistic work he loved so well and said he would hold revivals. Bishop Smith, after suitable reflection, said, "Well, I don't have enough religion to hold revivals, and I'm not smart enough to teach school. I'll just have to stay in and be a bishop."[10]

Opponents of term episcopacy often raise the question of where a bishop might serve when the term of office had expired. One obvious solution would be the one followed in the central conferences, where former bishops are returned to the annual conferences in which they were serving when elected. Some difficult practical issues remain concerning their status, such as the level of appointment to which they would be entitled, and the awkwardness of having such a person under the supervision of another bishop or a district superintendent. Although such problems could be resolved, the idea of mounting legislative efforts to adopt term episcopacy has yet to attract strong support.

The most apparent explanation for this lack of enthusiasm is that most of the desired practical benefits of term limits have been gained over the years by means that required no legislation. For example, the tenure of a bishop in one episcopal area was limited to twelve years in 1956 and reduced to eight years in 1976.[11] Bishop Lloyd C. Wicke once named the legislation enacting these limits the "Smith-Corson Rule." It was passed, he said, to ensure that the extended tenure that A. Frank Smith (twenty-one years), William Angie Smith (twenty-four years), and Fred Pierce Corson (twenty-four years) enjoyed in their respective areas could never be repeated.[12] Bishop James S. Thomas, former president of the Council of Bishops, endorsed this point in his contention that the real intent behind the study on episcopacy, authorized by the MC General Conference in

1960 and prepared by Murray Lieffer, was to find "a way to curb the power of some bishops; a way to see to it that no bishop would be resident in one area for twenty years and more."[13] Both Smith and Corson retired in 1960, the year the study was commissioned.

The 1976 (UMC) motion read, "A bishop shall not be recommended for assignment to the same residence for more than eight consecutive years. For strategic missional reasons only, a Jurisdictional Committee on Episcopacy on a two-thirds vote may recommend one additional four-year term in the same area."[14] In practice, the "missional" exception is invoked most frequently to solve problems faced by the Jurisdictional Committee on Episcopacy in assigning bishops who have only one additional quadrennium to serve before reaching the age of mandatory retirement. Few bishops are excited about moving to a new area when there are only four years to serve. Most are convinced it takes at least eight years to make any impact on an area. But the situation arises with some regularity, and it is always difficult to know how to address it.

Consider this case: Only one bishop, Janice Riggle Huie, was elected in the South Central Jurisdiction of The UMC in 1996. Bishops J. Woodrow Hearn (elected in 1984) and Raymond Owen (elected in 1992) had served for only one quadrennium in their respective areas and could be reappointed to complete their eight-year term and retire in 2000. Bishops Bruce Blake, Dan Solomon, and William Oden (all elected in 1988) had reached the eight-year limit and were moved to new areas; since they also will be retired in 2004, they have a full eight years to serve in their new assignment. But in 2000 the Committee on Episcopacy will have to assign two new bishops and determine whether to return Bishops Alfred Norris and Albert Frederick Mutti to their present assignments for a third quadrennium or to move them to serve only one quadrennium in a new area before they retire in 2004. The easiest solution for the committee would be to invoke "missional reasons." Similar situations exist in each jurisdiction nearly every quadrennium.

Mandatory Retirement

The ultimate practical limit to episcopal tenure is the provision for mandatory retirement. Legislation to impose it first passed in the MEC in 1912. It made retirement mandatory for bishops "at the close of the General Conference nearest his seventy-third birthday."[15] In 1928, the age was reduced to seventy and an optional age for voluntary retirement set at sixty-seven.[16]

Although the MECS was slower to enact similar legislation, it had been aware for some time that procedures were needed to remove aging and ineffective bishops from active service. In 1866 at the General Conference, which reorganized the church and set it on the road to recovery from the devastation of the Civil War, one of its first actions was to retire both Bishops Andrew and Soule and elect four younger leaders to take their place. Finally, in 1930 a motion was passed in the MECS which provided that "a Bishop may be superannuated on account of age or infirmity, at his own request, or on recommendation of the Committee on Episcopacy; *provided*, that no Bishop shall remain on the effective list longer than the General Conference nearest his seventy-second birthday; *provided further*, that the provision in regard to age retirement shall not become effective until the close of the General Conference of 1934."[17]

It certainly is incorrect to say that all bishops in either branch of Methodism went gladly into the golden years of their retirement. Bishop Thomas B. Neely appealed to the General Conference to prevent his retirement, but his request was not granted. Bishop James Cannon Jr., who, prior to his own election, had played an active role in forcing the retirement of eighty-year-old Bishop A. W. Wilson in 1914, waged an all-out campaign to avoid his own.

Cannon was a controversial and sometimes embarrassing figure in southern Methodism. Between 1928 and 1934 he received unflattering public attention in the press when called to appear before two Senate Committee hearings to answer charges of violating the Corrupt Practices Act because of his involvement in questionable dealings in the stock market. These dealings led him to be charged in the 1930 General Conference with "conduct unbecoming to a bishop." The General Conference actually investigated a number of charges, ranging from hoarding flour to adultery, but found Cannon not guilty in 1931. He was subsequently tried in the civil courts for violating the Corrupt Practices Act and again was found not guilty on 27 April 1934. Though this was just days after the General Conference of 1934 opened in Jackson, Mississippi, the Committee on Episcopacy chose to ignore his exoneration and voted 42-28 to remove him from the effective list of bishops by involuntary retirement. Cannon appeared before the committee, appealed their action, and successfully managed to reverse their decision by one vote: 38-37. He did better on the floor of the General Conference, which voted to retain him by a margin of 269 to 170.[18] Although Cannon was already seventy at the time, a provision in the new legislation governing retirement that was adopted as part of the Plan of Union to create the MC allowed him to serve another quadrennium. He was mandatorily retired at the last General Conference of the southern church, which met in Birmingham, Alabama, in 1938, and even then he protested the ruling. Cannon wrote: "I would never have agreed to accept the election [as a bishop] with an age limit attached."[19] He correctly pointed out that other ministerial members were not bound by such a rule and charged discrimination against the bishops.

The current rule in The UMC provides that at any time bishops may be involuntarily retired by a two-thirds vote of the Jurisdictional or Central Conference Committee on Episcopacy after thirty days' notice has been given when such action is found "to be in the best interests of the bishop and/or the Church." They may also be retired between sessions of the jurisdictional or central conference for reasons of health by a two-thirds vote of the Committee on Episcopacy and upon recommendation of one-third of the College of Bishops. A bishop may resign at any time. All bishops who reach the age of sixty-six on or before 1 July of the year in which the jurisdictional conference is held are mandatorily retired on 31 August of that year. Bishops who reach that age after 1 July are eligible to serve another quadrennium.[20]

Given these rules mandating retirement, a simple and effective strategy for limiting the period of episcopal service is readily available without any further legislative action by the General Conference. All that is required is that the delegates considering a candidate for election to the episcopacy know the candidate's exact age. When episcopal candidates are being discussed by delegations it is not infrequently heard that an otherwise promising candidate is "too young" to be elected. Generally this is not an assessment of ability or maturity but an expression of discomfort about the number of years the individual will have to serve.

The Appointive Power of the Bishops

Although most Methodists have never disputed the right of the bishops to make appointments, the potential for abuse of that power has always been a concern both to the body of preachers and to laypersons. The deepest source of the power of a Methodist bishop has from the beginning been the authority to station the preachers and to name the district superintendents. As McKendree wrote in 1820, "The power by which the Bishops are enabled 'to oversee the business of the church,' consists in the power of appointing and controlling the preachers, and especially the Presiding Elders, because they are authorized to exercise all the powers of General Superintendents in the bounds of their respective Districts, except that of ordination."[21]

The challenge has always been to find suitable ways to make bishops accountable in these actions. It cannot be disputed that their authority has sometimes led to autocratic practice. Writing of early Methodism in his *Essentials of Methodism*, Bishop Francis J. McConnell said, "Conditions in America were primitive, and the bishop was really the only church official who had a chance to know the whole field. In the nature of the case the pioneer system was autocratic, and in the human nature of the case the bishops were very likely to manifest autocracy in their bearing."[22]

It is also true that the understanding of the nature of the episcopal office, especially in the MECS, further enhanced the possibilities for autocratic administration. New bishops followed the practices of senior role models. Warren Candler's biographer says:

> During his youth and early manhood [Candler was born in 1857 and lived to be eighty-five] it was expected that bishops should be autocratic, and not often did the strong bishops of that period—and sometimes the feebler ones, which was worse—fail to rise to the occasion. . . . Democracy was slow in making its way into The Methodist Episcopal Church, South. . . . The prerogatives of this body were almost absolute. The most arbitrary bishop, in his most arbitrary moment, did not strain his authority; he rather restrained himself from using his authority to the limit. These prerogatives Bishop Candler inherited but did not create; he simply exercised what had been handed down to him with no connivance on his part. He was a strong man, with great confidence in his own judgment, with no excessive fondness for opposition, and with vast constitutional prerogatives. The stage was set for him to play the autocrat, and sometimes he acted the part remarkably well.[23]

The same could be said of many of his contemporaries and successors both past and present. While defending life tenure for bishops, John M. Moore asserted, "It is an admitted fact that the appointive power is autocratic, and has always been so—and has been considered best so—by the express will and requirement of the Church."[24] Bishop William Angie Smith ran the Oklahoma, New Mexico, and Oklahoma Indian Missionary Conference fairly but with an iron hand. He made it clear what he expected, and those who ignored his wishes could expect soon to be in trouble with the bishop. Like Candler, he did not expect to be opposed. Preachers in the Philadelphia area knew that when Bishop Corson entered the dining room at annual conference he expected to receive the special treatment of having them all rise.

By no means have all of the bishops been autocratic, and from time to time some have received the honor of election to the episcopacy with refreshing modesty and good humor. Bishop Earl Cranston wrote in his diary on 26 May 1896:

This day Charles C. McCabe and I, having been duly elected thereto after many ballots by General Conference, were solemnly set apart and no less democratically infected with "hotocratic tendencies" in the presence of the General Conference in a large assembly of reverend observers. . . . After the operation we were at once removed from contact with our codelegates and isolated with the colony of the infected, seated in a chair and bidden to speak only when we are spoken to from the seats of the immune and to go and come and do only as directed by a little black book—the decrees of all General Conferences in pocket edition—under penalty of all the woes written in the book and the sentence is for life.[25]

But such examples did not override the concern about potential abuse of episcopal power. Thus Bishop James S. Thomas observes that in the early 1960s Methodists were looking with some urgency for ways "to curb what seemed to them to be an arrogance and high-handedness in making appointments; an assurance that every preacher would be given 'due process,' and that this would be done by peers, not by the bishop . . . and the assurance that appointments would be made only after consultation." In 1972, these attitudes and feelings "literally exploded into a reaction against the vestiges of a monarchical episcopacy."[26] The result was the comprehensive legislation to require consultation in making the appointments.

Seniority

The rule of seniority always played a significant role among the bishops—even in their dealings with one another. While neither the College of Bishops (MECS) nor the Board of Bishops (MEC) ever had constitutional status, they exercised significant influence on their respective denominations. This gave particular power to those who held influence within these forums. From time to time this created problems, especially when strong senior members held presiding roles for many years. For example, according to custom, the presidency of the College of Bishops went to the senior bishop. This meant that Bishop Warren Candler was president for twenty years. In 1927 his colleagues made a change, perhaps as much directed by dissatisfaction with Candler as by a newly discovered commitment to democracy. They ousted Candler by voting to rotate the chairmanship. At the same time they replaced Bishop Collins Denny, who had served as secretary of the College continuously since his election to the episcopacy in 1910.[27]

These moves were reinforced by a new generation joining the College of Bishops. Bishop William C. Martin, elected at the last General Conference of the MECS in 1938, said that the election of Arthur Moore, Paul Kern, and A. Frank Smith in 1930 "gave a new image to the episcopacy." According to Martin, Bishops John M. Moore and Edwin Mouzon had already "been more relaxed at that point than some of the other bishops, such as Darlington, Denny, and Candler. But there came to be, under the leadership of these men— Moore [Arthur], Kern and Smith—without any fanfare of trumpets about it, just a changed attitude toward the way a bishop should treat his brethren in the cabinet or in the conference."[28] Martin's modesty kept him from considering himself a member of that group, but those who knew him would readily agree he joined them in the exercise of a more democratic form of administration during the twenty-six years he served in the episcopacy.

The Plan of Union creating the MC in 1939 gave the episcopal gathering constitutional status, now called the Council of Bishops. The presidency of this council is now a largely ceremonial position that is rotated through the bishops of the jurisdictions and central conferences. Their selection usually follows the old pattern of preferring a senior bishop. Each of the jurisdictions formed with the MC has its episcopal sub-gatherings in its College of Bishops. At least the

South Central Jurisdiction determines the presidency of its College by seniority, based on the year of election. Where more than one bishop has been elected in the same year, the ballot on which the election occurred determines who is senior. If more than one is elected on the same ballot, the bishop receiving the largest number of votes is senior. Even the list of retired bishops is in order of seniority, following the same guidelines.

The Bishops' Response

Although not all attempts at limiting episcopal power have been successful, real and significant changes have occurred through the years. As might be imagined, the bishops have consistently protested this erosion of their power—at times with justification. Their list of grievances is aptly summarized in an Episcopal Address to the 1912 MEC General Conference:

> As president of the General Conference the bishops are governed by rules adopted by the delegates, and their decisions in the chair may be reversed by the house on appeal. Formerly they had a discretionary voice as to the ordination of persons elected general superintendents, elders, or deacons. Now they have no such voice. Once the bishops could receive and suspend preachers; he could hear and decide all law questions and appeals, thus virtually holding power to exclude members. Now he has no such powers. Formerly the bishops nominated the most important standing committees. These are now elected by the district representatives. Once they chose their own residences, like other circuit riders. Now they are assigned to designated cities. All these modifications are proper safeguards against abuses of power, but in effect they leave our episcopacy weakened in administrative efficiency. . . . So the glamour of power falls away from the office and there remains—what? Simply a man entrusted with functions no more sacred than those of his brethren, and no higher except in the range of their contact with great interests; a man whose power for leadership must depend more upon his personal qualities than upon his office; a man approved only according to his fidelity to his trust and the confidence inspired by his behavior; a man always amenable—not to a court of his colleagues, but to the judgment of his brethren, both ministers and laymen in General Conference, who demand a two-thirds vote as to his fitness when elected, and only a bare majority to declare his unfitness any time thereafter.[29]

214

Some of these limitations were not new. Bishop Soule's Episcopal Address, delivered in 1844, already indicates some of them. In particular, he laments that "the Bishop can ordain neither a Deacon nor an Elder, without the election of the candidate by an Annual Conference: and in case of such election he has no discretional authority; but is under obligation to ordain the person elected, whatever may be his own judgment of his qualifications." But Soule also celebrates the fact that Methodists have been wise enough to impose some limits on their bishops.

> The office of a bishop or superintendent, according to our ecclesiastical system, is almost exclusively executive; wisely limited in its power, and guarded by such checks and responsibilities as can scarcely fail to secure the ministry and membership against any oppressive measures, even should these officers so far forget the sacred duties and obligations of their holy vocation as to aspire to be lords over God's heritage.[30]

The Asburian understanding of the role and work of bishops in the government of the church generally afforded those in the office in the southern church more authority than was granted to their northern counterparts. But in both branches the changes that the bishops often decried as a loss of power are more accurately seen as a reflection of the changing nature of the church and society than as a result of organized efforts to limit episcopal power. Moede summarizes these changes:

> The forces . . . had hewn out a new type of bishop in Methodism, a bishop fully responsive to the checks and balances of democratic government . . . but also localized, that is sensitive and sympathetic with the local needs of particular areas . . . a bishop whose influence has been drastically curtailed in both sectors of the church by his steady descent to *Promotor inter pares*, but, at the same time, following unique Methodist tradition, a bishop whose position represented what the church in its age felt would be most useful to the church.[31]

Lay Representation

There can be no doubt that few changes in the life of Methodism in America have influenced it more than the introduction of laypersons into the government of the church, especially as delegates of

215

General Conference and as members of boards and agencies. Laypersons' presence created a new climate for administration and directly influenced many changes. It was noted earlier that the desire to include laypersons in the government of the church led to the formation of the MPC. D. B. Dorsey advocated lay representation in a paper called *Mutual Rights* in 1828, resulting in his expulsion from the Baltimore Conference. This in turn led to the formation of "Union Societies," which finally united in the new denomination. It was not until years later that the movement to secure lay representation finally triumphed in both branches of (Anglo) episcopal Methodism.

It was necessary for those wishing to make the case for lay representation to establish first that laypersons had any right to be present in the conferences of Methodism, since power was vested in the body of preachers and had to be delegated by them. Discussion of this issue was overshadowed in the 1840s by the dilemma of slavery and the division of the church North and South. By 1852 the issue of lay representation was once again on the agenda of General Conference in both regions. By the 1860s the right of laypersons to be included had been generally accepted, sometimes because of practical necessity, and the arguments now shifted to demonstrate that their presence was in the best interest of the church. In simple terms, the climate of the society required it. Their expertise, experience, and financial support had already proved useful in the boards and agencies. The MECS desperately needed to include them for its 1866 reorganization to be successful. And conferences in the West took the lead in advocating their inclusion in the MEC.

The Oregon Conference adopted a report in 1858 that authorized the seating of three lay representatives from each district at its next session and requested the General Conference to do the same.[32] Special conventions were organized to promote the seating of lay representatives, and a newspaper, *The Methodist*, was begun in 1860 as the official organ for its advocates. The MEC General Conference of 1860 authorized a vote to determine the will of the church on the subject. All adult male members of the church were declared eligible to vote. Although the measure failed to win approval, new legislation passed that moved the denomination closer to its realization. Lay trustees were introduced into the quarterly conference. The MEC General Conference of 1868 was flooded with petitions favoring lay representation. Abel Stevens, who had changed his mind on the subject, spoke to a lay delegation convention in 1868 and argued that (1) the spirit and genius of early Christianity demanded this form of church government, and (2) their being excluded is contrary to the American style of polity. He declared that "progress is in the instincts of humanity; progress is the signal flag which waves in the front of the world—waves from the throne of God; progress is the law of all the living universe. He who would fix a system of Church or State government that could not change and advance must reverse the order of God and bind fast the destinies of humanity."[33]

George Crooks, editor of *The Methodist*, said that "between 1868 and 1872 the Church turned over; the minority grew into a majority; the judicious men, who meant to take no personal risks, came to the winning side."[34] The first lay delegates (all men) quietly took their seats at the General Conference of 1872. In 1900, a new constitution was written for the MEC that seated laypersons in the annual conferences as well.

The MECS made provision for lay representation when the church was reorganized in 1866. Laypersons took their seats in the General Conference of 1870 and soon afterward in the annual conferences. Once seated they demanded a greater role in all the affairs of the church and a more democratic style of leadership. Their preferences would be reflected in the style and content of episcopal practice.

Episcopal Leadership in the Boards of the Church

The influence that laypersons exercise through their work on the general boards and agencies of the denomination, as it is now organized, has just been mentioned. The bishops of the church also serve in these organizations, usually in the role of president. In certain instances they have had great influence through them, but their role is usually limited when compared to that of the executive of the organization—the general secretary. James Cannon was highly regarded for his work on behalf of temperance and with the Board of Temperance. Arthur Moore's leadership in the Board of Missions, both in the MECS and in the MC, was significant; the same was true of A. Frank Smith, who followed him. Other strong episcopal leaders have served in the Board of Education. William C. Martin was the organizer of the Commission on Promotion and Cultivation of the

217

MC and its first president. But unlike the bishops who serve four-year terms and are subject to re-election, the general secretaries serve extended terms and enjoy considerable independence in their administration. For example, Clarence True Wilson spent virtually all of his effective ministry as secretary of the Board of Temperance in the MEC. In their work with the large groups of preachers and laypersons who make up their boards, and in the oversight of large budgets and staff, general secretaries exercise power and influence that are independent of episcopal direction. Robert W. Goodloe wrote of the distinction between bishops and the general secretaries: "Bishops are 'itinerant, general superintendents'; Board Secretaries are localized managers of specific interests. . . . These secretaries are elected by the General conference, are directed in their work by the Board which they represent, and are responsible to the General Conference, not to the Bishops."

"In fact," Goodloe continues, "since 1860 there is a group of 'general managers' in The Methodist Church, and also a body of 'special managers'; and the general managers have no direct oversight of the special managers. And what might be very correctly observed, as the work of the special managers increases, the general managers of the church find their field correspondingly narrowed."[35]

In the Episcopal Address in 1934, Bishop John M. Moore noted the same development and expressed his concern and that of his colleagues. He told the delegates, "In the course of time, boards were organized and established by the General Conference to which the administration and the promotion of the great departmental interest of the Church were committed. This has reduced the general superintendency of the episcopacy almost entirely to the general supervision of the ministry."[36]

The situation has not improved since Moore spoke; and a study of the ministry, ordered by the General Conference of 1970, reached the conclusion that although "bishops and boards need not be in competition . . . unfortunately, often they are." It attributed the problem to "a fundamental breakdown in communication," and observed that the constantly changing membership of persons on the boards enables and encourages the permanent staff "to assume power beyond the description of their responsibilities."[37]

There can be no doubt that the increased power and influence of the boards and agencies of the denomination have provided yet another means by which episcopal power has been limited. The names of general secretaries of boards and agencies who have given long and honorable service to the church are as familiar as the names of all but the most prominent bishops—Harry Denman, Clarence True Wilson, Ralph Diffendorfer, Theresa Hoover, Tracey Jones, Tom Trotter, and Ewing Wayland, to name only a few.

CHAPTER 16

Unification: The Methodist Church and The United Methodist Church

The attempt to reunite episcopal Methodism began shortly after the MECS was organized in 1846. Lovick Pierce, a well-known and respected figure in the entire denomination, was sent to the General Conference of the MEC in 1848 as a fraternal delegate from the MECS. But he was refused admission, and left vowing never to return. Following the end of the Civil War the bishops of the MEC appeared to open the door to reunion when they declared, "The great cause which led to the separation from us of both the Wesleyan Methodism of this country and The Methodist Episcopal Church, South has passed away."[1] Although perhaps well intended, their statement ignored the substantial differences that existed between the groups that were not related to slavery. At this time the prevailing opinion among northern Methodists was that the South was schismatic and could restore the unity only by returning to the mother church. Serious negotiations were impossible from this starting point.

A meeting at Cape May, New Jersey, in 1876 marked a dramatic change. At that gathering, it was agreed that both branches of Methodism were recognized as legitimate representatives of episcopal Methodism in the United States, constituting one Methodist family though existing in distinct ecclesiastical connections. This removed the secessionist label and opened the door for constructive talks eventually leading to reunion. These were conducted in a variety of settings and groups until the Methodist Church became a reality in Kansas City, Missouri, on 10 May 1939.

The Reunion of Episcopal Methodism, 1939

The church was reunited in the most traditional Methodist manner—by being reorganized. The key to the plan of reorganization was the jurisdictional structure that was adopted in 1939, and that continued with modifications into The UMC when it was organized in 1968. The proposal for a jurisdictional organization was made in 1916 at a meeting of the Joint Commission on Unification. The basic plan of a united denomination, proposed by Edgar Blake, secretary of the Sunday School Board of the MEC, called for: (1) one General Conference with power to judge its own actions—an idea that was unacceptable in the South; (2) sectional conferences to distribute authority for local efficiency both in the United States and in central conferences overseas; and (3) a single jurisdiction (the Central Jurisdiction) to contain all of the African American congregations and clergy in the new church. Blake favored assigning bishops to areas because he thought it would ensure accountability, and he accepted the reality of localized episcopacy, which had already become established in both branches.[2] Despite its early opposition to sectionalism, the MEC had come to favor local autonomy. Blake's scheme became known as the "regional plan" and, with modifications, it was the core of the organization that finally was approved to create the MC. It was apparent in 1939 that the MEC had no great attachment to the jurisdictional structure, and there is little more enthusiasm for it today in what became the Northeastern Jurisdiction. They simply accepted the fact that jurisdictions were essential to bringing the southern church into the union.

If most in the MEC were lukewarm about the proposed regional structure, African American Methodists were at best frustrated, if not angered and disappointed by it. Not a single African American delegate to the Uniting Conference in Kansas City voted for the Plan of Union.[3] Many left the conference before the final vote was taken, and most of those who remained abstained from voting altogether. A majority of the approximately three hundred thousand African American Methodists involved in the union were in the MEC. Some

African American Methodists in the South had left to join other denominations after the organization of the MECS in 1846. Most remained in the MECS until the organization in 1870 of the Colored Methodist Episcopal Church (now Christian Methodist Episcopal Church). The MECS General Conference authorized the formation of this new denomination, organized its annual conferences, sanctioned the election of bishops to preside over them, and ordained those who were elected. Meanwhile, African American congregations in the MEC were segregated and organized into separate annual conferences over which only African American bishops presided. As has already been noted, while these bishops were elected by the General Conference, their authority was limited to annual conferences composed of African Americans. Although they had the status of general superintendents, they could not itinerate through the connection.

The fact that so many African Americans eventually joined the MC in 1939 is testimony to their loyalty and to the realization that the united church, despite its discrimination against them, was a preferable alternative to separating into what would likely remain small, weak African American churches. Speaking to the Uniting Conference, Matthew Simpson Davage, president of Clark College in Atlanta, argued, "There are too many of that sort now whose only word is a wail of want and whose only message is a piteous appeal for funds. . . . What manner of service could such an organization render to a people so greatly in need of help and guidance?"[4]

Union and Its Effect on the Episcopacy

The Plan of Union, which so obviously affected African American Methodists, also had significant though perhaps less obvious implications for the form and practice of episcopacy. In fact, nothing in the history of American Methodism so changed its episcopacy. While many recognized some of these implications, it is doubtful that anyone could have foreseen the full extent of the changes. There were frank discussions in the Joint Commission about the influence the plan would bring to the episcopacy. The analogy between the status of bishops in the central conferences and in the proposed jurisdictions was clear to everyone. Central conferences had bishops who were not general superintendents, elected for a term of service with limited jurisdiction. Although the Plan of Union

223

called for "general superintendents," they were also to be elected in jurisdictions for service in an assigned area, and eventually they would be restricted to a specified number of years in those areas, a form of term episcopacy.

MEC Bishops Richard Cooke and Frederick Leete spoke directly to the issue. Cooke told the Joint Commission at one of its meetings that "the kind and character of the Methodist episcopacy is hereby changed." He went on to ask the commissioners if they understood "that the fundamental character and the nature of Methodist episcopacy is hereby changed from an itinerant general superintendency to diocesan episcopacy limited to the jurisdiction from which he comes."[5] Bishop Leete pronounced the innovation nothing less than the end of general superintendency and urged the commission to acknowledge the fact by dropping the name altogether. "I dislike to see the name left," Leete said, "if the principle is gone."[6]

Both MEC bishops appeared to ignore the fact that Methodism was already well down the road to the end of general superintendency. In many ways the proposal to create the jurisdictional structure was only the final ratification of what had already taken place. Moreover, the delegates from the MECS favored these limitations. This significant modification in the essential understanding of the episcopal office was accomplished without laying a glove on the Third Restrictive Rule placed in the constitution to protect it. MPC delegates were inconsequential participants in these deliberations since they had no bishops and their concerns (lay membership in conference, consultation in appointments, and so on) had been met long before 1939.

The common wisdom defining the greater good of Methodism in America required the reunion of the three denominations, and the opposition of both African American Methodists and remaining proponents of the Asburian form of general superintendency were laid aside in favor of that objective. Once again Methodism took the course of meeting a need without any plan for addressing the consequences.

Ratification of the Plan of Union was not easy, however. It took the better part of twenty years to accomplish. The MECS had almost a century of separate existence when the MC was finally formed. In that period, it had grown and become the vehicle of antebellum southern culture, and many people—both lay and preachers—saw no reason for it to cease to exist. Up until the actual time of reunion a group of southern laypersons made an organized attempt to block it. Among the most outspoken opponents in the South were Bishops Warren A. Candler and Collins Denny. Bishop Denny, probably the finest legal mind in the connection, and his son Collins Denny Jr., an attorney, once attempted unsuccessfully to block reunion on a technicality by seeking relief from the civil courts. Bishop Denny was one of only two members of the Joint Commission on Unification in 1916 who was alive in 1939 when the Plan of Union was ratified.[7] He refused to attend the Uniting Conference in Kansas City, did not sign the documents creating the MC, and would not accept status as a bishop in the new church. He declined even to receive the pension to which he was entitled from it.

Despite such resistance the spirit of unification finally prevailed, in large part owing to the support of younger, progressive preachers and laypersons. The Plan of Union was formally accepted by the MPC and the MEC in 1936. A year later, the annual conferences of the MECS approved the plan by the necessary three-fourths majority and sent it to the General Conference, which gave its approval in 1938.

Many of the changes proposed by the reorganization were not new. Methodist bishops had not been elected by their peers since laypersons took their places in the General Conferences in the 1870s. Localized episcopacy was de facto in place and accepted. Bishops had first been assigned to cities and then to areas. Within those areas they rotated among the conferences and sometimes even alternated with other bishops in adjacent regions. But the trend was for bishops to remain exclusively within their areas and for the number of annual conferences they served to be reduced. This called for the election of more bishops. The MEC brought into union twenty-one active bishops, of whom were two missionary bishops. The MECS had twelve active bishops, seven of whom had been elected in May 1938, at the last General Conference before reunion. Since the MPC had no prior bishops, they met separately in Kansas City and elected John C. Broomfield and James H. Straughn as their contribution to the ranks. This brought the total number of active bishops in the newly organized MC to thirty-seven (plus seven central conference bishops from the MEC, with their more restricted status).

The Plan of Union called for establishing a Council of Bishops to meet at least once a year. This gave the organization of bishops constitutional status for the first time. The council became the formal place where bishops hold their membership in the church, since they are ineligible to be members of local congregations or annual conferences. The council was charged in the Plan of Union to "plan for the general oversight and promotion of the temporal and spiritual interests of the entire Church" and to carry "into effect the rules, regulations, and responsibilities prescribed and enjoined by the General Conference." While this charge of providing oversight of the entire church was official, it included little real power to carry out the mandate.[8] The council facilitates the work of the bishops, and its twice-yearly sessions are a significant event that few would willingly miss. But the fact remains, as Bishop Short has noted, that "no Methodist bishop has ever had the power to tell another bishop what to do, and no Methodist bishop is bound even by any action of the bishops meeting in council, except as he chooses so to be."[9]

A. Frank Smith was elected the first president of the Council of Bishops. G. Bromley Oxnam was elected secretary, a position he would hold for sixteen years and would make the most powerful position in the council. The presidency rotated from year to year and functioned in a largely ceremonial manner. As secretary, Oxnam served a four-year term and was eligible for re-election. In this role he exercised leadership and control throughout the early years of the council's existence. He is responsible for establishing many of the practices that continue today. In addition to keeping the *Minutes* (facilitated by his ability to take shorthand), he controlled the agenda (which he sometimes circulated only after the meeting was begun), influenced or made the assignment of the bishops to various committees, and determined who would represent the denomination on special occasions. He also established a procedure for keeping a permanent record of the work of the council housed at Drew University in Madison, New Jersey.

Oxnam assessed the importance of the secretary's position when at age sixty-four he decided to give it up. "This is a very hard decision to make," he said, "since this office has been and is the most influential position in the Church. Many have no idea of how influential it is."[10] His colleagues were among those who did understand. Bishop Arthur Moore said of Oxnam: "He was a high-grade organizer. You didn't have to prompt Bromley; you had to restrain him."[11] Roy Short, who followed Oxnam, also served as secretary of the council for sixteen years.

Retired bishops attend council meetings with the privileges of the floor but since 1940 have not been allowed to vote.[12] Bishop

A. Frank Smith seems to have been confused about the evolution of this practice. He said that the rule, adopted at the meeting of the council in Atlantic City in the fall of 1940, was suggested by Bishop Oxnam to quiet several retired brethren "who talked continually." It was to go into effect a year later, but when Bishop Ernest G. Richardson followed Smith as president, he ignored the rule. Bishop Smith remembered incorrectly that it was made part of the *Discipline* in 1948.[13] Retired bishops, including those from the central conferences, attend the meetings of the council at church expense and, in the current body, slightly outnumber the combined active members.

Many of the organizations that had been created in the two branches of Methodism with the intent or practical effect of limiting episcopal power were incorporated into the Plan of Union in 1939. The prime examples are groups that had been created in both the MEC (the Committee on the Judiciary) and the MECS (the Judicial Council) to rule on the constitutionality of acts of the General Conference and the bishops. Until the creation of the Judicial Council in 1934, issues of constitutionality in the MECS had been a prerogative of the College of Bishops. The custom was for its members to bring to the attention of their colleagues questions that arose during their administrations in order to seek help and advice. The current practice in The UMC is for every episcopal ruling to be reported and routinely reviewed by the Judicial Council, and it has become common practice for controversial decisions made by the bishops to be appealed to the Judicial Council.

After the organization of the MC was completed in May 1939, its bishops were assigned by the Uniting Conference to their areas. This necessitated the seven newly elected bishops from the former MECS being reassigned to new areas after only one year, creating considerable inconvenience and financial hardship. For example, Bishop William C. Martin had served the California Area of the MECS in 1938–39 and was transferred to the Omaha Area of the MC. The first General Conference of the new church was held in 1940, and its first three new bishops, William A. C. Hughes, Lorenzo H. King, and Bruce R. Baxter, were elected at meetings of the jurisdictional conferences that year.

One of the clearest concessions to regionalism in the Plan of Union was the transfer of the election of bishops from General Conference to jurisdictional conferences, with newly elected bishops having immediate authority to serve only in the jurisdiction where elected. Provisions in the *Discipline* do allow for the transfer of bishops between jurisdictions, but no active bishop has ever been transferred. The only attempt took place at the General Conference of 1940, when it was proposed to send Bishop Arthur J. Moore to the Washington, D.C., Area, but it could not be accomplished. There have been a few cases (Gerald Kennedy and Leontine Kelly, to name two) where bishops were elected by jurisdictions other than the one in which they were living and serving, but even this blurring of jurisdictional lines is quite rare.

Selecting a New Kind of Bishop

The most striking change in the episcopacy that came out of the 1939 merger was not in the number of bishops elected, although many more joined the ranks of the episcopacy, but in the type of person chosen. The process used in the selection will always influence the kind of person who will be chosen. If a person desires different results, one sure way to achieve them is to change the process.

During the MC's almost thirty years of existence, one hundred nine persons were elected to the episcopacy. Of those chosen, only thirteen were serving with boards or agencies at the time of their election; seven editors of church publications were chosen; only one was a district superintendent when elected. This means that the vast majority were pastors; the road to the episcopal office now went through the high-steeple congregations of the denomination. As a result, the already localized episcopal office became even more regionally defined. Methodist bishops after 1939 have seldom lived, been educated, or appointed outside the jurisdiction in which they were elected. This was the exact result desired by the former MECS in advocating this structure; they were unwilling to be led by outsiders.

The contrast with the previous practice of Methodism is instructive. Between 1784 and 1845 only fourteen Methodist bishops were elected. Since they served as "general superintendents" more truly than any group after (although only McKendree and Asbury actually attended all the annual conferences), their election required general support. The main role that provided broad exposure was presiding elder, and six of the first nine bishops had been presiding elders. With the 1845 split, this prominence of presiding elders rapidly declined.

Robert K. Hargrove was the only presiding elder elected in the entire history of the MECS, and only seven of the ninety-three general superintendents elected in the MEC between 1845 and 1939 were presiding elders.

What was the most frequent path into episcopal office in the MEC and the MECS during this period? It was not the local church. Since elections were conducted at General Conference, one had to gain visibility and prominence sufficient to attract its attention. This was most readily achieved in appointments outside the local church. Of the persons elected bishop in the two churches during this period, five were publishing agents, fifteen were missionary secretaries, twelve held other connectional assignments, and twenty-two (fifteen in the MEC and seven in the MECS) were editors of church papers at the time of their election. The most common setting for successful candidates in both branches of episcopal Methodism was in higher education—fifty-five were serving in educational institutions, often as presidents, when elected.[14]

The preferred route into the episcopal office changed dramatically with the adoption of jurisdictions, particularly in the South. The MECS had seldom elected bishops from its pastors until the years just prior to unification. By contrast, the southern jurisdictions of the MC seldom elected anyone but pastors. Of the ten persons elected bishop in the South Central Jurisdiction over the life span of the MC, only H. Bascom Watts (1952) was not currently a pastor, and he had only recently moved into the district superintendency from an appointment as pastor of Boston Avenue Church in Tulsa, Oklahoma.

New Process for Election to Bishop

The process by which bishops are elected was changed dramatically by the jurisdictional structure, and the change is largely responsible for the difference in the type of person who has been elected in both the MC and The UMC, especially in the latter. In preparation for this book, the author was advised by a bishop that to be elected today a person must meet three general criteria: (1) be nominated by and have the support of an annual conference, and if possible he/she should lead the delegation (of the thirty-eight persons who have been elected bishops in the history of the South Central Jurisdiction, twenty-four of them have led their delegations); (2) make a positive impression in the interviews by delegations that are now part of the selection process; and (3) have an annual conference that is willing to receive him/her as bishop, if elected.

The stipulation that any annual conference nominating a candidate for bishop should be willing to accept the person if elected is most contrary to traditional Methodist practice. In the face of our continuing constitutional commitment to itinerant general superintendency, this vividly demonstrates that bishops do not itinerate throughout the denomination and cannot be appointed without the approval of the annual conference to which he/she may be assigned. It has become popular to welcome a new bishop into an area with a celebration in which symbols of office, like the shepherd's crook or stole, and other representative gifts from various groups such as pastors, laypersons, women, and young people are presented. In some ways these occasions seem not only to welcome but also to signal the "acceptance" of the new episcopal leader, an idea that by no stretch of the imagination can be understood as characteristically Methodist. The Episcopal Church is less confusing since its service of installation for a new bishop begins with the person standing outside and knocking on the door of the church to ask permission to come inside. Perhaps Methodists ought to consider devising a comparable symbolic act.

One other criterion should probably be added to the suggested list of requirements for successful candidacy to the episcopacy—the candidate must not be too controversial. Under the present system it is hard to imagine that persons like Gilbert Haven (the outspoken opponent of slavery), Atticus Haygood (a college president with a vision for the future of African Americans in the South that was years beyond his time), Warren Candler (aristocratic and autocratic), James Cannon Jr. (a controversial and radical advocate of temperance), or Charles C. Selecman (so unpopular with one group in his own North Texas Annual Conference that their failed attempt to stop his election resulted in the selection of William C. Martin) could successfully negotiate the process and be elected.

The United Methodist Church, 1968

The United Methodist Church, created by the uniting of The Methodist Church and the Evangelical United Brethren Church, was formally organized at the Uniting Conference held in Dallas in the spring of 1968. As had been the case in 1939, a proposed Plan of Union had been approved by the respective churches in their General Conferences in 1966 (which met in Dallas to facilitate their discussions) and in their respective annual conferences the following year.

There were substantial differences between the two bodies despite their common heritage and substantial agreement on doctrine. The EUBC was quite small by comparison to the MC. It had thirty-two annual conferences in the United States with a total membership of 768,099 in 1968, while there were nearly 10 million members in the MC.[15] The two churches were also quite different in practice and government, with the EUBC generally having moved farther toward consultation and democratic process in its government than the MC. In particular, pastoral appointments were made for indefinite tenure; a Program Council was a significant organization in the annual conference; a General Council on Administration had the power to act on behalf of the General Conference between sessions and was charged with implementing its decisions; and persons filling positions on denominational administrative boards and agencies were limited to twelve-year terms (including the bishops), and were not eligible to serve on two boards simultaneously.

In the strictest sense the EUBC was grafted onto the structure of Methodist episcopal polity. In most cases the Methodist pattern was followed. Thus the Plan of Union could call for "a continuance of an episcopacy in The United Methodist Church, of like plan, powers, privileges, and duties as now exist in The Methodist Church and in The Evangelical United Brethren Church in all those matters in which they agree and may be considered identical."[16] In all other aspects—and there were some substantial differences, such as term limits on episcopal service and more democratic procedures with respect to the appointment-making process—the differences were negotiated. The active bishops in the EUBC were given life tenure in The UMC.

Electing a Bishop in The United Methodist Church

Electing a Methodist bishop has never been without political overtones, but after 1968 it became even more political because of the new procedure used. One has only casually to observe what happens, beginning with the election in the annual conference of delegates to general and jurisdictional conferences, to see that people enjoy meeting, talking, and negotiating.

Special interest groups form in the conferences to enlist support for their candidates. Mailings are made in advance of the jurisdictional conference and flyers introducing and profiling candidates appear on the desks of delegates before every session. Once the delegates are elected by their annual conference (the year prior to the jurisdictional conference), there are numerous meetings to determine if a favorite candidate can be elected, even to the point of deciding how many ballots will be cast for the candidate if it becomes obvious the cause is lost. Delegations from neighboring conferences meet to talk and interview persons who have been nominated by their annual conferences. Deals are offered in which support is promised for a candidate from one area in exchange for the assignment of a favorite episcopal leader who is slated to move. It is the epitome of the great American pastime of politics, which culminates only when the voting is completed.

Once the jurisdictional conference actually convenes, after the Committee on the Episcopacy has announced the number of persons to be elected (a number already well known by everyone), the first ballot is taken at the first plenary session. Lay and clergy delegates vote separately. Voting is now done electronically, which speeds the process as well as eliminates errors by tellers who formerly counted the votes by hand.[17] When the result of the ballot is returned to the conference, it becomes the "Order of the Day" and supersedes all other business. Sixty percent of the votes cast are necessary for election. In the South Central Jurisdiction, the rules of the conference call for the presiding officer to lead the conference in prayer, "invoking the guidance of the Holy Spirit," before every ballot after the first and then to recess the delegates for thirty minutes before taking the vote.[18] If the mandate to the presiding bishop is to invoke the Holy Spirit, the business of the recess is to determine how the delegates will vote—with or without spiritual intervention. Late-night or other meetings between delegations iron out strategies until the final ballot is counted. The process continues until the required number of bishops is elected, and the conference must remain in session until the task is finished. There are both lay and clergy members who exhibit remarkable talent for using the process to achieve their ends. At the 1996 meeting of the South Central Jurisdiction in Kansas City, one of the delegates told the author how many votes the leading candidate would receive before "peaking" and falling out of contention. His prediction proved to be exactly right.

There is little substantive business conducted at the jurisdictional conference other than the election of bishops. It begins with an address from the College of Bishops on the "State of the Church," but everyone is restless and anxious for this address to be over so they can move on to the elections. Between ballots, however, there is plenty of time to caucus, to hear promotional and inspirational speeches, to get reports from the agencies and leaders within the jurisdiction, and to be entertained by various groups. The College of Bishops holds its meetings during the sessions. Other items on the agenda include electing trustees to institutions in organizations controlled by the jurisdiction, naming persons to the various committees in the church that require jurisdictional representation, and awaiting the climax when the Committee on Episcopacy stations the bishops. It would be interesting to see what might happen at a jurisdictional conference without a bishop to elect, or what might result if it were determined to conduct the election on the Internet.

The logistics and the expense required to mount the jurisdictional conference are substantial. At the 1996 South Central Jurisdictional Conference, each of the three hundred thirty-two delegates was paid a lump sum of $248 for the duration of the conference for lodging and meals; travel was paid separately. Annual conferences provided subsidies to cover any remaining expenses.

Laypersons play a significant role in the jurisdictional structure. The leadership of the jurisdictional conference delegation, which is composed of an equal number of lay and clergy delegates, alternates between clergy and laypersons. Laypersons are represented in virtually every part of the church's organization in equal numbers with clergy. They have brought a new perspective to the deliberations of groups formerly led only by preachers. It should be acknowledged, however, that the persons who elect bishops today at the jurisdictional conferences do not fit the profile of either average Methodist clergy or laypersons. In the study of the episcopacy done in 1964 it was reported that delegates at general and jurisdictional conferences "are older, better educated, and come from larger churches, paying larger salaries, located in larger towns and cities."[19] Although the study itself is dated, those characteristics have not changed. It is simply impossible for many interested laypersons to be away from their work for the two weeks or more required to serve as delegates to the general and jurisdictional conferences. Admittedly, since the delegations to the jurisdictional conference are larger, and since its meetings are shorter in duration, there is wider representation among its members. But within the denomination there is a cadre of persons, both lay and clergy, who tend to be elected to attend these meetings over and over. They fit the profile noted above. They are also the ones who are usually nominated to serve on national boards and agencies.

The Profile of a Bishop, Changing Again

What impact have the changes in the process of the selection of bishops just described had on the profile of successful candidates for bishop in The UMC? It has continued one trend noted in the MC and reversed another. The MC tendency (by contrast with the precedent in the MEC and MECS) to favor electing as bishop those with prominent pastoral experience has continued, while the relative absence of former district superintendents among MC bishops (particularly by contrast with the prominence of presiding elders in the initial decades of the MEC) has been reversed.[20] It is likely because of the recognition of the increased promotional and managerial tasks of today's episcopal leader that persons whose experience, talents, and personality lend themselves to these functions are often favored for the episcopacy. Pastors of large congregations remain the most popular choices. But twenty-one of the persons elected UMC bishops so far were district superintendents at the time of their election, and forty-seven more had served in the office at least once prior to their election. A survey taken in the Council of Bishops in 1982–83 revealed that on average the bishops had spent 19.8 years as pastors of local congregations and 4.73 years as district superintendents.[21] The pattern remains the same today. Of the eighteen bishops elected in 1996, three, all of whom had formerly been district superintendents, were in connectional assignments; one, who previously had many years of service in a large congregation, was a seminary president; and fourteen were pastors or district superintendents when elected.

A conference assignment can heighten the visibility needed to be a viable candidate for bishop in The UMC. Among the connectional appointments, the new position, Director of the Conference Council on Ministry, created after the merger in 1968, has yielded the most bishops. Seventeen persons were elected to the episcopacy from connectional appointments, and six were directors of these councils.

By comparison with predecessor groups, academicians are generally less frequently chosen as bishops in The UMC. The clearest exception to this generalization is with successful African American candidates. Cornelius Henderson, the president of Gammon Theological Seminary in Atlanta, was elected in 1996; and his predecessor at Gammon, Alfred Norris, was elected in 1992. Otherwise, only Bishops Fred Wertz, Earl Hunt, Alsie H. Carlton, William R. Cannon, Don W. Holter, Wayne K. Clymer, James M. Ault, Mack Stokes, and Bruce Blake had served in educational institutions prior to election.

If academicians have been less successful, women and ethnic minorities have benefited from the current procedures. Coming into the merger, all Methodist bishops were males, and about the only minorities were persons elected for the central conferences or to serve the (Black) Central Jurisdiction. By contrast, in 1996 The UMC Council of Bishops contained fifty active bishops serving assignments in the United States. In addition, there are eleven active bishops in Africa, one in Eurasia, three in Europe, and three in the Philippines. Seventy-six retired bishops belonged to the council. Among the active bishops in the United States were ten African Americans, two Hispanics, two Asian Americans, and nine women. Three women and four African Americans were elected in 1996 alone.

The first Asian American, Wilbur W. Y. Choy, was elected bishop in the Western Jurisdiction in 1972, and Elias Galvan, the first Hispanic, was elected in 1984. The first woman to be elected to the episcopacy was Marjorie Matthews in 1980. Matthews, a second-career person with a Ph.D. degree, was only able to serve one quadrennium because of her age. She had been a district superintendent before her election. Eleven more women have been elected since Bishop Matthews. Of these, the majority were in connectional assignments—three were pastors and three were district superintendents. It would appear that women have not yet consistently attained the "high steeple" pulpits in The UMC that could springboard them into the episcopacy.

The current procedure for electing bishops has also affected the age makeup of the Council of Bishops. Although most bishops elected have been in their fifties, some younger bishops have been chosen in The UMC. A. James Armstrong, Sharon Brown Christopher, and Joseph H. Yeakel were all forty-four when they were elected. Susan Morrison was forty-five. The average age of persons elected in 1992 was fifty-four; in 1996 it was slightly younger—fifty-two. In practical terms this means that most bishops serve for three quadrenniums. The oldest persons elected so far in The UMC are Don Holter (sixty-eight), J. Chess Lovern (sixty-seven), and Cornelius Henderson (almost sixty-two). The youngest member of the council in 1996 was Alfred Johnson, who was forty-six; Roy Sano was the oldest, at sixty-five. Six bishops were in their forties, and twenty-three were in their sixties.[22]

Making Appointments with Consultation

Just as striking as the changes in the profile of the bishops of The UMC are modifications in traditional Methodist polity that have been adopted. The greatest modification related to episcopal authority came in 1976 and concerns the making of pastoral appointments. The presence of the EUBC, with their pattern of more democratic practices, was influential in this development, as well as a strong long-term sentiment favoring the change. The General Conference of 1972 authorized a "Study Commission on the Episcopacy and the District Superintendency." This time the desire for significant reform evident in 1964 had intensified until, according to Bishop Thomas, "Methodists intended to radically revise the episcopal office and make it more accountable."[23] While affirming the historic role of the bishop to "make and fix the appointments," this study recommended a number of significant changes that were adopted by the General Conference of 1976. This legislation created a process by which assigning clergy to their stations was enlarged to require a consultative interaction between bishop, cabinet, district superintendent, clergy, and congregation.[24]

According to the new process, "Appointments are to be made with due regard to the gifts and graces of pastors, to the needs, characteristics, and opportunities of congregations, and to program and missional strategy of conferences and without regard to origin, sex, or color." The required consultation is defined as meaning "conferring with the parties affected by the process of appointment-making. Consultation is not unilateral decision-making or notification.

236

Consultation is both a continuing process and a more intense involvement during the period of change in appointment." This consultative process "may be initiated by a pastor, a Pastor-Parish Relations Committee, a district superintendent, or a bishop." When a change is "imminent," consultation must take place. After it has been done, "the bishop and the Cabinet shall consider all requests in light of criteria developed for each charge and each pastor." All appointments must be considered by the entire cabinet and the bishop until a "tentative" decision is made. Further consultation is then used to determine if the tentative conclusion can be supported, and once a final decision is reached "the announcement of that decision shall be made to all parties directly involved in the consultative process . . . before a public announcement is made."[25] The usual practice now is for all appointments to be made and announced prior to the meeting of the annual conference. This has eliminated the suspenseful moment in every annual conference when preachers, their kin, and members sat with bated breath awaiting the reading of the appointments which, until the announcement, were known only to the bishop and the district superintendents.

Although the process created in 1976 is cumbersome and works to a greater or lesser degree in the various contexts to which it is applied, there remain some problems that it has not significantly changed. Since the middle of the nineteenth century bishops have lamented in numerous Episcopal Addresses the propensity for larger churches to influence unduly the appointment process. Meanwhile, smaller congregations believe that no matter what is said about consultation they will get whomever the bishop and cabinet decide to send. This has not changed. However, the new process has reduced the temptation to arbitrariness and imposed limits on the degree to which judgments in the appointive process are above question. Asbury would not have been at home in such a situation, nor would hosts of his successors, especially in the MECS during the late-nineteenth and early-twentieth centuries.

This, of course, raises the question of episcopal accountability. By the *Discipline* bishops are subject to the Committee on Episcopacy in the jurisdictional conference—and finally to the General Conference—for their conduct and administration. Their rulings are also all reviewed by the Judicial Council. Yet the study commissioned by the General Conference in 1972 revealed considerable ambiguity on the part of the bishops about their accountability to the church.

The writers reported that "probably on no score was there greater disagreement among the bishops. It almost looked like utter confusion."[26] The commission also asked the bishops about their sense of accountability to the Council of Bishops and to one another personally. The Study Commission on Episcopacy and District Superintendency reported, "There seems to be a tendency that bishops do not hold each other accountable for the work they do, each in his own area. And when they are together, they are reluctant to police themselves."[27] This has been a problem in one form or another at least since McKendree threatened to bring charges against Bishops George and Hedding for refusing to itinerate. It is a matter that still warrants attention.

CHAPTER 17

The Episcopacy in Today's Church

The story of the episcopacy in American Methodism has been one of evolution and change, in response to the various challenges that have confronted its mission. The challenges that United Methodism faces on the edge of the twenty-first century are easy enough to identify but complicated and difficult to resolve. In addressing them there is good reason to remember, respect, and honor the past, but there are also cherished practices that must be set aside in order to preach the gospel successfully to a new age. This chapter will consider some of the challenges as they relate to the critical question of how leadership should be exercised in United Methodism as it moves into the twenty-first century.

The Challenge of General Superintendency in a Global Church

Over the course of this study we have watched the original commitment of American Methodism to an itinerant general superintendency being transformed by degrees into acceptance of a diocesan episcopacy. By the time that Roy Short was elected to the episcopacy of the MC in 1948, he could see the impact. "The time has come when there are bishops who have never held conference sessions other than those of their own area. Some of them for their entire episcopacy have had only one area, and that oftentimes is an area composed of a single conference."[1]

This changed situation of individual bishops inevitably affected the Council of Bishops' self-understanding of its nature and mission. Bishop Short, who served as the secretary of the council for sixteen years, wrote in 1979 in his history of its work: "The council . . . has become less of a general superintendency, except in a collective sense. It has become increasingly a body of area administrators meeting to plan together for the entire church."[2] Bishop James S. Thomas, who was elected in 1964 and was an active member of the council for twenty-four years, echoed Short's observations: "There is little evidence to indicate that the Council was a group of General Superintendents with large concern for and authority in the whole Church." In Thomas's long experience, "the Council was a warm fellowship of leaders with great influence in their individual Conferences but with little sense of a 'General Superintendency,' except in the transfer of pastors across state and jurisdictional lines."[3]

This lack of awareness of the dimension of general superintendency is quite significant in view of the fact that The UMC is a global organization existing in an increasingly globally conscious age. This reality has not yet been sufficiently addressed. One has only to attend the sessions of any UMC General Conference to see how North American interests and concerns dominate its agenda and deliberations, and to hear United Methodists from other nations protest the lack of awareness and sensitivity to their special interests or needs. Broadening the scope beyond UMC borders, it remains an irony to British Methodists that the headquarters of "world Methodism" should be located in a place as isolated as Lake Junaluska, North Carolina.

The global dimension of The UMC needs to be taken seriously not only by the bishops of the central conferences but by their counterparts in the United States as well. Outside of General Conference, the only place where representative world leaders of United Methodism and its affiliate bodies are routinely present is in the Council of Bishops. The bishops who compose its membership are given the specific mandate in the 1996 *Discipline* to share the responsibility for "the supervision of the whole Church."[4] They are collec-

240

tively "general superintendents" charged with leading a world church. But it is not clear that the council has in place practices or structures to help accomplish this important task.

Earlier chapters traced the struggle in both the MEC and MECS to find appropriate ways to provide episcopal oversight to areas outside the United States—ways that not only served the "missionary" areas but also created a deeper appreciation for world Methodism among the bishops and in the American church. By 1939, with the adoption of jurisdictional structures in the new MC, most of the truly interactive models were replaced with what was essentially diocesan episcopacy. The members of the Council of Bishops sensed this loss and took some steps to address it. In 1943, at the insistence of G. Bromley Oxnam, the council began to require all of its active members to make a visit outside their own country at least once a quadrennium.[5] Since none of the active bishops at that time had experience in another country, Oxnam's intention was to acquaint his colleagues with the church as it functioned in other lands in order for the council better to direct it. Upon their return, the members presented an oral report to the council and prepared a written version for inclusion in the *Minutes*. This practice has continued, and a few bishops have become globe-trotters, managing to be gone a great deal of the time. That is especially true of those who are associated with the missionary outreach of the church. But it is doubtful that the brief overseas visitation of most bishops is sufficient to prepare them for effective global leadership.

The Challenge of Focus in an Expanded Office

If lack of overseas travel can diminish a bishop's ability to contribute to the general superintendency of the church, an overabundance of travel for other purposes often has the same affect. With its greatly expanded administrative structure, bishops in The UMC are required to travel constantly in order to fulfill their obligations as officers and representatives of the various denominational boards and agencies, to carry out the program of the church within the areas to which they are assigned, and to represent the church in ecumenical efforts and cooperative endeavors with non-church agencies. Many bishops find themselves away from home a great deal of the time in the exercise of these numerous duties related to their office.

241

While Asbury was also on the road continuously, to the point that it is hard to talk of his even having a "home," much of the travel of current bishops is for purposes very different from Asbury's itinerant general superintendency. Neither does it resemble in any significant way the practice of bishops in the nineteenth century. Travel "through the connection at large," as the 1798 *Discipline* described it, was related almost exclusively to the itinerant ministry and was required to fulfill the recognized duties assigned to the bishops' presiding in the conferences, fixing the appointments of the preachers, and ordaining bishops, deacons, and elders. Bishops today find it hard to focus on these historic tasks because of the plethora of other administrative roles that they have inherited in the bureaucracy of the modern denomination.

Not all of the additional work of Methodist bishops today is administrative. There has been a conscious effort to combine the classic model of episcopacy with the unique Methodist form that it was given by Asbury. This has resulted in adding to their uniquely Methodist duties the classic mandates "to guard the faith, order, liturgy, doctrine and discipline of the Church; to seek and be a sign of the unity of the faith; to exercise the discipline of the whole Church, to supervise and support the Church's life, work and mission throughout the world, and to lead all persons entrusted to their oversight in worship, in the sacraments, and in their mission of witness and service in the world."[6] While this broadening of the understanding of episcopacy is welcome, it increases the importance of finding a focus in handling the numerous duties thrust upon bishops in The UMC today.

Looking back over his long years of episcopal service, Bishop Thomas said, "Today's Methodist bishop is seriously in danger of suffering an identity crisis."[7] Is the bishop's role that of a general superintendent with responsibility for a global church or a diocesan executive expected to attend to and promote local issues? What has become of the traditional role of Methodist bishops to promote and defend an itinerant system of ministry that now is changed and threatened by circumstances over which the bishop has no control? Is the bishop today only a facilitator in the process of appointment-making? And in The UMC, on the eve of the twenty-first century, how does one understand the historic role the bishops have assigned to them to be pastors, teachers, and administrators? Most of those who serve in the office are left to carve out niches for themselves

242

suited to their gifts, personal preferences, and understanding of the office. There are no job descriptions for UMC bishops, and the church provides little orientation when they are elected. The adjustment must be made by trial and error or with the help of a mentor.

For individuals who find it difficult to manage time or work, a bishop's life can easily be filled to overflowing by responding to the demands made by other persons. When others are allowed to set the agenda, attending to the ordinary chores that arise in any episcopal area—occasions such as dedications of new facilities; celebrations of special days and events; writing a weekly column for the newspaper; preaching or speaking in local congregations; plus attending an endless round of meetings to promote and interpret various causes endorsed by the denomination—will fill every waking minute. Every bishop must attend and preside at the various annual conference committee and board meetings; is asked hundreds of times "to say a word of greeting" in one group or another; talks with scores of people in and out of the office, most of whom have something they want or need the bishop to do; answers stacks of mail; and spends hours in the car, on airplanes, and on the telephone. Prior to the availability of economical air travel, most bishops did their office work and reading on the train. Meetings of national boards and agencies, to which all are assigned, often require being out of town for extended periods of time. In addition, there are the unforeseen "plaster falling from the ceiling" events that disrupt any schedule by demanding immediate attention, intermingled with regular meetings of the cabinet, and boards of trustees or executive committees of institutions on which a bishop is required to serve ex officio.

Despite the now-mandated "study leave," which provides three months each quadrennium, bishops find little time for reflection, reading, or study—sometimes even less for family life or recreation. When first elected and assigned, they begin their new work immediately. There is no time to adjust. For many years it has been customary for a new bishop to visit every charge in the area upon arrival. It is often a whirlwind tour. Bishop Oxnam's biographer described his "get acquainted" tour of the Boston area. "Because of Oxnam's meticulous record keeping, we know that the tentative allocation of twenty minutes per church was more theory than fact. On occasion only one minute was given to a church and one minute to a parsonage. Often only two or three minutes could be spared. The twenty-six churches and ten parsonages in the Vermont Conference on

9 September 1939, received an average of six minutes."[8] Some bishops may do better on these rounds, but each always has less time to spend than the task requires. And all bishops struggle to find the proper focus for balancing their many responsibilities.

The Challenge of Addressing Timely Issues

Outside of participation in the activities of denominational agencies, which would be understood by most of the bishops as a major part of their work in the general superintendency of the church, there are few tangible evidences of episcopal leadership in the church as a whole. One of them is the Episcopal Address that opens the General Conference every four years. All the bishops participate in its preparation, although one member of the council is elected to write the address and deliver it to the conference. While preparing it is a long and difficult task, the assignment is considered a high honor. Suggestions for topics to be covered and advice from others who have had the experience are solicited before the writing begins. Once in draft form, the address is brought back to the council and discussed. For many years the final version read at the General Conference was signed by all the active bishops, but that practice has been discontinued. The Episcopal Address serves both as a summary of the "state of the church" and as an action agenda. In its earliest form it set the agenda for the deliberations of the General Conference. It is unique in that it provides the bishops an opportunity to express their views on timely issues to the entire church.

From the time of its organization the Council of Bishops has also sought to provide direction and leadership to the church as a whole through special statements addressing current topics. In the first year of its existence, on the eve of World War II, the council sent a "Message on the World Situation" (1939); in 1986, in a paper titled "In Defense of Creation: The Nuclear Crisis and a Just Peace," they again addressed issues of peace. They have recently spoken on the subject of church renewal in "Vital Congregations, Faithful Disciples" (1990), and on "Children and Poverty: An Episcopal Initiative" (1996). Between 1939 and 1978 the Council of Bishops addressed the denomination in this manner twenty-two times.[9] Richey is correct in regarding these pronouncements as representing the attempt of the bishops "in a united fashion" to give "theological leadership to the Church."[10] But they carry nothing like the historic weight of pronouncements from the bishop of Rome to the Catholic Church. At most, these comments of United Methodist bishops have only the force that respect for their opinions and the power of their arguments may have among their constituents. There is little evidence that they have influence outside of Methodism. Finding the most effective way to exercise the teaching office remains a challenge for the Council of Bishops as the church enters the next century.

The Challenge of Finding an Effective Structure

It has become clear within the Council of Bishops that an integral part of strengthening their teaching office is developing a more effective structure for accomplishing its work. For most of its existence since the 1939 merger the de facto defining purpose of the council has been to provide a "warm fellowship" for the member bishops.[11] The dinner that opens its regular session, one to which spouses are invited, is informally known as the Family Dinner. This provision of support and encouragement is a significant function, since the council is the place in which bishops hold their membership in the church. But its "family" tone fosters a very specific style of operation. It is considered best not to make "family disagreements" public. Thus it was expected that the members of the council would always speak publically with one voice, and they were reluctant to take up divisive and significant issues in the life of Methodism—even in executive session. For years it was an honored practice that no bishop in the council would call for the question in order to stop its debate.[12]

This style of operation seems unrealistic and even undesirable in providing leadership to address the present challenges of a diverse global church. It is not too surprising that fractures have begun to appear in the fellowship of the "family of the council." For example, just prior to the General Conference of 1996 a group of fifteen bishops issued a statement openly disagreeing with the denomination's position on homosexuality without telling their colleagues in advance. The manner in which they chose to send their message to the denomination had a greater impact on the bishops than the message itself. It was regarded by many of their colleagues as a betrayal of trust. There are certain to be continuing disagreements among the bishops, and the bishops are actively searching for ways to address these differences more openly and seek true consensus.

In addition to promoting more open dialogue, efforts have been made to organize the Council of Bishops more effectively to address larger concerns in the life of the church. As originally organized in 1939, the council had three officers: president, vice president, and secretary.

The presidency was (and remains) a largely ceremonial role that was rotated among the jurisdictions and central conferences, with the person elected often being the senior member of its college of bishops. The president had little ability or time to build influence and accomplish agendas because he or she served a non-renewable term of one year. By contrast, the position of secretary was allowed a four-year term with no limit on renewals, which enabled this person (if so inclined, as was Bishop Oxnam) to build considerable influence over agendas. Two additional bishops joined the three officers to compose the executive committee of the council. The remaining members of the council were divided into two standing committees: Reference, and Law & Administration. This was not a structure designed to foster broad proactive leadership for the church as a whole.

A new group of bishops who joined the council in 1964 (Walter Kenneth Goodson, Dwight Loder, William McFerrin Stowe, and James S. Thomas) recognized the limitations of the current structure and pressured the council to undertake a study of possible revisions.[13] Based on this study, the council was reorganized in 1972 into four standing committees related to teaching, pastoral, administration, and relational concerns. The power of the seniority system was challenged and a new executive committee composed of representatives from each jurisdiction and standing committee was created, reducing the power that could be exercised by any individual member of the council. The secretary of the council continued to serve a four-year term, but in 1995 a recommendation was passed that limited the secretary to one term in office. This removed any possibility that the office will ever again have the power it did during the life of Bishops Oxnam and Short. Some sessions of the council were opened for the first time to the public, and a greater effort was made to inform the church of its deliberations. It is now fair to say that the council meetings are open except for the time when it declares itself to be in executive session.

Since the organization of the standing committees, "covenant groups" composed of nine or ten bishops each have been introduced, as has a Committee on Role, Vision, and Leadership, and another on Council Life and Work. At the November 1996 meeting of the council, the Committee on Council Life and Work proposed the creation of Permanent Discussion Groups, designed to allow the bishops to participate in discussions on topics of common interest in small groups. Previously, these items would have been taken up in one of the standing committees and brought back to the entire council for action. Today the standing committees, though still in existence, meet less frequently and have less influence in the body as a whole.

While these structural changes may help the Council of Bishops to interact more genuinely within the body, they do little to strengthen episcopal leadership and teaching authority within the church as a whole. One potential way to move in this direction would be to designate one of the bishops a "presiding bishop." But there seems to be little support for this in the council or in the General Conference. Even the proposal to allow the Council of Bishops to have a full-time secretary was defeated by the General Conference of 1972 (which had adopted the other revisions of the council).[14] As Bishop James Thomas remembered the mood of this General Conference, "No one dared to raise the possibility of a presiding bishop."[15]

Despite this reticence, the idea of a presiding bishop has continued to be entertained by some. It offers some clear benefits, especially between sessions of the General Conference, since there is no individual or group with authority to speak for or represent the church. Those who have been attracted to the concept have envisioned a designated episcopal leader who could speak for the church within the guidelines and policies adopted by the General Conference. In November 1989, Jack M. Tuell presented a confidential proposal to the Council of Bishops to introduce legislation before the General Conference to create the office of presiding bishop. The change would require the action of both General Conference and the annual conferences, since it would be necessary to amend the constitution. In Bishop Tuell's plan, the presiding bishop would be given a four-year term. Along with other responsibilities, the presiding bishop would "serve as spokesperson for The United Methodist Church within the context of the positions of the General Conference." The first rationale Tuell gave to support his proposed change was the need for more unified leadership in the face of urgent national and international issues; the second was to respond to the request of the denomination for its bishops to provide greater leadership; and the final rationale was to enable The UMC to become a "more effective participant in the long-range strategies of ecumenism." Bishop Tuell's proposal ran into stiff opposition in the South Central and Southeastern Jurisdictions, and the measure failed to pass even in the Council of Bishops.[16] Thus, the only "official" voice of the denomination remains the General Conference.

There was, however, a provision introduced into the *Discipline* in 1976 that allows a bishop to be assigned by the council to undertake a special mission on behalf of the entire church. Paragraph 507.3 empowers the Council of Bishops to "assign one of its members for one year to some specific churchwide responsibility deemed of sufficient importance to the welfare of the total Church."[17] Retired bishop Wayne Clymer was the first to be assigned to work as a liaison between the council and the seminaries of the church. Bishop Felton May was released from his area for one year to lead an effort to address the problem of alcohol, drugs, and substance abuse on behalf of the church; at the end of his term the assignment was extended for a second year. In 1996, the council created a new position to address the third of Bishop Tuell's concerns. On the recommendation of the Committee on Council Life and Work, retired bishop William Grove was given the title of "ecumenical officer," with the task of representing the church in ecumenical opportunities and leading his colleagues in addressing them. This was done to facilitate long-term discussions with other denominations where continuity is important. Perhaps these are small steps that will someday lead to establishing the position of presiding bishop.

The Challenge of the Appointment Process

Through the years the most consistent work of Methodist episcopal leaders has been "stationing" the preachers. Their authority for this role was given by the body of preachers itself. But that authority has been greatly diminished by the process of consultation that now must be followed. One result is that the traditional role of Methodist bishops, expressed by no one better than its first bishop, Francis Asbury, to model, defend, and promote the itinerant system of ministry, has been compromised.

Indeed, the expectations of consultation have placed the itinerant system under tremendous pressure. Many pastors do not expect to itinerate, and do not itinerate. That is especially true in the larger congregations of the denomination where long pastorates have become the rule. If these preachers are unable to continue for longer periods of time in a pastorate, they may seek employment in alternative forms of ministry such as a staff assignment in a large congregation, or work with a board or agency of the church. The number of "appointments beyond the local church" over which the bishop exercises little real control has grown. The mobility that was the hallmark of the Methodist itinerant system is now limited. The "shock troops" of early Methodism are now garrisoned.

The greatest impact on the itinerant system of ministry, however, is not the consultative process but the profile of Methodist preachers. The clergy are older. The average age of United Methodist seminary students today is past thirty-five. About 40 percent of them are women. The typical seminarian of the 1950s—a male, freshly graduated from college—is hard to find among them. Once graduated, their mobility is limited by the fact that the large majority of the spouses of Methodist preachers, male and female alike, are employed.

Nostalgic appeals to the past, pressure from Boards of Ordained Ministry, or even demands for faithfulness and commitment to the "covenant" of ministry from the bishops cannot change the circumstances in the real world of today's ministry. Clergy may be willing to go wherever sent, but their commitment often is not shared by a spouse who will be required to surrender a well-paying and satisfying job and take a child out of a fine school in order to move one hundred fifty miles to a small town to obey the directive of the bishop. Many preachers have never lived in rural areas, have strong preferences for urban living, and do not welcome assignments to the town or country congregations that are so typical in The UMC. As a result, the itinerant system today is neither the itinerancy of years past, nor a call system common to groups like Baptists or Presbyterians. In some ways it lacks the advantages of either. And if itinerant ministry has changed, so has the understanding of the role of the episcopal office, which is historically central to its operation.

The situation today is in stark contrast to that of my childhood in a Methodist parsonage. My memory is still vivid of sitting in the sanctuary of the host church at annual conference and waiting with bated breath to hear the bishop, who seldom appeared in the area for any other reason, read the appointments. He and the cabinet met during the conference sessions, and there were always plenty of rumors to keep the conversation lively in the halls. It was one of the aspects of the annual conference that was fun. The "kitchen cabinet" was actively in session too. When Sunday came we knew that, with or without consultation or foreknowledge, all of us were committed to be bound by the episcopal decision about to be announced. The congregations were expected without question to receive or lose us. Our lives and theirs were literally in the hands of the bishop and the presiding elders. Three years in the same appointment was considered a long pastorate, so we and one-third of our friends expected to move at least that often. Some wanted to move, but others longed desperately to stay. Pastors and a few laypersons sat with pen or pencil poised over the list of churches printed in the conference journal to note the changes as they were read. One friend missed an appointment, punched the preacher next to him and asked, "Who went to Merkel?" He was astounded by the answer: "You did." We stood together when it was over, sang the doxology—not everybody sang—and went home either to begin a new conference year in a familiar place or to pack. Thursday was moving day, and the new assignment began on Sunday. We moved in trailers or trucks in the dead of winter, since the conference in those days was held in November. For the children Monday was often the first day in a new school.

Today's annual conference lacks this drama, since the appointments are announced well in advance. Bishops lack the freedom and power once enjoyed by their predecessors to make appointments as they see fit, and as a result it is more difficult to implement their priorities for conference or local church. The larger the congregation involved in the appointment, the more difficult the task. No matter what episcopal priorities may be declared to be—Bishop Bruce Blake in the South Central Jurisdiction during the last quadrennium outlined his priorities as (1) the mission of the church, (2) the needs of the local congregation, (3) the well-being of the preacher, in that order—in the final analysis it is a negotiated process.

For years every large congregation was deeply involved in the making of its appointment. Their preferences have always mattered. Nineteenth-century bishops, as well as their modern counterparts, were concerned about the exercise of improper influence. Today, congregations of every size expect the same authority. Most want the same kind of pastor—between the ages of forty and fifty, male, married, an exciting preacher, a good manager, hardworking, and personable. At the same time, smaller congregations must deal with economic constraints that may make it impossible for them to afford the services of a seminary-trained, full member of the annual conference. By the time a local congregation pays salary at the minimum amount set by the annual conference, provides the required housing, utilities, travel allowance, medical insurance, and pension for the preacher, plus the apportionment for the Ministerial Education Fund, it will have little left in its budget for operation or program. Several years ago, when the price of fuel oil went up dramatically, a friend in the Northeast observed that the cost of heating oil was doing more for the ecumenical movement in upstate New York than anything ever done by the church. Economic realities cannot be overlooked.

Almost all of the conferences now face a shortage of full-time pastors. The influx of preachers into the conferences at the end of World War II have reached retirement age. As a result, the bishop and the district superintendents are confronted with the necessity of appointing more local preachers or bi-vocational ministers to congregations. In both early American and English Methodism, there existed a hierarchy of pastors. That situation ironically exists again today. Full-time local pastors, essential to the ministry of the denomination, most of whom have received their education in the Course of Study Schools run by seminaries for the church, have been relegated to second-class citizenship in the hierarchy of the annual conferences. It remains to be seen whether the new order of deacon will be given a similar status.

The increased complexity of the appointment process, combined with the burgeoning episcopal workload, has magnified the difficulty for UMC bishops today to fulfill the historic role of being "shepherds of the shepherds of the sheep." Most bishops have continued to consider it an essential part of their duty to care for and nourish the pastors under their supervision, but practical realities must be faced. For the entire period of his episcopal service from 1938 to 1964, William C. Martin acknowledged special occasions in the lives of his preachers and their families—telegrams or letters of congratulations and condolence went out regularly. He kept a record of children in parsonage families and recognized their accomplishments. Often he called on them in the hospital when they were ill.[18] This level of pastoral involvement is a thing of the past. Bishops may not have the opportunity even to know all the families of pastors under their direction. Pastors do not expect such personal attention from their bishop and would be surprised to receive it.

It is unusual for preachers facing difficult decisions to seek the counsel of the bishop or district superintendent initially. It is more common to schedule an appointment when matters are near resolution to inform the bishop after the decision has been made. This is in part a concession to busy schedules, but there is no escaping the reality that no matter how sincere the intent to relate as a "pastor to pastors," to function as a "shepherd of the sheep," the authority to change and direct the lives of persons creates a gulf between bishop and pastor. The same can be said of the relation of pastors to district superintendents, who are—as they have always been—an extension of episcopal power.

The Challenge of Weakening Connectionalism

Just as UMC bishops today are challenged by the changing expectations of preachers, they are challenged by the changing sense of "connectionalism" within the churches. In the beginning this term was simply a way of describing those persons who considered themselves to be "in connection" with Wesley or the Methodists in America, a means of identification. Later it was accepted generally to mean "Doing together what cannot be done separately." Included in this category were projects like education, foreign missions, and the like. The way to "share" in such projects was originally by voluntary giving. But this method was often uneven, so the process was "rationalized" into a system of standardized apportionments to share the load. Whatever the benefits of this move, the result is that connectionalism today is equated almost exclusively with appointments and apportionments enforced on local congregations by the imposition of power from above.

When it is defined in these economic terms, it is easy to identify ways in which the principle of connectionalism is being challenged and weakened. One clear way is the growing practice of registering disagreement with a policy or perceived political commitment of the church by withholding the relevant portion of apportionments. An early example of this occurred during the 1960s when denominational membership in the National and World Councils of Churches sparked resistance from conservatives in local churches and they withheld their support. Today, some congregations have withheld all or part of their contributions to the General World Service apportionment because they are opposed to the interpretation of the nature of the missionary task and practices of the General Board of Global Ministries. Theologically conservative elements led by the Good News caucus in The UMC some years ago organized their own missionary agency and congregations, and individuals in sympathy with their concerns provided funds to support it. Some of this money undoubtedly was diverted from the denomination.

Other money is diverted from the denomination simply because individual congregations in The UMC are increasingly placing a higher priority on local programs and needs than on those that serve the larger "connection." For example, a large congregation in San Antonio, Texas, failed to pay its apportionments in full because it made a deliberate choice to fund the $133,000 cost of its day care operation rather than contribute to the denomination. The impact of such decisions upon the bishops is clear: bishops are forced to spend a great deal of their time promoting the benevolent causes of the church, and encouraging their payment.[19]

The challenge of the "focus on the local" in today's society affects more than finances. It calls into question the very value of denominational identity. Prospective members of a local congregation today are less attracted to churches because of their denominational affiliation. They come for other reasons. They want to know how affiliation with a local congregation can enhance their lives and enrich them as individuals. The senior pastor of a large United Methodist congregation described them as wanting "a good music program, good preaching, and a way to relate." This leads pastors to play down denominational affiliation because the persons they are seeking to attract are interested only in what the local church can offer. And the congregations that they attract often contain only a minority raised in (and valuing) the Methodist tradition.

The sense of the Methodist "connection" is further diminished by the reality that an increasing number of UMC pastors have not grown up or been educated as Methodists, either. For almost two decades, half of the seminary graduates entering UMC ministry have been trained in theological schools that are not affiliated with The UMC. For a first-year seminary student who is thirty-eight years old and married with children, the price of a theological education is far more important in the choice of seminary to attend than the school's historical ethos or even its quality as an educational institution. If it is close to home, cheaper, accredited, and approved by the Board of Ordained Ministry in an annual conference, it will attract UMC students. As a result, Methodist pastors today may be almost as lacking in their knowledge of the denomination's history and ethos as those sitting in their pews who came primarily to hear the music. They will be leading congregations whose members were attracted to their church by its location, the presence of a program like a day care center, the style or time of worship, contemporary music, or (hopefully) a dynamic preacher. In such a context it is ultimately the bishops who must be concerned about the importance and means of keeping the churches in their care "Methodist."

The Challenge of Diminished Public Influence

With the tremendous amount of time and energy going into the various other tasks that we have considered, it may come as small surprise that studies of the episcopacy have shown that UMC bishops have little involvement in the communities in which they live, and as a result they have little influence beyond the boundaries of the church. This was not always the case. From the mid-nineteenth to the mid-twentieth centuries, Methodist bishops were extremely influential in cultural and political matters at local, regional, and national levels.

Consider the case of Bishop A. Frank Smith. He had been pastor of First Methodist Church in downtown Houston for eight years when he was elected to the episcopacy of the MECS in 1930. Although he was assigned to the Missouri-Oklahoma area, he never moved from Houston. At unification in 1939, he was reassigned to the Houston area and served there until his retirement. This meant that he was a presence in the city of Houston for forty years. Bishop Smith was a strong supporter of institutions like the Methodist Hospital in Houston and Southern Methodist University in Dallas (where he chaired the Board of Trustees for twenty-six years). But his influence is best illustrated by his support of his alma mater, Southwestern University in Georgetown.

During the Great Depression of the 1930s, Southwestern University was attempting to get federal assistance for its library.

Because there was a federal program designed to assist city and county libraries, school administrators managed to have the Cody Library on the campus designated as the city-county library for Georgetown and Williamson County, which had no library. Campus land on which the library was located was donated to the city and leased back to the university for one dollar a year. Bishop Smith saw the application through with the aid of his good friend and fellow Houstonian, Jesse Jones, who then was head of the Reconstruction Finance Corporation in Washington. After the grant was approved, however, a "New Dealer" lawyer (as Bishop Smith described him) learned that Southwestern was a church-related college and got the application rescinded. Smith spoke immediately to his friend, Senator Morris Sheppard, whom he managed to meet "by accident" on the train to St. Louis. After reaching Washington, Smith went to see the "Philadelphia lawyer" who had vetoed the appropriation. While Smith was discussing the matter with him, Senator Sheppard came into the office. Sheppard said, "I just came by here to tell you to give my good friend Bishop Smith anything he wants." He walked out the door with the final words, "Let me know, Bishop." The papers approving the grant were signed without further delay.[20] Because of his many years in Houston and the Southwest, there were few Methodists of wealth and influence whom Smith did not know and upon whom he could not call for support.

Bishop William C. Martin enjoyed a similar place in Dallas. He was pastor of First Methodist Church in the city for seven years before being elected to the episcopacy in 1938. In 1948, he was assigned to the Dallas–Fort Worth area and remained there for the next sixteen years as an active bishop, and then became a member of the faculty of the Perkins School of Theology for four more. Altogether he lived in Dallas for almost thirty years. Among his friends, church members, and acquaintances were a number of individuals for whom streets and other landmarks in the city are named today. Although Martin was careful never to abuse his power, his influence was significant.

Today, no episcopal leader either serves in the office long enough or is allowed to remain in one episcopal area long enough to establish such a base of power. Even strong personalities like Bromley Oxnam who reside in important centers of government or commerce like Washington, D.C., or New York City have little ability to influence either commerce (business) or political affairs. Oxnam, while secretary of the Council of Bishops, attempted to expose the bishops to business and governmental leaders. He arranged for the council to spend a week in Washington to confer with leaders in the Roosevelt administration, including the president. It was done again during the Eisenhower administration. In 1954, he arranged for the bishops to spend a week with leaders of the United Nations. The bishops heard and talked with Secretary General Dag Hammarskjöld, Benjamin Cohen, Ralph Bunche, and John P. Humphrey.[21] But Oxnam's biographer recounts that Oxnam was frustrated at his inability to access the seats of political power to which he thought he was entitled as the Methodist bishop in the Washington area. If that was the case in the "religious" 1950s, how much more in our post-Christian era. The challenge of how bishops can help the church exercise influence in our society is a pressing one.

Ironically, one of the biggest distractions from this task of influencing society today is that bishops are continually beset by society's legal influence upon the church. Whereas legal action against any religious body was at one time rare, today the church at all levels, like other institutions, is vulnerable to charges of sexual harassment, professional misconduct, financial maladministration, false advertising, and other breaches of the law. It is certainly not unusual to find a bishop who has been sued. During the financial crisis involving the Pacific Homes retirement center operated by the Methodists in California, the plaintiffs attempted unsuccessfully to tap the deep pockets of the entire denomination. In a recent well-publicized case of sexual harassment in Fort Worth, Texas, charges were filed against the preacher, an associate pastor, the congregation, annual conference, its bishop, and former bishop, plus the South Central Jurisdictional Conference. One role (and challenge) new to the office of bishop is the protection of the annual conferences from possible legal action.

The Challenge of the Jurisdictions

There is one final challenge that confronts those concerned with promoting effective episcopal oversight in The UMC for the twenty-first century: the jurisdictional structure. This structure was created in the 1939 merger to protect regionalism and to keep African American churches and clergy separate from their Anglo counterparts in the Central Jurisdiction. With the 1968 merger the Central Jurisdiction was finally abolished. Its last bishops were elected at a special session of the jurisdictional conference that met in 1967. Prior to that, African American congregations were integrated into Anglo annual conferences, and the first appointments were made of African American bishops to predominantly Anglo areas. Bishop Prince Taylor was assigned to the New Jersey area, and Bishop James S. Thomas to the Iowa area.

Should the other jurisdictions be merged just as was the Central Jurisdiction? The jurisdictional system today is clearly underutilized in all but the South Central and Southeastern Jurisdictions. In the system's almost sixty years of operation, it has never functioned as envisioned in the original design. When the system has been studied, as it was in 1964, the conclusions about it and its usefulness have usually been negative. In the age of shrinking middle management, perhaps the time has come to consider its elimination, or at least to ask serious questions about its purpose.

There is little doubt that a strong case can be made that episcopal leadership in The UMC would be enhanced if bishops were transferred across jurisdictional lines to enable them to serve wherever their talents and experience seem best suited. It is hardly logical that one of two active Hispanic bishops in the church today serves the Nebraska area. Prior to the meetings of the jurisdictional conferences in 1996, fourteen active bishops signed a statement indicating their willingness to serve in jurisdictions other than their own. This might be a suitable compromise to another alternative—electing bishops at the General Conference. If the past is a reliable guide, there is no question that the denomination would have a different kind of episcopal leader if its bishops were elected there. At the same time, it is highly unlikely this change would be considered so long as the jurisdictional structure exists.

As the church approaches a new millennium, it seems time for these issues to be put on the table. There is a sense that the denomination as a whole lacks leadership. The office of bishop is in a state of transition, and the direction it will take in the future is uncertain. The process used to choose the bishops has a crucial role to play in the type of person who will be chosen. If a different sort of leader is required, a new process is necessary. In reflecting on his own years of service, Bishop Thomas said:

Like the Church itself, The United Methodist bishop is going through an identity crisis. Until further light comes he or she must see the office as the president of an Annual Conference, but also, more importantly, the president of a congress of organization, each insisting upon its share of autonomy until it gets into deep trouble.[22]

Unless the church is satisfied to allow this limited form of leadership to continue, the time has come to return again to find ways to recast and renew the office that has played such a crucial role in the history of American Methodism.

Abbreviations

Bangs, *History*   Nathan Bangs, *A History of the Methodist Episcopal Church*, 12th ed., 4 vols. (New York: Carlton & Porter, 1860).

Buckley, *History*   James M. Buckley, *Constitutional and Parliamentary History of the Methodist Episcopal Church* (New York: The Methodist Book Concern, 1912).

Clark, *Hedding*   D. W. Clark, *Life and Times of the Rev. Elijah Hedding* (New York: Carlton & Phillips, 1855).

Drew, *Coke*   Samuel Drew, *The Life of the Rev. Thomas Coke, L.L.D.* (New York: Lane & Tippett, 1847).

EUBC   The Evangelical United Brethren Church (1946–68).

General Conferences *The General Conferences of the Methodist Episcopal Church from 1792–1896*, ed. Lewis Curts (Cincinnati: Curts & Jennings, 1900).

General Superintendency *Study of the General Superintendency of the Methodist Church* (Nashville: Co-ordinating Council, The Methodist Church, 1964).

259

JGC/MEC 1796–1856	*Journals of the General Conference of the Methodist Episcopal Church, 1796–1856*, 3 vols. (New York: Carlton & Phillips, 1856). Conference year indicated in parentheses.
JGC/MEC	Refers to the *Journal of the General Conference of the Methodist Episcopal Church* for the year indicated (after 1856).
JGC/MECS	Refers to the *Journal of the General Conference of the Methodist Episcopal Church, South,* for the year indicated.
JLFA	*The Journal and Letters of Francis Asbury*, ed. Elmer T. Clark, 3 vols. (London: Epworth; and Nashville: Abingdon Press, 1958).
Lee, *Short History*	Jesse Lee, *A Short History of the Methodists* (Baltimore: Magill and Clime, 1810). Note: the reprint edition of Lee also is dated 1810, but has different pagination.
Letters (Telford)	*The Letters of the Rev. John Wesley, A.M.*, ed. John Telford, 8 vols. (London: Epworth, 1931).
MC	The Methodist Church (1939–68).
McTyeire, *History*	Holland N. McTyeire, *A History of Methodism* (Nashville: Publishing House of the Methodist Episcopal Church, South, 1904).
MEC	The Methodist Episcopal Church (1784–1939).
MECS	The Methodist Episcopal Church, South (1845–1939).

Minutes 1784	*Minutes of several Conversations between the Rev. Thomas Coke, LL.D., the Rev. Francis Asbury and others, at a Conference, Begun in Baltimore, in the State of Maryland, on Monday, the 27th of December, in the Year 1784. Composing a Form of Discipline for the Ministers, Preachers and Other Members of the Methodist Episcopal Church in America* (Philadelphia: Charles Cist, 1785).
Minutes MEC	*Minutes of the Methodist Conferences, Annually Held in America; from 1773 to 1813, Inclusive* (New York: Daniel Hitt, Thomas Ware, 1813; John C. Totten, printer).
MPC	The Methodist Protestant Church (1830–1939).
MQR	Refers to the quarterly theological journal of the Methodist Episcopal Church under its fluctuating names.
MQRS	Refers to the quarterly theological journal of the Methodist Episcopal Church, South.
Neely, *Bishops*	Thomas B. Neely, *The Bishops and the Supervisional System of the Methodist Episcopal Church* (New York: Eaton & Mains, 1912).
Neely, *Conference*	Thomas B. Neely, *A History of the Origin and Development of the Governing Conference in Methodism, and Especially of the General Conference of the Methodist Episcopal Church* (Cincinnati: Curts & Jennings, 1892).
Neely, *Missions*	Thomas B. Neely, *The Methodist Episcopal Church and Its Foreign Missions* (New York: The Methodist Book Concern, 1923).
Organization MECS	*History of the Organization of the Methodist Episcopal Church, South, with the Journal of Its First General Conference* (Nashville: Publishing

House of the Methodist Episcopal Church, South, 1925).

Paine, *M'Kendree* Robert Paine, *Life and Times of William M'Kendree*, 2 vols. (Nashville: Publishing House of the Methodist Episcopal Church, South, 1872).

Richey, *Conference* Russell E. Richey, *The Methodist Conference in America* (Nashville: Kingswood Books, 1996).

Spellman, "Superintendency" Norman Spellman, "The General Superintendency in American Methodism, 1784–1870" (Unpublished Ph.D. diss., Yale University, 1960).

Tigert, *History* Jno. J. Tigert, *A Constitutional History of American Episcopal Methodism*, 3rd ed., revised and enlarged (Nashville: Publishing House of the Methodist Episcopal Church, South, 1908).

Tigert, *Methodism* Jno. J. Tigert, *The Making of Methodism: Studies in the Genesis of Institutions* (Nashville: Publishing House of the Methodist Episcopal Church, South, 1898).

UMC The United Methodist Church (1968–).

Works *The Works of John Wesley*; begun as "The Oxford Edition of the Works of John Wesley" (Oxford: Clarendon Press, 1975–83); continued as "The Bicentennial Edition of the Works of John Wesley" (Nashville: Abingdon Press, 1984–); 15 of 35 vols. published to date.

Works (Jackson) *The Works of John Wesley*, ed. Thomas Jackson, 14 vols. (London, 1872; Grand Rapids: Baker, 1979).

Notes

Introduction

    1. Minutes 1784, 4.

1. American Episcopacy

    1. After noting that the preface to the *Discipline* of 1790 gives precedence to the work of Embury, McTyeire notes that the error "as to the precedence of the two men in forming Societies and building churches might easily be made" since Sam's Creek in Maryland was "not so conspicuous as John Street, in New York, nor so often visited." McTyeire, *History*, 271.

    2. The original letter to Wesley does not exist, but Frank Baker has written extensively about it and reconstructed its contents. See Frank Baker, *From Wesley to Asbury* (Durham: Duke University Press, 1976), 73-79.

    3. Russell E. Richey, "Culture Wars and Denominational Loyalties: A Methodist Case Study," *Quarterly Review* 18 (1998): 3-17.

    4. Asbury, journal (3 September 1781), JLFA 1:411. See also ibid. (22 December 1772), 1:60.

    5. H. K. Carroll, *Francis Asbury in the Making of American Methodism* (New York: The Methodist Book Concern, 1923), 73.

    6. Bangs, *History* 1:70.

    7. Asbury, journal (21 November 1771), JLFA 1:10.

    8. Ezra Squier Tipple, *Francis Asbury, the Prophet of the Long Road* (New York: Methodist Book Concern, 1916), 242.

9. Baker, *Wesley to Asbury*, 118.

10. Asbury, journal (7 August 1771), *JLFA* 1:3: "On the 7th of *August*, 1771, the Conference began at Bristol, in England. Before this, I had felt for half a year strong intimations in my mind that I should visit America . . . At the Conference it was proposed that some preachers should go over to the American continent. I spoke my mind, and made an offer of myself. It was accepted by Mr. Wesley and others, who judged I had a call."

11. Asbury, journal (27 October 1771), *JLFA* 1:6. Also Lee, *Short History*, 38.

12. Asbury, journal (10 October 1772), *JLFA* 1:46: "I received a letter from Mr. Wesley, in which he required a strict attention to discipline; and appointed me to act as assistant."

13. Bangs, *History* 1:74. "October 10, 1772, Mr. Asbury says he received a letter from Mr. Wesley, in which he required a strict attention to the general rules, and also appointing him general assistant.

14. Lee, *Short History*, 40-41, says the title given by Wesley was "assistant in America" and explains there were three forms of preachers: "1, Helpers, 2, Assistants, 3, General Assistants. . . . The *Assistant*, was the oldest preacher in the circuit, who had charge of the young preacher, and of the business of the circuit."

15. Ibid., 45. Lee says there "were six or seven travelling preachers at it, most of whom were Europeans." Buckley is more specific and writes, "All in attendance were natives of Europe; they were Thomas Rankin, Richard Boardman, Joseph Pilmoor, Francis Asbury, Richard Wright, George Shadford, Thomas Webb, John King, Abraham Whitworth, and Joseph Yearby" (Buckley, *History*, 16). It is an interesting coincidence that there were also ten preachers present at Wesley's first session of conference in 1744.

16. Asbury, journal (3 June 1773), *JLFA* 1:80.

17. Asbury, journal (19 March 1776), *JLFA* 1:181.

18. Lee, *Short History*, 64.

19. Asbury, journal (13 March 1778), *JLFA* 1:263-64.

20. Lee, *Short History*, 67.

21. Ibid. The conference began on April 28. Asbury reported that all of the seventeen northern preachers were present (*JLFA* 1:300). Bishop Neely says that "for a time there was no person actually bearing the title of General Assistant" and that Asbury had not been reappointed by Wesley after the departure of Rankin (Neely, *Bishops*, 45).

22. Lee, *Short History*, 67.

23. *Minutes MEC* (1779), 20. In answer to "Quest 4, 'What preachers act as assistants?'" the name of Francis Asbury heads the list.

24. Neely, *Conference*, 148.

25. Richey, *Conference*, 27.

26. Spellman, "Superintendency," 85.

27. Lee, *Short History*, 70. See also Asbury, journal (28 April 1779), *JLFA* 1:300: "As we had great reason to fear that our brethren to the southward were in danger of separating from us, we wrote them a soft, healing epistle."

28. Neely, *Conference*, 153.

29. Drew, *Coke*, 64. Drew says that Asbury was released from his confinement because of John Dickinson of Pennsylvania. "From Mr. Dickenson [*sic*] he received such letters of recommendation as enabled him to appear in public, and finally to travel through the states without molestation."

30. Asbury, journal (9 May 1780), *JLFA* 1:349.

31. Ibid., 350.

32. Lee, *Short History*, 73.

33. Asbury, journal (10 May 1780), *JLFA* 1:350.

34. Neely, *Conference*, 171.

35. *Minutes MEC* (1782), 37. Also Lee, *Short History*, 80-81. At the conference in Baltimore, 24 April 1781, Asbury reports several preachers from Virginia and North Carolina were in attendance. "All but one [Strawbridge] agreed to return to the old plan, and give up the administration of the ordinances: our troubles now seem over from that quarter . . ." (*JLFA* 1:402).

36. Wesley, letter to the American preachers through Jesse Lee (3 October 1783), *Letters* (Telford) 7:190-91. See also Asbury, journal (24 December 1783), *JLFA* 1:450.

37. Neely, *Conference*, 211.

38. Quoted in James O. Andrew, "Bishop Asbury," *MQRS* 13 (1859): 8.

39. Wesley, letter to James Barry (3 July 1784), *Letters* (Telford) 7:225.

2. Wesley's Ordination for America

1. It is not possible to know exactly when Wesley made the decision to ordain persons for work in America. His journal contains an

entry dated 1 September 1784—the day of his ordination of Richard Whatcoat and Thomas Vasey as deacons—which says, "Being now clear in my own mind, I took a step which I had long weighed in my mind, and appointed Mr. Whatcoat and Mr. Vasey to go and serve the desolate sheep in America" (*Works* 23:329-30). Coke was ordained a general superintendent one day, and Whatcoat and Vasey elders the next.

2. Tigert, *Methodism*, 139.

3. The source for this is Drew, *Coke*, 71. Wesley's published Journal entry for 14 February 1784 mentions nothing of this, and his manuscript diary notes only that he saw Coke at 11:00 that day (see *Works* 23:476).

4. Buckley, *History*, 39. Wesley's willingness to innovate in the face of necessity as the movement grew in England had caused him to organize societies, to use lay preachers, to preach out of doors, to build meeting places, and to issue a Deed of Declaration to secure this property to the Methodists. See also Drew, *Coke*, 71-72.

5. Wesley, "Of Separation from the Church" (30 August 1785), *Works* (Jackson) 13:256.

6. Frank Baker, *John Wesley and the Church of England* (Nashville: Abingdon Press, 1970), 259-60. He wrote to the bishop in August 1780, "I mourn for poor America, for the sheep scattered up and down therein. Part of them have no shepherds at all, particularly in the northern colonies; and the case of the rest is little better, for their own shepherds pity them not" (*Letters* [Telford] 7:30-31).

7. Wesley, letter to Barnabas Thomas (25 March 1785), *Letters* (Telford) 7:262.

8. Luke Tyerman, *The Life and Times of the Rev. John Wesley, M.A., Founder of the Methodists* (New York: Harper and Brothers, 1872) 3:428.

9. Ibid., 429. Thomas Coke, letter to John Wesley (9 August 1784).

10. Ibid.

11. Thomas Jackson, "The Life of the Rev. John Wesley," in Wesley, *Works* (Jackson) 5:19.

12. Frank Baker, *Representative Verse of Charles Wesley* (Nashville: Abingdon Press, 1962), 368.

13. Thomas Jackson, *The Life of the Rev. Charles Wesley, M.A.* (London: John Mason, 1841), 391.

14. Ibid., 392.

15. Wesley, letter to Charles Wesley (19 August 1785), *Letters* (Telford) 7:284-85.

16. Charles Wesley, letter to John Wesley (8 September 1785), quoted in Tyerman, *Life and Times of John Wesley* 3:446. John defended Coke by replying, "I believe Dr. Coke is as free from ambition as from covetousness." And he bluntly acknowledged their disagreement. "You say I separate from the Church; I say I do not. Then let it stand." Wesley, Letter to Charles Wesley (13 September 1785), *Letters* (Telford) 7:288.

17. Wesley, letter to "Our Brethren in America" (10 September 1784), *Letters* (Telford) 7:238-39.

18. See Wesley, journal (4 August 1788), The *Journal of the Rev. John Wesley, A.M.*, ed. Nehemiah Curnock, 8 vols. (London: Epworth, 1909–16) 7:422. The entry is but one that shows the question was on his mind.

19. Ibid.

20. Spellman, "Superintendency," 63.

21. Tyerman, *Life and Times of John Wesley* 3:430.

22. Wesley, letter to "Our Brethren in America" (10 September 1784), *Letters* (Telford) 7:238.

23. Wesley, journal (20 January 1746): "I set out for Bristol. On the road I read over Lord King's Account of the Primitive Church. In spite of the vehement prejudice of my education, I was ready to believe that this was a fair and impartial draught. But if so, it would follow that bishops and presbyters are (essentially) of one order, and that originally every Christian congregation was a church independent on all others!" (*Works* 20:112).

24. Wesley, letter to Westley Hall (27–30 December 1745), *Works* 26:173-74; reprinted in journal (27 December 1745), *Works* 20:109-10.

25. Wesley, letter to James Clark (3 July 1756), *Letters* (Telford) 3:182.

26. Edward Stillingfleet, *The Irenicum, or Pacificator: Being a Reconciler as to Church Differences* (Philadelphia: M. Sorin, 1842), 438-40.

27. Wesley, letter to James Clark (3 July 1756), *Letters* (Telford) 3:182.

28. Stillingfleet, *Irenicum*, 222-23. He goes on to say, "Ordination doth not belong to the power of order but to the power of jurisdiction, and therefore is subject to positive restraints, by prudential determinations. By this we may understand how lawful the

exercise of an episcopal power may be in the church of God, supposing an equality in all church officers as to the power of order" (ibid., 233).

29. Wesley, letter to Charles Wesley (8 June 1780), *Letters* (Telford) 7:21.

30. Wesley, letter to Barnabas Thomas (25 March 1785), *Letters* (Telford) 7:262.

31. Henry D. Rack, *Reasonable Enthusiast* (Nashville: Abingdon Press, 1992), 292. Richard P. Heitzenrater takes a more traditional position. "Wesley had for some time been convinced, by the same arguments of King and Edward Stillingfleet, that he also had the right to ordain, but he had felt that it was not expedient to break with the traditional order of the Church." See Heitzenrater, *Wesley and the People Called Methodists* (Nashville: Abingdon Press, 1995), 286.

32. Baker, *Wesley and the Church of England*, 263.

33. Tyerman, *Life and Times of John Wesley* 3:431-32.

34. See chapter 7 in Baker, *Wesley to Asbury*, 105-17.

35. Ibid., 116-17.

36. *Minutes of the Methodist Conferences from the First Held in London by the Late Reverend John Wesley, A.M. in the Year 1744* (London: Thomas Cordeaux, Agent, 1791–1836): 1:259-60.

37. Ibid., 278-82.

38. Ibid., 321-27. See also James E. Kirby, "A Study of British Methodist Conference Minutes 1791–1836 with Special Reference to the Status and Meaning of the Sacrament of the Lord's Supper for Methodist Societies" (unpublished STM thesis; Perkins School of Theology, Dallas, Texas, 1959).

3. American Episcopal Methodism

1. Drew, *Coke*, 99.

2. Ibid., 92.

3. See Asbury, journal (14 November 1784), *JLFA* 1:471.

4. Drew, *Coke*, 97-98.

5. Ibid., 99-100.

6. Asbury, journal (14 November 1784), *JLFA* 1:471-72.

7. Ibid., 471.

8. Spellman, "Superintendency," 77.

9. James O. Andrew, "Bishop McKendree," *MQRS* 13 (1859): 164.

10. Neely, *Conference*, 251-52.

11. See Tigert, *History*, 191-92.

12. Richey, *Conference*, 35-36.

13. Lee, *Short History*, 94.

14. There is some disagreement about the date. Coke's biographer sets the time as "Christmas-eve" while Jesse Lee records it began on December 27. Lee is probably following the date assigned in the printed *Minutes* prepared later by Coke and Asbury. See Drew, *Coke*, 102; and Lee, *Short History*, 94. Asbury's journal says, "Continued at Perry Hall until Friday, the twenty-fourth. We then rode to Baltimore, where we met a few preachers" (*JLFA* 1:474).

15. Lee, *Short History*, 94.

16. *Minutes 1784*, 3.

17. Lee, *Short History*, 95.

18. *Minutes 1784*, 3.

19. Thomas Ware quoted in Buckley, *History*, 49. Asbury wrote in his journal: "It was agreed to form ourselves into an Episcopal Church, and to have superintendents, elders, and deacons" (*JLFA* 1:474).

20. Lee, *Short History*, 94-95. Lee does not include Asbury among the elders and deacons despite the fact that Asbury was elected and ordained to both orders before being consecrated a superintendent.

21. Asbury, journal (18–24 December 1784), *JLFA* 1:476.

22. Drew, *Coke*, 102-3. This account does not explain Lee's report that only three deacons were elected—John Dickins, Caleb Boyer, and Ignatius Pigman. The elders, according to Lee, were Freeborn Garrettson, William Gill, Le Roy Cole, John Hagerty, James O. Cromwell, John Tunnel, Nelson Reed, Jeremiah Lambert, Reuben Ellis, James O'Kelly, Richard Ivey, Beverly Allen, and Henry Willis. Garrettson and Cromwell were ordained for Nova Scotia, and Lambert for Antigua (Lee, *Short History*, 94-95).

23. Drew, *Coke*, 103.

24. Asbury, journal (18–24 December 1784), *JLFA* 1:474. Wording from Asbury's ordination certificate. He was ordained deacon on 25 December and elder on 26 December.

25. Leroy M. Lee, *The Life and Times of the Rev. Jesse Lee* (Richmond: John Early, 1848), 149. Lee's *Short History* records that Asbury was not alone in the practice. "Some of the Elders, introduced the custom of wearing gowns and bands, but it was opposed by many of the preachers, as well as private members, who looked upon it as needless and *superfluous*" (Lee, *Short History*, 107).

26. *Minutes 1784*, 7.

27. Ibid.

28. Ibid.

29. Wesley, letter to Thomas Coke (6 September 1786), *Letters* (Telford) 7:339.

30. Lee, *Short History*, 126.

31. John Emory, *A Defense of Our Fathers* (New York: Phillips & Hunt, 1879), 126. Emory also includes (pp. 127-28) copies of letters written by Thomas Coke, Philip Bruce, and Richard Whatcoat in 1796 that attest that it was James O'Kelly who opposed the nomination of Whatcoat. Asbury, they said, was not opposed.

32. Lee, *Short History*, 127. They concluded the matter by writing Wesley "a long and loving letter" in which they requested him to come to America.

33. Ibid., 125.

34. Ibid. Text of the certificate, signed by Coke and witnessed by three members of the conference—John Tunnil, John Hagerty, and Nelson Reed.

35. In a letter to an unknown recipient on 31 October 1789, Wesley wrote of Asbury, "He quietly sat by until his friends voted my name out of the American *Minutes*. This completed the matter and showed that he had no connexion with me" (*Letters* [Telford] 8:183). A dozen years after the incident, Asbury remembered: "I never approved of that binding minute. . . . At the first General Conference I was mute and modest when it passed, and I was mute when it was expunged" (Asbury, journal [28 November 1796], *JLFA* 2:106).

36. Wesley, letter to Richard Whatcoat (17 July 1788), *Letters* (Telford) 8:73.

37. Asbury, journal (19 March 1776), *JLFA* 1:181.

38. Lee, *Short History*, 127.

39. *Minutes MEC*, 77.

40. Lee, *Short History*, 128. Lee reports that at the next conference "they asked the preachers if the word *Bishop* might stand in the minutes; seeing that it was a scripture name, and the meaning of the word *Bishop*, was the same with that of *Superintendant* [*sic*]."

41. *Minutes MEC*, (1785) 51, (1786) 56, (1787) 62. In 1787 the question is modified slightly to read: "Who are the superintendents of our church for the United States?" The answer is also modified to read: "Thomas Coke (when present in the States) and Francis Asbury" (ibid., 62). It was modified again in 1788 to "Who are the bishops of

our church for the United States?" and changed again in 1789 to "Who are the persons that exercise the Episcopal Office in the Methodist Church in Europe and America?" (ibid., 69, 77).

42. Spellman, "Superintendency," 93.

43. Asbury, "Valedictory Address to William M'Kendree" (5 August 1813), *JLFA* 3:477: "Mr. Wesley . . . ordained Thomas Coke, bishop, or general superintendent, and Francis Asbury was elected by the General Conference held in Baltimore, Md., December, 1784, general superintendent; was first ordained deacon and elder; on December 27, bishop, or general superintendent. . . ."

44. Asbury, "Last Will and Testament" (6 June 1813), *JLFA* 3:472: "Francis Asbury . . . Superintendent and Bishop of the Methodist Episcopal Church in America."

45. Asbury, letter to Joseph Benson (15 January 1816), *JLFA* 3:544-45: "With us a bishop is a plain man, altogether like his brethren, wearing no marks of distinction, advanced in age, and by virtue of his office can sit as president in all the solemn assemblies of the ministers of the gospel . . . raised to a small degree of constituted and elective authority above all his brethren." Thomas Neely (*Bishops*, 58) says that in Wesley's vocabulary "*Superintendent* was the same as bishop, but he preferred *Superintendent*, possibly to avoid the appearance of prelatical episcopacy."

46. Wesley, letter to Asbury (20 September 1788), *Letters* (Telford) 8:91. Asbury wrote in his journal on 15 March 1789, "Here I received a *bitter pill* from one of my greatest friends. Praise the Lord for my trials also—may they all be sanctified"(*JLFA* 1:594). It was the last letter Asbury ever received from Wesley.

47. "Debates in the General Conference, 1844," in *JGC/MEC 1796–1856* 2:131-32.

48. The Restrictive Rules appear in the *JGC/MEC 1796–1856* (1808) 1:82-83. They can also be found in the *Book of Discipline of The United Methodist Church*, 1996, 26-27.

4. The Bishops and the Conference

1. Abel Stevens, *History of the Methodist Episcopal Church in the United States of America* (New York: Phillips and Hunt, 1884) 3:11-12.

2. Tigert, *History*, 243; and *Minutes MEC* (1789), 33.

3. Tipple, *Prophet of the Long Road*, 255.

4. Lee, *Short History*, 150. O'Kelly began systematic opposition to the idea immediately upon his return from the first session (see Tigert, *History*, 248).

5. Tigert, *History*, 248.

6. Lee, *Short History*, 151.

7. Ibid., 158-59.

8. Asbury, journal (12 January 1790), *JLFA* 1:620.

9. Ibid. (3 December 1789), *JLFA* 1:614.

10. Tigert, *History*, 246.

11. Asbury, journal (14 June 1790), *JLFA* 1:642.

12. Asbury, journal (1 December 1790), *JLFA* 1:657.

13. L. M. Lee, *Life of Jesse Lee*, 270. Asbury records in his journal (7 July 1791): "This day brother Jesse Lee put a paper into my hand, proposing the election of not less than two, nor more than four preachers from each conference, to form a general conference in Baltimore, in December, 1792, to be continued annually" (*JLFA* 1:687).

14. Paine, *M'Kendree* 1:113. The decision not to send a delegate to replace O'Kelly, who was determined not to attend, came on Thursday, 4 November. McKendree writes: "Met the preachers in conference at Brother Young's; twenty-two preachers present, and by nine o'clock agreed to send no member to Council, but stand as we are until next conference" (ibid., 128).

15. Asbury, journal (23 February 1791), *JLFA* 1:667-68. McKendree's diary confirms what Asbury says: "Mr. O'Kelly had already, by letters, prejudiced Dr. Coke against it, and . . . he had been untiring in his efforts to array the Virginia preachers against it" (Paine, *M'Kendree* 1:128).

16. Asbury, journal (25 April 1791), *JLFA* 1:672.

17. Snethen's journal is quoted in Tigert, *History*, 252.

18. Bangs, *History* 1:338.

19. As a child growing up in a parsonage, I was fully aware that the bishop was an "unseen and mystical" presence in our lives. He had the power to assign us wherever he chose, but that was done once a year when he came out from Dallas to attend the sessions of the conference, and stood on Sunday afternoon to read the appointments. In the interim, which was most of the year, presiding elders, who rotated from one district to another and stayed perennially in office, ran the conference.

20. "Minutes," General Conference of 1792, *General Conferences*, 6-7.

21. Asbury, letter to Stith Mead (20 January 1801), *JLFA* 3:196.

22. Lee, *Short History*, 176-77.

23. Paine, *M'Kendree* 1:138.

24. Lee, *Short History*, 193.

25. Asbury, journal (25 May 1784), *JLFA* 1:460.

26. Lee, *Short History*, 178.

27. Ibid.

28. Asbury, journal (30 October 1792), *JLFA* 1:733-34.

29. Ibid. (8 November 1792), 734.

30. See Paine, *M'Kendree* 1:139.

31. "Minutes," General Conference of 1792, *General Conferences*, 6-7.

32. Quote in R. W. B. Lewis, *The American Adam* (Chicago: University of Chicago Press, 1955), 42.

33. Andrew, "Bishop Asbury," *MQRS* 13 (1859): 2.

34. William Phoebus, *Memoirs of the Rev. Richard Whatcoat, Late Bishop of the Methodist Episcopal Church* (New York: Joseph Allen, 1828), 34.

35. *The Doctrine and Discipline of the Methodist Episcopal Church in America with Explanatory Notes by Thomas Coke and Francis Asbury* (Philadelphia: Henry Tuckniss, 1798), 40.

36. Neely, *Bishops*, 130.

37. Lee, *Short History*, 265.

38. See Tigert, *History*, 288.

39. *JGC/MEC 1796–1856* (1800) 1:35.

40. Ibid., 36. A summary of the discussion is found in *General Conferences*, 61.

41. Lee, *Short History*, 251.

42. Ibid., 266.

43. Tigert, *History*, 283.

44. Tigert, *Methodism*, 10.

45. Lee, *Short History*, 345.

46. Thomas Coke, letter to Walter Fountain (1 June 1805), in *JLFA* 3:319.

47. Coke, letter to the New York Conference (6 January 1806), in *JLFA* 3:334-39.

48. See *JGC/MEC 1796–1856* (1800) 1:35-36.

49. "Minutes," General Conference of 1792, *General Conferences*, 7.

50. Lee, *Short History*, 234.

51. *Minutes MEC* (1800), 60; and *JGC/MEC 1796–1856* (1800) 1:34.

52. *Minutes MEC* (1800), 65.

53. See Lee, *Short History*, 290; *JGC/MEC 1796–1856* (1804) 1:52, 56.

54. Bangs, *History* 2:143.

5. The General Conference and the Episcopacy

1. Lee, *Short History*, 297-98.

2. *JGC/MEC 1796–1856* (1808) 1:71-72.

3. *JGC/MEC 1796–1856* (8 May 1800) 1:34.

4. Neely, *Conference*, 70.

5. *JGC/MEC 1796–1856* (1808) 1:77.

6. Ibid., 78-79.

7. Ibid., 79.

8. Tigert, *History*, 302.

9. Charles Elliott, *The Life of the Rev. Robert R. Roberts* (New York: Lane & Tippett, 1844), 157-58.

10. *JGC/MEC 1796–1856* (1808) 1:80. "Moved by John M'Claskey, and seconded by Ezekiel Cooper, that seven be added to the superintendency." A number of other motions had been made recommending the election of from one to seven additional bishops.

11. Quoted in Tigert, *History*, 303.

12. *JGC/MEC 1796–1856* (1808) 1:82-83.

13. Tigert, *History*, 303.

14. Elliott, *Life of Rev. Roberts*, 157-58: "At the next meeting of the whole committee, although the plans of Ezekiel Cooper and Joshua Soule were both before the committee, Mr. Soule's was adopted by all the members, with some slight modifications."

15. "Restrictive Rules," *JGC/MEC 1796–1856* (1808) 1:82-83.

16. L. M. Lee, *Life of Jesse Lee*, 442: "There was some opposition to this report in the committee, but it was more general and decided in the Conference. In both, Mr. Lee was the most prominent opponent. His favourite measure now was to compose the body by seniority rather than by election. . . . It was under the force of his arguments, as we have been assured by very high authority, the report was defeated."

17. *JGC/MEC 1796–1856* (1808) 1:83.

18. Tigert, *History*, 306.

19. Bishop McKendree's "Essays on Our Church-Government," Paine, *M'Kendree* 2:367.

20. Paine, *M'Kendree* 2:368.

21. *JGC/MEC 1796–1856* (1808) 1:84.

22. Ibid. Lee's biographer says: "This defeat was a source of surprise and sorrow to the friends of the measure," and credits Lee with its defeat (see L. M. Lee, *Life of Jesse Lee*, 442).

23. Neely, *Conference*, 356.

24. Paine, *M'Kendree* 1:191.

25. This and the next two quotes are from *JGC/MEC 1796–1856* (1808) 1:88.

26. L. M. Lee, *Life of Jesse Lee*, 442-43.

27. Tigert, *History*, 312.

28. *JGC/MEC 1796–1856* (1808) 1:89. See also Paine, *M'Kendree* 1:191.

29. *JGC/MEC 1796–1856* (1808) 1:95.

30. Tigert, *History*, 323.

31. Neely, *Bishops*, 139.

32. Neely, *Conference*, 383.

33. Ibid., 379.

34. Tigert, *History*, 329-30. In either case the results were the same.

35. Neely, *Conference*, 376-77.

36. *JGC/MEC 1796–1856* (1808) 1:76.

6. After Asbury: Redefining the Episcopacy

1. Asbury, journal (6 May 1808), *JLFA* 2:569-76.

2. This story is included in Andrew, "Bishop M'Kendree," *MQRS* 13 (1859): 168. Andrew was presiding in the session of the annual conference in which the story was told.

3. Ibid., 165.

4. Paine, *M'Kendree* 1:260-61. McKendree's letter is dated 8 October 1811. It is interesting that no record of this exchange appears in Asbury's journal or letters.

5. Asbury, journal (22 October 1815), *JLFA* 2:794: "My eyes fail. I will resign the stations to Bishop M'Kendree—I will take away my feet."

6. Henry Smith to Robert Paine; quoted in Paine, *M'Kendree* 1:263.

7. *JGC/MEC 1796–1856* (1812) 1:100.

8. Paine, *M'Kendree* 1:264.

9. Ibid., 270-71.

10. William McKendree's "Episcopal Address" in Paine, *M'Kendree* 1:269.

11. *JGC/MEC 1796–1856* (1812) 1:101. The conference had earlier voted itself the power to organize as a committee of the whole (ibid., 100), and for the first time seated alternate delegates elected by the New England Conference (ibid., 99).

12. Ibid., 102.

13. Ibid., 103.

14. Ibid., 114.

15. Paine, *M'Kendree* 2:356.

16. Ibid.

17. Ibid., 363-64.

18. Ibid., 367.

19. The number is based on an estimate by Nathan Bangs, that Asbury held an average of seven conferences each year (Bangs, *History* 2:400).

20. Paine, *M'Kendree* 1:307.

21. Paine, *M'Kendree* 1:311. It appears in a number of places.

22. *JGC/MEC 1796–1856* (1816) 1:137. .

23. Ibid., 142.

24. Ibid., 135.

25. Ibid.

26. Ibid., 164.

27. Ibid., 140. The vote was 42 in favor and 60 against. This was the largest majority ever recorded.

28. Ibid., 161.

29. Russell Richey argues that both the General Conference and the episcopacy share the teaching office (magisterium) of the church; see Richey, "The Legacy of Francis Asbury: The Teaching Office in Episcopal Methodism," *Quarterly Review* 15 (1995): 145-74.

30. Tigert, *History*, 335.

31. Paine, *M'Kendree* 1:362.

7. Bishops and Presiding Elders: Limiting Episcopal Power

1. Richey, *Conference*, 83.

2. McTyeire, *History*, 570 n.

3. *JGC/MEC 1796–1856* (1820) 1:207.

4. Ibid., 213.

5. Tigert, *History*, 339. Cites Capers manuscript account of the event to support this assertion. It was also a source used by Bishop Paine in his *Life of M'Kendree*, and by Robert Emory, *The Life of the Rev. John Emory* (New York: George Lane, 1841), 146.

6. Paine, *M'Kendree* 1:409.

7. *JGC/MEC 1796–1856* (1820) 1:221.

8. See Paine, *M'Kendree* 1:410-11.

9. The record of these events, from which the summary in the remainder of this section is drawn, can be found in *JGC/MEC 1796–1856* (1820) 1:222-38.

10. Quoted from the original letter in the possession of Paine, *M'Kendree* 1:420-21.

11. Ibid., 418.

12. Ibid., 419. The sequence is confused because the *Minutes* report, first of all, that the resolution was passed on 20 May; Soule's letter, the original of which Paine claimed to have in his possession when writing the biography of McKendree, has a postscript dated May 18 that was written at the request of McKendree to prove that Soule was willing to submit himself to the authority of the General Conference. This could not have happened before the actual legislation was passed and Soule made his decision to resign. McKendree's letter is dated May 22, which does not pose a problem.

13. McKendree's journal, in Paine, *M'Kendree* 1:422.

14. Ibid., 423.

15. *JGC/MEC 1796–1856* (1820) 1:229.

16. Paine, *M'Kendree* 1:418-19. It is also contained in Tigert, *History*, 342-43.

17. The account of their action is from William Capers of South Carolina, and quoted in Paine, *M'Kendree* 1:412.

18. The next was Wilbur Fisk, who was elected in 1836 against his wishes and while out of the country. He refused to be ordained because of his work and for reasons of poor health.

19. Paine, *M'Kendree* 1:429-30. "The Conference was in great trouble. The majority had, for the sake of peace, adopted a measure which, upon reflection, they believed unconstitutional. They harmonized with the man whom they had chosen for their Bishop, and desired his ordination, though they believed he would not obey the law. Yet they hesitated to repeal the law, for fear of dissensions and

strife. The resignation of the Bishop elect was designed to relieve them."

20. Quoted in Tigert, *History*, 348.

21. R. Emory, *Life of John Emory*, 147.

22. *JGC/MEC 1796–1856* (1820) 1:238.

23. Paine, *M'Kendree* 1:426.

24. William McKendree, "To the Annual Conferences of The Methodist Episcopal Church, Commencing with the Ohio Conference, to Be Held in Lebanon, September 6, 1821," in Tigert, *History*, 366-67. Tigert characterizes this letter as "one of the most important documents in our constitutional history."

25. Tigert, *History*, 354.

26. *JGC/MEC 1796–1856* (1824) 1:270. In fact, McKendree's biography reports that "seven out of twelve of them declared the resolutions unconstitutional, but, for the attainment of peace, and in compliance with the wishes of the senior Bishop, gave their consent for their introduction, conformably with the constitution at the next General Conference. . . . The other five Conferences refused to accept the change as a constitutional measure because they were unwilling to acknowledge the want of power in the General Conference to effect it. They laid the address upon the table, and there let it lie—virtually refused to act on it, and thus tacitly avowed their determination to carry the change into effect" (Paine, *M'Kendree* 1:458).

27. R. Emory, *Life of John Emory*, 148 n. McKendree's journal reports, "It was satisfactorily ascertained that seven of the twelve Annual Conferences judged the suspended resolutions unconstitutional. . . . But the five other Conferences, in which the steady friends and most powerful advocates of the proposed change were found, refused to act on the address, and thereby prevented its adoption in a constitutional way, and, of course set in for another vigorous contest at the next General Conference" (Paine, *M'Kendree* 1:440). The text of McKendree's address is found in Paine, *M'Kendree* 1:444-58.

28. Tigert, *History*, 370.

29. Ibid.

30. Paine, *M'Kendree* 1:441.

31. *JGC/MEC 1796–1856* (1824) 1:267. Bishop Paine preserves a document signed by all the bishops, Thomas Douglass, and William Capers, which appears to indicate that the resolution introduced by Pierce and Winans was, in fact, written by the bishops themselves (see Paine, *M'Kendree* 2:36-37).

32. *JGC/MEC 1796–1856* (1824) 1:277.

33. Tigert, *History*, 355.

34. *JGC/MEC 1796–1856* (1824) 1:281. Clark, *Hedding* (p. 300) recounts that one brother was pulled from the pulpit by a messenger sent from the conference to bring him back to cast a vote. "Here he arrived, panting for breath and bathed with perspiration, just after the decision in favor of postponement had been announced."

35. Tigert, *History*, 384.

36. *JGC/MEC 1796–1856* (1824) 1:285.

37. Ibid., 297. See also Paine, *M'Kendree* 2:39-40.

38. Paine, *M'Kendree* 2:37.

39. Tigert, *History*, 371. It is ironic, however, that a "down easterner" from Maine, Joshua Soule, the author of the constitution, eventually went with the southern branch of the church because he believed it conformed most strictly to the constitution when division came in 1844.

40. Paine, *M'Kendree* 2:49.

41. Joshua Soule to William McKendree (6 May 1821), quoted in Tigert, *History*, 365.

42. R. Emory, *Life of John Emory*, 151.

43. Ibid., 152.

44. Ibid., 164.

8. Modifying the General Superintendency

1. *JGC/MEC 1796–1856* (1824) 1:301-2.

2. Paine, *M'Kendree* 2:48.

3. Hedding's biography says that the meeting was held in Baltimore, not Philadelphia (Clark, *Hedding*, 324).

4. *Minutes MEC 1773–1813* (1780) 1:25.

5. *JGC/MEC 1796–1856* (1800) 1:44.

6. Ibid. (1804) 1:63.

7. Ibid. (1808), 93. A motion made by Stephen G. Roszel, Baltimore Conference, and seconded by Thomas Ware of the Philadelphia Conference.

8. *JGC/MEC 1796–1856* (1816) 1:169-70.

9. *JGC/MEC 1796–1856* (1836) 1:475.

10. Quoted in McTyeire, *History*, 546.

11. Clark, *Hedding*, 325. He does not mention the assignment of conferences.

12. Capers was elected on the second ballot, defeating Wilbur Fisk by a margin of 82 to 72; *JGC/MEC 1796–1856* (1828) 1:339.

13. Quoted in Tigert, *History*, 390-91.

14. Ibid., 392.

15. McKendree to George and Hedding (19 April 1826), quoted in Tigert, *History*, 392. Tigert (*Methodism*, 16) claimed to have in his possession a handwritten copy of charges that McKendree drew up against Bishop George and expected to present to the General Conference of 1828. Tigert also says that the relations between McKendree and George had been strained since 1820, but declines to be specific about the cause. It is certainly possible, however, in the case of naming a delegate, that George honestly believed that the language of the resolution passed in the General Conference of 1824 did not require them to make a selection.

16. Ibid., 393.

17. Hedding's biography mentions serious illness in 1824 and 1825, but nothing is reported in 1826 (Clark, *Hedding*, 320). In 1827, Hedding managed to be away from home nine months without any mention of illness (ibid., 332).

18. Tigert, *History*, 398.

19. Ibid.

20. Andrew, "Bishop McKendree," *MQRS* 13 (1859): 166.

21. Thomas Hamilton Lewis, *Handbook of the Methodist Protestant Church* (Baltimore: 1925), 36.

22. Ibid., 37.

23. *JGC/MEC 1796–1856* (1828) 1:332.

24. Ibid., 353-54.

25. Tigert, *History*, 403.

26. Paine, *M'Kendree* 2:402.

27. Report #8, Committee on Episcopacy, *JGC/MEC 1796–1856* (1832) 2:408-9.

28. *JGC/MEC 1796–1856* (1832) 1:419.

29. Ibid., 419-20.

9. The Road to Division

1. R. Emory, *Life of John Emory*, 288.

2. Although ballots are cast in the same way, today persons are nominated for the office by their annual conferences and go through

a series of interviews before the meeting of the jurisdictional conference at which they are actually elected.

3. *JGC/MEC 1796–1856* (1836) 1:478.

4. Ibid., 474.

5. Ibid., 476.

6. Jesse T. Peck, "General Conference of 1844," *MQR* 52 (1870): 167.

7. "Address of the Bishops," *JGC/MEC 1796–1856* (1840) 2:134.

8. Reprinted in Bangs, *History* 4:260.

9. *JGC/MEC 1796–1856* (1836) 1:443.

10. Spellman, "Superintendency," 246, quoting *JGC/MEC 1796–1856* (1836) 1:438.

11. *JGC/MEC 1796–1856* (1836) 1:475.

12. Clark, *Hedding*, 493.

13. Ibid., 494.

14. Ibid., 495-96.

15. Ibid., 481.

16. Ibid., 497.

17. Ibid., 505.

18. The following summary draws from ibid., 507-9.

19. Ibid., 508.

20. Ibid., 510.

21. Ibid., 532.

22. Ibid., 497-98.

23. Ibid., 525-26.

24. Charles Baumer Swaney, *Episcopal Methodism and Slavery* (New York: Negro Universities Press, 1969), 71.

25. Ibid., 93.

26. For the following summary and quotes, see "Episcopal Address," *JGC/MEC 1796–1856* (1840) 2:134-39.

27. Ibid., 148.

28. Ibid., 120-21.

29. John Nelson Norwood, *The Schism in the Methodist Episcopal Church 1844* (Alfred, N.Y.: Alfred University Press, 1923), 50.

30. Spellman, "Superintendency," 257.

31. Timothy L. Smith, *Revivalism and Social Reform* (Nashville: Abingdon Press, 1957), 188.

32. The full text of the "Westmoreland Petition" can be found in *JGC/MEC 1796–1856* (1840) 2:167-71; the resolution is on p. 171.

10. Division, 1844

1. Donald G. Mathews, *Slavery and Methodism* (Princeton: Princeton University Press, 1965), 212.

2. *JGC/MEC 1796–1856* (1840) 2:60.

3. Orange Scott, *Zion's Herald* (15 June 1842), quoted in Mathews, *Slavery and Methodism*, 229.

4. Jesse Hamby Barton Jr., "The Definition of the Episcopal Office in American Methodism" (unpublished Ph.D. diss., Drew University, 1960), 108.

5. *JGC/MEC 1796–1856* (1844) 2:29.

6. See "The Baltimore Conference," *Christian Advocate and Journal* (23 October 1844), for details summarized in this and the next two paragraphs.

7. *JGC/MEC 1796–1856* (1844) 2:33-34.

8. R. Alexander to Littleton Fowler (30 August 1844). Letters of Littleton Fowler, Bridwell Library, Perkins School of Theology, Dallas, Texas.

9. "Debates in the General Conference, 1844," in *JGC/MEC 1796– 1856* 2:73.

10. On the other hand, this may have been an unnecessary step since under the laws of Georgia, a woman's property at the time of her marriage continued to be her own afterward. See George G. Smith, *The Life and Letters of James Osgood Andrew* (Nashville: Southern Methodist Publishing House, 1883), 337. Andrew's written statement containing information about the trust, requested by the Committee on Episcopacy, is printed in the *JGC/MEC 1796–1856* (1844) 2:63-64.

11. Smith, *Life of Andrew*, 258.

12. Ibid., 342-43.

13. *JGC/MEC 1796–1856* (1844) 2:58.

14. Ibid., 63.

15. Ibid., 64.

16. "Debates in the General Conference, 1844," in *JGC/MEC 1796– 1856* 2:83.

17. *JGC/MEC 1796–1856* (1844) 2:65-66. The argument that Andrew was unable to function as an itinerant general superinten- dent because he would not be welcome in certain conferences ignored the fact that long before 1844 none of the bishops itinerated through all the conferences.

18. Peck, "General Conference of 1844," *MQR* 52 (1870): 179.

19. Ibid., 181.

20. See "Debates in the General Conference, 1844," in *JGC/MEC 1796–1856* 2:86.

21. Spellman, "Superintendency," 270.

22. Quoted in the "Pastoral Address" of the 1846 General Conference of the MECS (in *Organization MECS*, 494). It is also contained in Charles Elliott, *History of the Great Secession from the Methodist Episcopal Church in the Year 1845* (Cincinnati: Swormsteadt & Poe, 1855), 228. Elliott adds an editorial comment that is important: "The resolution was passed without reference to any but traveling and local preachers, or members, having no reference, as it has no pertinency, to the Episcopacy. At a future day this became the stronghold in favor of a slaveholding Episcopacy."

23. "Debates in the General Conference, 1844," in *JGC/MEC 1796–1856* 2:148-49.

24. William A. Smith, who defended Francis Harding, wrote in a private circular in 1836: "It is true the Conference voted promptly against the wild schemes of the abolitionists. Unfortunately, however, it is equally true that a large majority voted on the principles of abolitionism in the election of Bishops, thus favoring the unrighteous prejudices of abolitionists, and proscribing from this highest office in the Church men admitted, in private conversations, to possess superior qualifications to those appointed, simply because of their connection with slavery" (quoted in Peck, "General Conference of 1844," 173). The individual Smith probably had in mind was William Capers, who took his name out of the election in 1832 because he was a slaveholder.

25. "Debates in the General Conference, 1844," in *JGC/MEC 1796–1856* 2:148.

26. Ibid., 150.

27. Ibid.

28. Peck, "General Conference of 1844," 184.

29. "Episcopal Address," *JGC/MEC 1796–1856* (1844, Appendix) 2:154.

30. Ibid., 155. This was certainly not something that would have been conceded by Asbury and Coke, who claimed a higher authority, based on Scripture, giving them veto power over the decisions of the preachers.

31. Bishop Soule speaking to the conference on 29 May 1844,

"Debates in the General Conference, 1844," in *JGC/MEC 1796–1856* 2:168-69.

32. Ibid.

33. The following summary and excerpts from Hamline's speech come from "Debates in the General Conference, 1844," in *JGC/MEC 1796–1856* 2:128-34.

34. Alfred Griffith speaking to his motion, in ibid., 83.

35. Ibid., 131-32. This same idea had been presented by Ezekiel Cooper in 1808 and rejected in favor of Soule's wording of the Third Restrictive Rule of the constitution.

36. Ibid., 132.

37. Ibid., 133.

38. "Debates in the General Conference, 1844," in *JGC/MEC 1796–1856* 2:83.

39. *JGC/MEC 1796–1856* (1844) 2:194.

40. Ibid., 195.

41. "Debates in the General Conference, 1844," in *JGC/MEC 1796–1856* 2:74.

42. *JGC/MEC 1796–1856* (1844) 2:54.

43. Ibid., 81. James Porter, a New England Conference delegate, later explained that after a caucus it was decided that if Bishop Andrew were allowed to remain in place, the New England Conferences would secede in a body and invite Bishop Hedding to preside over them. Hedding could not be reached with this information before he signed the document. See James Porter, "General Conference of 1844," *MQR* 53 (1871): 234-50. See also McTyeire, *History*, 636 n.

44. "Debates in the General Conference, 1844," in *JGC/MEC 1796–1856* 2:89.

45. Ibid., 90.

46. Ibid., 106.

47. *JGC/MEC 1796–1856* (1844) 2:109, 111.

48. Ibid., 117-18.

49. Bishop Andrew to William Wightman (6 July 1844), quoted in Barton, "Episcopal Office in American Methodism," 112. The bishops actually made two plans. In the one they published, Andrew was given no work. Thomas A. Morris wrote in February 1845 to explain that since Andrew was not present and they did not know his wishes, not wishing to infringe on his freedom, they had omitted Andrew. "Whether you would take part of the oversight or not was a question

which the final action of the General Conference devolved on yourself to decide. Of course we could not decide for you, and as you
were absent and unapprised of the final state of the case, you could
not then and there decide for yourself. . . . Hence, the published
'Plan' and the 'Revised Plan' in anticipation of your decision to
take work." Thomas A. Morris to James Andrew (19 February 1845),
quoted in Smith, *Life of Andrew*, 364.

50. Barton, "Episcopal Office in American Methodism," 122.

11. The Methodist Episcopal Church, South

1. "Debates in the General Conference, 1844," in *JGC/MEC 1796–1856* 2:200.
2. Ibid., 204.
3. Mathews, *Slavery and Methodism*, 269.
4. Quotations in this and the next two paragraphs come from "Debates in the General Conference, 1844," in *JGC/MEC 1796–1856* 2:218-19.
5. Ibid., 219.
6. Ibid., 222.
7. Ibid., 223.
8. Quoted in *Organization MECS*, 148.
9. Ibid., 146-47, 150.
10. Ibid., 154.
11. Ibid., 242.
12. Ibid., 245.
13. Ibid., 252.
14. Ibid., 288.
15. Mathews, *Slavery and Methodism*, 269-70.
16. Ibid., 271.
17. The quotation is from the Plan of Separation adopted by the General Conference, and quoted in *Organization MECS*, 293.
18. "Pastoral Address to the Methodist Episcopal Church, South, 1846," quoted in *Organization MECS*, 491.
19. "Report on the State of the Church, Methodist Episcopal Church, 1848," *JGC/MEC 1848–1856* (1848) 3:154.
20. Ibid., 156. They judged the Plan of Separation to be a *peace measure* that was never intended "to sanction a division of said Church," and beyond the intentions of the General Conference (ibid., 160).

21. The road to reunion led to a reorganization, not a return. Any idea of "returning to mother church" was unacceptable. See John M. Moore, *The Long Road to Methodist Union* (New York: Abingdon-Cokesbury Press, 1943).

22. Quoted in Bond's editorial "To Dr. Capers," *Christian Advocate and Journal* (9 October 1844).

23. Remaining quotes in this paragraph from Thomas E. Bond, "To Bishop Andrew," *Christian Advocate and Journal* (25 September 1844). The editorial to which Andrew was objecting was written during the General Conference on 29 May 1844.

24. "The Theory and Practice of the M. E. Church in Respect to the Authority of the General Conference over Bishops or General Superintendents," *Christian Advocate and Journal* (14 August 1844).

25. Mathews, *Slavery and Methodism*, 272.

26. The bishops declared in their "Pastoral Address" that they "felt perfectly at liberty to declare the Plan of Separation . . . null and void" (*JGC/MEC*, 1848, 175). This was despite the fact that it was clearly stated when the plan was adopted that only the provisions related to the Restrictive Rules had to be voted on by the annual conferences, and its failure to pass would not defeat the entire proposal.

27. Ruling of the United States Supreme Court in the Book Concern case, quoted in Buckley, *History*, 283.

28. "Report of the Committee on Organization," in *Organization MECS*, 316.

29. *JGC/MECS*, 1846, quoted in *Organization MECS*, 375.

12. The MECS: Defending the Asburian Ark

1. Asbury, journal (27 May 1774), *JLFA* 1:116.

2. Richey, *Conference*, 81.

3. *Doctrine and Discipline of the Methodist Episcopal Church*, 1792, 38-39.

4. Ibid., 39. This was changed in 1804 to restrict only their function as bishops. They were allowed to continue in the ministry. *Doctrine and Discipline of the Methodist Episcopal Church*, 1804, 18.

5. Richey, "Legacy of Francis Asbury," 150.

6. Paine, *M'Kendree* 1:456.

7. Spellman, "Superintendency," 213.

8. William Capers, "Dr. Capers' Reply to A. C.," *New York Christian Advocate* (16 October 1844).

9. "Committee on Organization," Louisville Convention, 1845, quoted in *Organization MECS*, 313.

10. Ibid., 318.

11. Ibid., 321.

12. Paul F. Blankenship, "Bishop Asbury and the Germans," *Methodist History* 4.3 (April 1966): 10-11.

13. Neely, *Bishops*, 228-29.

14. Norman Spellman refutes the idea that the South's adherence to the Asburian tradition of co-equal episcopacy was sectional and associated with the larger concern over slavery by noting that the MPC, far more radical in its anti-Asburian stance, was primarily a southern movement, and was both anti-bishop and pro-slavery (see Spellman, "Superintendency," 242).

15. *Organization MECS*, 163.

16. Herbert Stotts, "History of the Episcopacy," *General Superintendency*, 39.

17. *JGC/MECS*, 1854, 356.

18. Spellman, "Superintendency," 318.

19. *JGC/MECS*, 1870, 282.

20. Ibid., 286.

21. Ibid., 287.

22. See ibid., 285. McKendree had argued that "the General Conference is not the proper judge of the constitutionality of its own acts. . . . If the General Conference be the sole judge in such questions, then there are no bounds to its power" (see Paine, *M'Kendree* 2:37). Spellman argues that Soule affirmed the same limitations: "Therefore, when Soule spoke of the General Conference as the 'highest judiciary of the church,' he spoke of an authority that was delegated, not inherent; restricted, not absolute—the General Conference was a 'constitutional tribunal'" (Spellman, "Superintendency," 216).

23. See Stotts, "History of the Episcopacy," *General Superintendency*, 44.

24. *Organization MECS*, 282.

25. Mark K. Bauman, *Warren Akin Candler: The Conservative as Idealist* (Metuchen, N.J.: Scarecrow Press, 1981), 67.

26. See Robert W. Sledge, "A History of the Methodist Episcopal Church, South, 1914–1939" (Ph.D. diss., University of Texas at Austin, 1972), 135-37. Published as *Hands on the Ark: The Struggle for*

Change in the Methodist Episcopal Church, South, 1914–1939 (Lake Junaluska: Commission on Archives and History, The United Methodist Church, 1975).

27. Quoted in ibid.

13. The MEC: Evolving the Form of Episcopacy

1. See Moede, *Office of Bishop*, 129ff.

2. See John F. Marlay, *The Life of Thomas A. Morris* (Cincinnati: Hitchcock and Walden, 1875), 140, 165.

3. Henry B. Ridgaway, *Life of Edmund S. Janes* (New York: Phillips and Hunt, 1882), 154.

4. Matthew Simpson to Ellen Simpson (27 July 1853), autograph letter signed. Rose Memorial Library, Drew University.

5. Matthew Simpson to Ellen Simpson (13 September 1863), autograph letter signed. Rose Memorial Library, Drew University.

6. Matthew Simpson to Ellen Simpson, Manchester, New Hampshire (7 April 1860), autograph letter signed. Rose Memorial Library, Drew University.

7. Ivan Lee Holt, *Eugene Russell Hendrix* (Nashville: Parthenon Press, 1950), 16.

8. *General Superintendency*, 40.

9. Report #18, Committee on Judiciary, *JGC/MEC*, 1928, 509.

10. "Debates in the General Conference, 1844," in *JGC/MEC 1796–1856* 2:131-32.

11. Quoted in Moede, *Office of Bishop*, 131.

12. For a brief summary of its history, see Prince A. Taylor Jr., *The Life of My Years* (Nashville: Abingdon Press, 1983), 93-113. Taylor presided over the conference for a number of years before becoming one of the first African American bishops to be assigned to a predominantly White area, New Jersey.

13. *JGC/MEC 1796–1856* (1836) 1:473.

14. *JGC/MEC 1796–1856* (1840) 2:100. The mission conferences of Liberia, Germany, Switzerland, and India were not declared to be annual conferences until the General Conference of 1868 (see *JGC/MEC*, 1868, 497).

15. "Proceedings of the General Conference," The Methodist Episcopal Church, 8 May 1852, reported in the *Zion's Herald and Journal*. See also "Report of Committee on Missions–Bishop of Liberia," *JGC/MEC*, 1852, 3:193-94.

16. Neely, *Bishops*, 163.

17. See *JGC/MEC 1796–1856* (1852) 3:67-68

18. "Episcopal Address," *JGC/MEC 1796–1856* (1856) 3:198.

19. *JGC/MEC 1796–1856* (1856) 3:145.

20. Ibid., 146-47.

21. Neely, *Missions*, 125.

22. *JGC/MEC 1796–1856* (1856) 3:177.

23. See Neely, *Missions*, 124.

24. These are found in Neely, *Missions*, 128-29 and in the *JGC/MEC*, 1888, 300-301.

25. Neely, *Missions*, 129-31.

26. Ibid., 126.

27. "Episcopal Address," *JGC/MEC 1796–1856* (1844) 2:156.

28. "Episcopal Address," *JGC/MEC 1796–1856* (1852) 3:182-83.

29. See James Cannon Jr., *Bishop Cannon's Own Story: Life as I Have Seen It* (Durham: Duke University Press, 1955), 240.

30. Neely, *Missions*, 255.

14. Localizing Episcopacy, North and South

1. Bishop E. M. Marvin made the first episcopal visit to the Orient in 1876. E. M. Marvin, *To the East by Way of the West* (St. Louis: Bryan, Brand & Co., 1878). See also James Cannon III, *History of Southern Methodist Missions* (Nashville: Cokesbury Press, 1926), 94. One must consider that they may have been motivated by concern to avoid electing persons of color to the episcopacy.

2. Quoted in Wade Crawford Barclay, *History of Methodist Missions. Part Two, the Methodist Episcopal Church, 1845–1939* (New York: Board of Missions of the Methodist Church, 1957) 3:177-78.

3. Alfred W. Wasson, *The Influence of Missionary Expansion upon Methodist Organization* (New York: The Commission on Central Conferences of the Methodist Church, n.d.), 11.

4. *JGC/MEC*, 1884, 349.

5. Interview with Bishop Hardt. During one of his episcopal visits to Indonesia, Bishop John Wesley Hardt took $5,000 as a donation from the Oklahoma Annual Conference to print the *Discipline*. He was never aware that it was done.

6. Report #1, Committee on Judiciary, *JGC/MEC*, 1928, 497.

7. See Report #18, Committee on Judiciary, *JGC/MEC*, 1928, 509.

8. *JGC/MEC*, 1928, 716.

9. 73, *The Doctrines and Discipline of the Methodist Episcopal Church, South*, 1934, 47.

10. Report #48, Committee on Judiciary, *JGC/MEC*, 1932, 632. The ruling was made in response to the question of the constitutionality of term episcopacy in the central conferences.

11. They did not actually gain the right to vote on all matters until 1956 (see 444, *The Book of Discipline of the Methodist Church*, 1956, 152). Prior to that time they had "the privilege of full participation with vote . . . whenever the interests of his Central Conference or the interests common to all Central Conferences [were] involved" (555, *The Book of Discipline of the Methodist Church*, 1952, 149).

12. This was changed by Ruling 164 of the Judicial Council of the Methodist Church in 1960. It allowed them to attend all meetings of the Council of Bishops with expenses paid.

13. Report #17, Committee on Judiciary, *JGC/MEC*, 1936, 475.

14. Report #21, Committee on Episcopacy, *JGC/MEC*, 1912, 536.

15. *JGC/MEC*, 1872, 321.

16. *JGC/MECS*, 1882, 165-66.

17. *JGC/MEC*, 1884, 369.

18. Moede, *Office of Bishop*, 142.

19. Neely, *Bishops*, 298.

20. *JGC/MEC*, 1904, 517.

21. Ibid., 315.

22. 407.1, *The Book of Discipline of The United Methodist Church*, 1996, 250.

23. *JGC/MEC*, 1908, 456.

24. Report #5, Committee on Episcopacy, *JGC/MEC*, 1908, 456; and Report #7, Committee on Episcopacy, *JGC/MEC*, 1908, 457.

25. Neely, *Missions*, 234.

26. "Episcopal Address," *JGC/MEC*, 1916, 161.

27. Ibid., 481.

28. "Episcopal Address," *JGC/MECS*, 1918, 322.

29. "Episcopal Address," *JGC/MEC 1796–1856* (1852) 3:183.

30. "Episcopal Address," *JGC/MECS*, 1922, 340.

31. *JGC/MECS*, 1930, 384.

15. Limiting Episcopal Power

1. *General Superintendency*, 112. The nature of superintendency was, for the first time, defined in 1976 as "residing in the office of

bishop and extends to the district superintendent, with each possessing distinct responsibilities" (501, *The Book of Discipline of The United Methodist Church*, 1976, 212).

2. Report #6, Committee on Judiciary, *JGC/MEC*, 1924, 476.

3. Report #14, Committee on Episcopacy, *JGC/MEC*, 1916, 478.

4. *JGC/MEC*, 1884, 146.

5. Stotts, "History of the Episcopacy," *General Superintendency*, 91.

6. "Episcopal Address," *JGC/MECS*, 1934, 383.

7. Report #18, Committee on Judiciary, *JGC/MEC*, 1928, 509.

8. "Episcopal Address," *JGC/MECS*, 1934, 382.

9. Ibid., 383.

10. The story is told in Norman W. Spellman, *Growing a Soul, the Story of A. Frank Smith* (Dallas: SMU Press, 1979), 200.

11. 507, *The Book of Discipline of The United Methodist Church*, 1976, 215.

12. Bishop Lloyd C. Wicke made this comment while teaching my graduate class on episcopacy at Drew University. The Oklahoma Conference and the Oklahoma Indian Mission Conference had one of the Smith brothers as its bishop for almost half a century.

13. James S. Thomas, "Some Personal Reflections upon the Evolution of the Council of Bishops," 1. Prepared for me in 1993 (hereafter cited as Thomas, "Personal Reflections").

14. 507, *The Book of Discipline of The United Methodist Church*, 1976, 215.

15. 210.2, *The Book of Discipline of the Methodist Episcopal Church*, 1912, 149. There was no similar provision for ministers.

16. 245, *The Book of Discipline of the Methodist Episcopal Church*, 1928, 218.

17. 120, *The Book of Discipline of the Methodist Episcopal Church, South*, 1930, 72.

18. Cannon, *Bishop Cannon's Story*, xxvi.

19. Ibid., xiii.

20. 409, *The Book of Discipline of The United Methodist Church*, 1996, 251-54.

21. Paine, *M'Kendree* 1:447-48.

22. Francis John McConnell, *The Essentials of Methodism* (New York: The Methodist Book Concern, 1916), 78.

23. Alfred M. Pierce, *Giant Against the Sky* (New York: Abingdon-Cokesbury Press, 1943), 98.

24. "Episcopal Address," *JGC/MECS*, 1934, 384.

25. Quoted in Stotts, "History of the Episcopacy," *General Superintendency*, 92.

26. Thomas, "Personal Reflections," 1-2.

27. See Sledge, "History of the Methodist Episcopal Church, South," 140.

28. An interview with Bishop Martin, conducted by Robert W. Sledge and quoted in Spellman, *Growing a Soul*, 204.

29. "Episcopal Address," *JGC/MEC*, 1912, 186-88.

30. "Episcopal Address," *JGC/MEC 1796–1856* (1844) 2:154.

31. Moede, *Office of Bishop*, 156-57.

32. "Lay Co-Operation," *Christian Advocate and Journal* (7 October 1858), author unknown.

33. Abel Stevens, "Speech Made at Lay Delegation Convention in Newark," *The Methodist* (7 March 1868).

34. George R. Crooks, *Life of Bishop Matthew Simpson* (New York: Harper and Brothers, 1890), 430.

35. Goodloe, "Office of Bishop in the Methodist Church," 178.

36. "Episcopal Address," *JGC/MECS*, 1934, 377.

37. Egon W. Gerdes and Ellis Larsen, *Sharing a Royal Priesthood. First Report to the Study Commission on Episcopacy and District Superintendency in Joint Session with the Council of Bishops of The United Methodist Church Meeting in Los Angeles, 16-19 April 1974* 2:49.

16. Unification: The MC and The UMC

1. Quoted in William Warren Sweet, "The History of the Agitation for Union," an address given to the Working Conference on the Union of American Methodism, Evanston, Illinois, 1916. *A Working Conference on the Union of American Methodism* (New York: Methodist Book Concern, 1916), 42-43.

2. Edgar Blake, "A Suggested Working Plan for Methodist Union," in *A Working Conference*, 444.

3. James S. Thomas, *Methodism's Racial Dilemma: The Story of the Central Jurisdiction* (Nashville: Abingdon Press, 1992), 49.

4. Matthew S. Davage, "Methodism—Our Heritage and Our Hope," *Daily Christian Advocate* (9 May 1939), 475.

5. *Proceedings of the Joint Commission on Unification of the Methodist Episcopal Church and the Methodist Episcopal Church, South.*

Proceedings at Savannah, Georgia, 23 January–6 February 1918 (New York: The Methodist Book Concern, 1920) 2:574.

6. *Proceedings of the Joint Commission* 2:581.

7. The other person was Professor C. M. Bishop, a member of the Southern Methodist University School of Theology faculty at the time of his service on the Joint Commission.

8. 36, Article III, "The Plan of Union" in *Doctrines and Discipline of the Methodist Church*, 1939, 30.

9. Roy H. Short, *Chosen to Be Consecrated* (Lake Junaluska: Commission on Archives and History of The United Methodist Church, 1976), 28.

10. Quoted in Robert Moats Miller, *Bishop G. Bromley Oxnam, Paladin of Liberal Protestantism* (Nashville: Abingdon Press, 1990), 213.

11. Quoted in Spellman, *Growing a Soul*, 231.

12. See 337, *Doctrines and Discipline of the Methodist Church*, 1940, 105.

13. See Spellman, *Growing a Soul*, 230.

14. "Thus, McVey cites a thirty-year period in which, of the twenty-eight men elected to the episcopacy, only three were called directly from the pastorate. Most of the bishops of this period came to their office from a college presidency, or from the secretary-ship of one of the boards of the church." Moede, *Office of Bishop* (New York: Abingdon Press, 1964), 124-25. See also Short, *Chosen to Be Consecrated*, 76.

15. J. Bruce Behney and Paul H. Eller, *The History of the Evangelical United Brethren Church* (Nashville: Abingdon Press, 1979), 395.

16. "Division Three—Episcopal Supervision," Article I, the Plan of Union, The United Methodist Church, 1967, 17.

17. At the South Central Jurisdiction Conference in New Orleans in 1988, a teller forgot that he had placed a handful of ballots in his pocket when the count was made. Everyone recognized immediately that the total number of votes cast had gone down dramatically, but the election of Bruce Blake was announced, since he had a majority of the votes counted. Later, when the missing ballots were discovered, the conference was faced with determining the legality of Blake's election.

18. Rule 20, *Journal of the South Central Jurisdiction of The United Methodist Church*, Kansas City, Missouri, 14–18 July 1996, 110.

19. *General Superintendency*, 102.

20. For more on the sparsity of pastors elected to the episcopacy prior to 1900, and of presiding elders elected after 1840, see Short, *Chosen to Be Consecrated*, 76; and Frederick DeLand Leete, *Methodist Bishops, Personal Notes and Bibliography* (Nashville: Parthenon Press, 1948).

21. James K. Mathews, *Set Apart to Serve: The Role of the Episcopacy in the Wesleyan Tradition* (Nashville: Abingdon Press, 1985), Appendix B, 297-305.

22. Council of Bishops, "Mandatory Retirement Dates for United Methodist Bishops," November 1996.

23. Thomas, "Personal Reflections," 2.

24. The constitution of The United Methodist Church has since 1968 stipulated "the bishops shall appoint, after consultation with the district superintendent, ministers to the charges" (52, Article X).

25. This paragraph summarizes *The Book of Discipline of The United Methodist Church*, 1976, Section VIII, 527-29.6, pp. 228-29.

26. Gerdes and Larsen, *Sharing a Royal Priesthood* 2:53.

27. Ibid., 55.

17. The Episcopacy in Today's Church

1. Roy Short, *History of the Council of Bishops of The United Methodist Church, 1939–1979* (Nashville: Abingdon Press, 1980), 281.

2. Ibid., 280.

3. Thomas, "Personal Reflections," 2. Russell Richey observed that "the bishops made themselves into a great family; they had come to use their gatherings for social and peer-support functions. They became a family of regional superintendents" (Richey, "Legacy of Francis Asbury," 164).

4. II, 404.1, *The Book of Discipline of The United Methodist Church*, 1996, 248.

5. Short, *History of the Council of Bishops*, 34.

6. Ibid.

7. Thomas, "Personal Reflections," 3.

8. Miller, *Bishop Oxnam*, 203.

9. Bishop James K. Mathews, secretary of the Council of Bishops, compiled these under the title "Messages of the Council of Bishops of the Methodist Church, The United Methodist Church During Its First Forty Years, 1939–1978." Typescript, n.d.

10. Richey, "Legacy of Francis Asbury," 165.

11. See Thomas, "Personal Reflections," 2.

12. In his response to this chapter, Bishop Thomas remembered that in 1988 he broke that tradition by calling for the question and was told by an older bishop that he "should have known better." When the council was first organized, following the practice in the College of Bishops of the MECS, the members addressed one another in the meetings as "Bishop." The meetings today, however, are more informal.

13. Author's interviews with Bishops Stowe, Loder, and Thomas.

14. An attempt in 1943 to pay the secretary of the council an additional $25 a month for his services was denied by the Council on World Service. Short, *History of the Council of Bishops*, 33.

15. Thomas, "Personal Reflections," 3.

16. Confidential document to the Council of Bishops, November 1989.

17. 507.3, "Special Assignments," *The Book of Discipline of The United Methodist Church*, 1976, 215.

18. Bishop Martin's papers are in the archives of the Bridwell Library, Perkins School of Theology, Southern Methodist University.

19. Eugene Kennedy has described the different perspectives among leaders in the Catholic hierarchy, whom he names "Culture One Catholics," and those in the pews of the parish who comprise "Culture Two." They do not have the same priorities, and their loyalties are different. The same distinction, I believe, applies to Methodists. See Eugene C. Kennedy, *Tomorrow's Catholics, Yesterday's Church: The Two Cultures of American Catholicism* (New York: Harper & Row, 1988).

20. Spellman, *Growing a Soul*, 293-94.

21. See an account of their visit in William C. Martin's 1954 diary. Archives of the Bridwell Library, Perkins School of Theology, Southern Methodist University.

22. Thomas, "Personal Reflections," 4.

Index

abolition. *See* slavery

African American Methodists, 10, 43, 193; Allen leaves Old St. George's Church, 16; bishops, 185-86, 190, 223; Central Jurisdiction, 222-23; Central Jurisdiction abolished, 256-57; and Methodist Church, 222; missions to, 104

African Methodist Episcopal Church, 16, 101

agencies. *See* boards

Allen, Richard, 16, 101

Andrew, James O., 107, 143; becomes a slaveholder, 131-132; elected a bishop (1832), 109; and Francis Harding, 129; joins MECS, 153, 169; not guilty of wrongdoing, 136-137; omitted from Plan of Episcopal Visitation, 144; urged to stay in office, 133. *See also* slavery

annual conferences, 45, 51, 140, 231, 250; appeals to, 94-96; bishops given authority to create, 68; and the Constitution, 95; draw own regulations regarding slavery, 103; duties and rights of, 120-21; end of as constitutional unit, 109; General Conference and, 123; and lay representation, 216; and MECS, 165; power vested in, 74; proliferation of, 53

Armstrong, A. James, 177

Asbury, Francis, 56, 242, 248; appointment to America, 15, 264 n. 10; assistant in America, 13, 18; and Coke, 39, 40; compromise with Virginia Methodists (1780), 22; The Council, 51-52, 55, 165; describes a Methodist bishop, 276 n.

29; election as bishop, 40, 271 n. 43; as general assistant, 23; hiding in Delaware, 20, 265 n. 29; and itinerancy, 162; and itinerant general superintendency, 17; independence from Wesley, 9; influence on shape of episcopacy, 162; joins Wesley's Methodists, 18; leader of American Methodism, 13, 23; leaves city to preach in country, 17; model of episcopacy and itinerant ministry, 89, 159-63; and number of bishops, 82; ordination of , 44; power as bishop, 16; plan to resign, 60; primacy as bishop, 60-61, 161; and Thomas Rankin, 18-20

Baltimore Conference, 96, 126, 133. *See also* Harding

Bangs, Nathan, 156; Asbury as general assistant, 18; election of presiding elders, 84,88; history, 64; Plan of Separation, 147

Bascom, Henry B., 141, 145, 169

binding minute: approved (1784), 43; Abury's role in rescinding, 46; rescinded (1787), 47, 270 n. 35

bishops, 270 n. 40; accountability to General Conference, 137; elected for African American conferences, 185-86; age of, 236; authority to appoint preachers, 60; autocratic tendencies, 211-12 (MECS); and boards, 217; of central conferences, 194; criteria for

297